Religious Orthodoxy and Popular Faith
in European Society

Religious Orthodoxy and Popular Faith in European Society

Edited by Ellen Badone

PRINCETON UNIVERSITY PRESS

PRINCETON, NEW JERSEY

Copyright © 1990 by Princeton University Press
Published by Princeton University Press, 41 William Street,
Princeton, New Jersey 08540
In the United Kingdom: Princeton University Press, Oxford

Library of Congress Cataloging-in-Publication Data

Religious orthodoxy and popular faith in European society / edited by
Ellen Badone.
    p.   cm.
  Bibliography: p.
  Includes index.
  ISBN 0-691-09450-0 (alk. paper)
  ISBN 0-691-02850-8 (pbk. : alk. paper)
  1. Europe—Religious life and customs. 2. Christianity—Europe.
3. Europe—Religion—20th century. I. Badone, Ellen.
BR735.R454   1990
274—dc20   89-35353

This book has been composed in Linotron Caledonia

Princeton University Press books are printed on acid-free paper,
and meet the guidelines for permanence and durability of the
Committee on Production Guidelines for Book Longevity of the
Council on Library Resources

Printed in the United States of America by Princeton University Press,
Princeton, New Jersey

    10 9 8 7 6 5 4 3 2 1
(Pbk.) 10 9 8 7 6 5 4 3 2 1

Contents

Notes on Contributors

Ellen Badone is an Assistant Professor in the Department of Religious Studies and an Associate Member of the Department of Anthropology at McMaster University.

Ruth Behar is an Associate Professor in the Department of Anthropology at the University of Michigan, Ann Arbor.

Stanley Brandes is a Professor in the Department of Anthropology at the University of California, Berkeley.

Caroline Brettell is a Visiting Associate Professor in the Department of Anthropology at Southern Methodist University.

Jill Dubisch is a Professor in the Department of Sociology and Anthropology at the University of North Carolina, Charlotte.

Jane Schneider is a Professor at the City University of New York and Executive Officer of the Ph.D. Program in Anthropology.

Lawrence J. Taylor is an Associate Professor in the Department of Anthropology and Sociology at Lafayette College.

Religious Orthodoxy and Popular Faith
in European Society

CHAPTER 1

Introduction

Ellen Badone

DURING the Easter season in 1987 a battle of wills between the bishop of Versailles and the parishioners of the Church of St. Louis in Port Marly, a Paris suburb, made headlines in the *New York Times* (Bernstein 1987). The conflict had all the ingredients of a media drama: a church building occupied by the faithful, police storming the sanctuary with riot sticks to drag men, women, and children from their pews, and, finally, reoccupation of the church by parishioners who broke through police barricades with a battering ram at Easter Sunday Mass. At issue was the right of the congregation to continue celebrating the Latin mass with the pre-Vatican II liturgy.

Served until 1985 by an elderly and traditional priest, St. Louis was the only remaining parish in the area offering the mass in Latin. With the death of this priest, the bishop ruled that his replacement must conform to the Vatican II liturgical directives. However, the congregation of St. Louis had other ideas. Refusing to accept the modernizing priest, they invited instead a Benedictine monk opposed to contemporary Catholic reforms who agreed to continue the Latin rite. The initial occupation of the church, which began in November 1986, was undertaken to prevent the officially appointed priest from performing his duties. Not surprisingly, this outbreak of civil disorder led eventually to the intervention of the mayor and local police force. By Easter the three classic protagonists of religious conflicts throughout postrevolutionary French history—the church establishment, the laity, and the secular state—were all party to the unfolding drama in Port Marly. The situation was further complicated by conflict within the church establishment between the orthodox, modernizing bishop and the renegade, traditionalist Benedictine, a sympathizer of Archbishop Lefebvre's Integrist movement.

Despite their particularly forceful and at times violent expression, the emotions behind the incidents at Port Marly are not unique. Rather Port Marly represents but a single example—albeit perhaps an extreme one—of the ongoing tension between "official," orthodox, or clerical and "popular," "folk," or lay definitions of religion in Europe. A concern to document, evoke, and interpret this tension, both from historical and contemporary vantage points, unites the seven papers in the present volume.

All of the contributors to the book are social-cultural anthropologists, and all of them have acquired through fieldwork an intimate and richly textured understanding of the religious experience of priests and parishioners in European communities. The ethnographic contexts evoked in the following pages range from the Mediterranean to northern Europe and include both Roman Catholic and Greek Orthodox religious traditions. In these papers the voices of ordinary people speak for themselves. We hear elderly peasants in rural Spain and Portugal engaged in theological debates, while those in Brittany and Ireland recount stories about the supernatural powers of priests which can be employed for good or evil. This emphasis on multivocality and the use of folklore texts, combined with an approach which highlights key symbols[1] including cultural performances such as pilgrimages and *festas*, provides a common theoretical orientation throughout the book. Here we see people actively and creatively shaping their religious domain, sometimes in collaboration with "official" ritual specialists, often in open rebellion against such specialists or voicing pointed criticisms of them.

All of the case studies presented in this book share a focus on what has, by many researchers, been called "popular religion." As a scholarly category, "popular religion" is problematic. In many of the disciplines that deal with it—history, sociology, anthropology, and religious studies—the question of whether the "popular" constitutes a distinct domain of the religious field has been posed. As Peter Brown points out, the notion of a "two-tiered" religious system composed of elite and popular sectors can be traced back at least to the eighteenth century, when Hume contrasted the monotheism of the enlightened few with the implicitly polytheistic tendencies of the uninstructed "vulgar" masses. According to Hume, throughout history the popular classes have failed to perceive the design of a single deity in the rational order of the universe because of their lack of training for abstract contemplation and their anxious tendency to personalize as gods the unknown forces that govern human fortune and misfortune (Brown 1981:13–22; Hume 1956). Taken up by later scholars, this "two-tiered model" has continued to characterize the religion of the masses as lacking in internal dynamism (Brown 1981:18). In opposition to the religion of the elite, popular religion is also frequently "presented as in some ways a diminution, a misconception or a contamination of 'unpopular religion'" (Brown 1981:19). Categorizations of this kind, which make it difficult to conceive of the popular as a meaningful religious realm in its own right, have led some scholars to advocate abandoning the concept of popular religion entirely (Christian 1981a; Schmitt 1976).

Sensitive to the problems associated with its usage, the authors of the present volume employ the term popular religion with caution. In these papers "popular religion" can be read as referring to those informal, un-

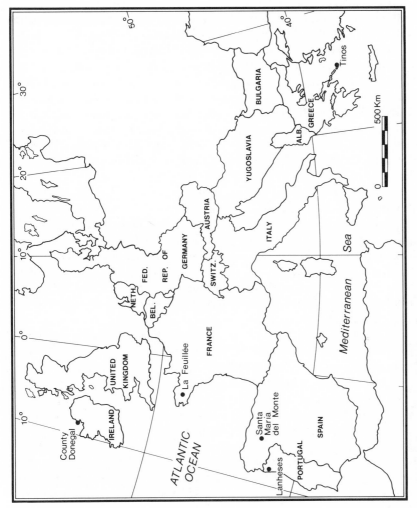

Locations of communities discussed in text.

official practices, beliefs, and styles of religious expression that lack the formal sanction of established church structures. Implicit in this definition is an opposition between the informal system and the formal structures. Yet, as several of the papers in this volume point out, the relationship is more than simply oppositional. Rather than viewing official and popular religion as monolithic entities, immutable and distinct, it is more fruitful to focus on the dialectical character of their interrelationship. It is this approach that informs the work of the Italian historian Carlo Ginzburg. As he shows in his study of the cosmology and religious ideas of a sixteenth-century Friulian miller, there are mutual, reciprocal influences between popular and dominant levels within a culture (Ginzburg 1980). Earlier anthropological work inspired by Redfield depicted "great" and "little" religious traditions as relatively autonomous and discrete spheres, with interaction between the two conceived primarily in terms of a downward percolation of concepts from "great" to "little" (Redfield 1956). Ginzburg, in contrast, building on a framework developed by Bakhtin, argues for a circular movement of ideas between cultural levels.

Redfield's work is in the tradition of the "two-tiered" models of religion that Brown seeks to escape. Like the term popular religion itself, the great tradition-little tradition distinction has helped to perpetuate the misconception that popular religion is always rural, primitive, unreflective, and traditional, as opposed to the urban, civilized, intellectual, and modern religion of the elite (Christian 1981a:178). As William Christian has demonstrated, at least in certain regions and periods of European history the same "local" religious style has been shared by members of all social classes, whether they be literate or illiterate, rural or urban dwellers. For Christian the term popular religion can only be legitimately applied when it refers to "religion as practiced" rather than "religion as prescribed" (Christian 1981a:178). It is in this sense also that the authors of the papers in the present volume understand the term.

Seeking to specify some of the general features of "religion as practiced," Christian suggests that it is both rooted in particular historical communities and geographical localities and that it is often conservative, resisting changes imposed by nonlocal authorities (Christian 1981a:178). Clearly, the Port Marly Catholics fighting for their Latin mass share the latter characteristic. Here the tension between orthodoxy and popular religion takes the form of a traditionalist backlash against reforms initiated by a church hierarchy that is perceived to be diluting the principles of the faith. However, popular religious movements are not necessarily conservative in their approach to liturgy and doctrine or in their political orientation. Many of the popular movements labelled as heresies during the twelfth and thirteenth centuries pressed for reform in reaction to the wealth and worldliness of the medieval church. The Waldensians, for example, rejected the legitimacy of the clergy and the rituals they performed, repudiated church teachings on Purgatory, and advocated a radically subversive mixture of moral purity, austerity, and adherence to the Scriptures, which they read in the vernacular (Lambert 1977). Nonetheless, in many cases popular religion emphasizes fidelity to the past. For this reason "religion as practiced" frequently clings to elements of "religion as prescribed" which, to the church establishment, have lost their significance. In Christian's analysis "so-called 'little tradition' is often merely 'great tradition' that has taken root in a particular place and lasted longer than its time" (Christian 1981a:178).

Since "religion as practiced" is often oriented toward the past, a historical perspective is invaluable for the understanding of its rituals and beliefs. Although it is essential to avoid the antiquarian approach that catalogues folk religious practices as simple "survivals" of an earlier era, it is nonetheless the case that popular religious traditions in Europe integrate elements from diverse historical periods. Moreover, the churches' definitions of religious orthodoxy, and hence the category of the unorthodox, have varied widely over time. To cite but one example among many, the elaborate processions encouraged by post-Tridentine Catholicism are now condemned by the clergy in the aftermath of Vatican II, generating confusion and resentment among the faithful (Brandes 1976). Likewise, since the 1950s Catholic teachings on Hell and Purgatory have changed dramatically.

In France the work of historians who have approached popular religion as a key to *mentalités* in the past provides especially useful source material for the anthropologist or student of comparative religion. Representative works in this tradition include those of Delumeau (1977, 1983), Le Goff (1984), Le Roy Ladurie (1979), Schmitt (1983), and Vovelle (1973).[2] As mentioned earlier, related research has been carried out in Italy by Ginzburg (1980, 1983). Among anglophone historians Natalie Davis has been particularly influential in bringing popular religion to the forefront of academic concern (Davis 1974, 1975a, 1975b, 1975c, 1977, 1981, 1982). Other useful works in English documenting European popular religion in historical contexts include those of Bossy (1970, 1973, 1983, 1985), Larner (1984), Moeller (1971), Obelkevich (1979), Sabean (1984), Scribner (1984), and Sperber (1984). In the present volume Jane Schneider reviews many of these historical case studies, which provide evidence for her analysis of the "disenchantment" of religious belief under the influence of the Reformation and Catholic Counter-Reformation.

While historical studies help contextualize popular religion in terms of a long-term diachronic perspective, anthropologists have privileged access to the words and lives of contemporary religious specialists and lay persons. For historians the records of inquisitorial proceedings are often the primary source enabling the reconstruction of past popular belief, as is the case in the work of Ginzburg (1980, 1983), Le Roy Ladurie (1979), and Schmitt (1983). Such materials have a distinct disadvantage, however, in that they were elicited in an atmosphere of fear, with the intent of eradicating heretical beliefs. The ethnographer, in contrast, is able to pose questions in a noninquisitorial setting.[3] Moreover, he or she may also choose not to ask questions at all but merely to observe religion as practiced and lived. This gives the anthropologist the possibility of achieving a more subtle and three-dimensional understanding than that afforded exclusively by historical documents. However, the two approaches can be fruitfully integrated, as the work of Christian (1972, 1981a, 1981b) and Lisón-Tolosana (1983) attests.

The study of popular Christianity has been especially active in predominantly Roman Catholic countries such as France and Italy. In France, starting in the 1930s, the work of sociologist and canon law expert Gabriel Le Bras was instrumental in reorienting the perspective of studies on religion toward a concern with popular belief and the significance of regional variations in religious practice (Le Bras 1955–1956, 1976). Likewise, his contemporary, the medievalist Delaruelle, himself a member of the clergy, played an important role in directing research attention toward the history of popular faith (Delaruelle 1975). However, as Schmitt (1976:943) notes, one difficulty stemming from Delaruelle's work lies in its portrayal of popular religion as emotionally oriented, superficial, and prelogical. This attribution of psychological "otherness" or irrationality to popular religion recurs in the work of other researchers, as Lanternari (1982:138–139) points out.

Too often the religious practices of ordinary lay people, conceptualized as magic or superstition, are assumed to be oriented solely toward practical or materialistic ends. Invocations to specific saints are made, for example, to cure a malady or to ensure that misfortune strikes one's neighbors rather than one's own family and crops. Such pragmatic, magical forms of devotion are explained as responses to a hostile and uncertain environment, over which peasants and working-class people can exert little technological control. In contrast, "true" religion, that of theologians and the clerical elite, is assumed to be concerned exclusively with ethics and spirituality.[4]

This interpretation of popular religion is unproductive for two reasons. First, it ignores evidence from ethnographic studies that popular religion is indeed concerned with ethical issues. Freeman, for example, makes this clear in her work on religion in the Castilian community of Valdemora. Despite the absence in Valdemora of the highly developed sense of individual sin and preoccupation with personal salvation central to orthodox post-Tridentine Catholicism, Valdemorans have clearly defined ideas of Christian virtue. To be a "good Christian" in Valdemora is closely bound up with fulfillment of one's duties to the community and respect for one's neighbors (Freeman 1968:42–43).

The assumption that popular religion is simply pragmatic and magical is misleading for a second reason. It is based on a narrow conception of religion which parallels that espoused by the established churches. As Natalie Davis rightly asks, "Can we learn as much as we would like about the *meaning*, *modes* and *uses* of popular religion to peasants and city dwellers, if we judge it by the standards of Chancellor Jean Gerson, Cardinal Carlo Borromeo, or even the generous Erasmus?" (Davis 1974:308–309). Increased understanding of popular religion can only be achieved with the expanded definition of the religious realm called for by Europeanist anthropologists Freeman (1978:120–121) and Riegelhaupt (1973:835), which includes as "religious" those beliefs not recognized by the church concerning phenomena such as omens, supernatural curing, and the power of amulets or specific shrines.[5] Instead of viewing these types of belief as evidence for the failure of the folk to achieve a true religious understanding, it is necessary to interpret them as parts of consistent symbolic systems whereby individuals and communities make sense of their world.

Hildred Geertz (1975) underscores the same point in her review of Keith Thomas's *Religion and the Decline of Magic* (1971). Taking issue with Thomas's distinction between religion, defined as a "term which covers the kinds of beliefs that are comprehensive, organized and concerned with providing general symbols of life," and magic, defined as "those beliefs which are specific, incoherent and primarily oriented to providing practical solutions to immediate problems,"[6] she argues that this separation of categories was probably not recognized by the majority of ordinary people in the Elizabethan England that Thomas describes. So-called "magic" practices, like those Thomas would classify as "religious," can only be understood in terms of a coherent, culturally and historically particular cosmology and world view (Geertz 1975:83).

REGIONAL CULTURAL VARIATION

The present collection builds on the important contributions assembled by Wolf (1984) which examine the relationships between religion and power in Mediterranean contexts. Whereas Wolf's collection sought to compare and contrast these relationships in Latin Christianity, Judaism, and Islam, this volume is concerned exclusively with Christianity. At the same time the geographic coverage of the present collection encompasses studies based on ethnographic fieldwork in northern Europe alongside the Mediterranean. The papers in this volume thus reflect the unity of

Europe within the Roman Catholic and Eastern Orthodox Christian tradition, despite the regional differences traditionally recognized by anthropologists. Nonetheless, the juxtaposition of papers on Irish and Breton Catholicism with those on religion in Spain, Portugal, and Greece provokes questions about regional religious variation. The most obvious source of variation is the division between Eastern Orthodoxy and Roman Catholicism, which despite their common origin have undergone radically different trajectories of historical development since the schism that divided them after A.D. 1054.

Unlike the Roman Catholic church, which constitutes a single international body with the Pope at its head, the Eastern Orthodox church is a loosely affiliated collection of local or nationally based churches, with no single administrative hierarchy. Likewise, there is no single, authoritative collection of Eastern Orthodox canon law, as in the Roman Catholic tradition. Canon law differs among the various Orthodox national churches. Moreover, Orthodoxy has historically been more flexible than Roman Catholicism in its approach to dogma and in the application of canon law. At present there is a widely recognized need for reform of Orthodox canon law, since many of the ancient canons are difficult to follow under contemporary conditions (Benz 1963:42–43, 69, 72; Ware 1963:11–16, 212–214).

In contrast to Eastern Orthodoxy, Roman Catholicism gives greater prominence to legalism, since the church is conceived "as a spiritual legal institution which Christ founded by virtue of divine law" (Benz 1963:45). In the West this legalistic outlook contributed to the expansion of canon law, to the strengthening of the political authority of the papacy, and to the extension of ecclesiastical power to the secular domain. The legalism of the Roman Catholic tradition has also influenced its eschatology, giving primacy to the concepts of Judgment, divine justice, and, after the twelfth century, to the need for sinners to pay off their debts to God through a period of suffering in Purgatory. In contrast, the concept of Purgatory has never been widely accepted in Eastern Orthodoxy. Sin, in the Orthodox tradition, is conceived less as debt that must be expiated before or after death, than as a diminution of the divine image which is held to exist in every human being. Attitudes toward sin thus emphasize the renewal, healing, or perfection of the soul (Benz 1963:43–47, 51; Ware 1963:259, 295–296).

Another extremely significant difference between Catholicism and Eastern Orthodoxy pertains to the role and social status of the parish priest. While bishops must be celibate, Orthodox parish clergy are permitted to marry. However, only members of celibate monastic orders are eligible for promotion to high ecclesiastical office, and in the past only monks received extensive academic training. As a result, there has traditionally been a gap in education, salary level, and social status between the higher and parish-level clergy (Benz 1963:72–73; Ware 1963:298). Parish priests in Orthodox communities have therefore tended to be closer than priests in Catholic settings to their parishioners in terms of wealth, social power, education, and marital status.

The character of the relationship between priest and parishioner in Eastern Orthodoxy is reflected in the sacrament of repentance or confession. In the Roman Catholic confession the priest adopts a judgmental role, traditionally sitting while the penitent kneels, whereas in Eastern Orthodoxy both parties sit or stand. Likewise, many versions of the Eastern Orthodox formula for absolution present the priest as sharing the sinful nature of the penitent. In contrast to the Roman Catholic formula, in which the priest absolves the lay person's sins, the liturgy of most Orthodox churches stresses that only God can forgive the common failings of both priests and other sinners (Benz 1963:50; Ware 1963:295–296; Zernov 1961:251–253).

It is clear that the dynamics of relations between church and state as well as those between clergy and laity differ widely between eastern and western Europe. Within Roman Catholic Europe, however, these relationships also vary. Many contemporary differences in the character of Catholicism between countries and regions in western Europe are the product of centuries of historical development and local interactions between civil and clerical authorities. The present volume represents a preliminary effort at coming to terms with the regional diversity of European Catholicism, but much work remains to be done in this area.

Nonetheless, a few clear contrasts between the Mediterranean and northern Europe can be outlined at this point. Relative to southwestern Europe, Ireland is notable for its low level of anticlericalism and high degree of male participation in regular devotions. Moreover, Catholicism in Ireland and in other parts of the Atlantic Fringe has been noted for its special preoccupation with eschatological issues, the welfare of the souls, and mortuary rituals (Christian 1972:94; see also Arensberg 1959:207–216; Badone 1989; Douglass 1969; Evans 1957:289–294; Goldey 1983; Ott 1981; Pina-Cabral 1980, 1986; Vallée 1955). Studies of northern Europe have emphasized the impact of the moral rigor of Catholic teachings, particularly in those areas influenced by Jansenism (Scheper-Hughes 1979). While the post-Tridentine church attempted everywhere to purify ritual occasions by eliminating profane activities such as courtship, dancing, and communal feasting, the festive aspects of Catholicism seem to have remained more pronounced in the Mediterranean than in northern Europe. However, this generalization does not hold true in all contexts. Riegelhaupt (1984) noted a prevailing sadness in Salazarist Portugal, which she suggests may be related to the inability of individuals to find meaning and consolation in Catholic symbols.

THE PRESENT VOLUME: THEORETICAL CONCERNS

The theoretical considerations that have guided previous anthropological work on religion in Europe continue to inform the papers in this volume. Among these issues the impact of the Counter-Reformation on European popular religion has been of primary importance. From the perspective of historians such as Bossy (1970) and Delumeau (1977) the rural population of Europe was only superficially Christianized before the post-Tridentine reforms of the sixteenth and seventeenth centuries. It is this theme that is explored and elaborated by Jane Schneider in Chapter 2. Taking Weber (1958a) as her point of departure and following recent historical scholarship which views the Counter-Reformation and the Protestant Reformation as analogous social and religious processes, Schneider examines the impact of these twin movements for reform on the world view of European Christians. She argues that just as the Reformation set in motion the development of religious "rationalization," so too did the Counter-Reformation contribute to the "disenchantment" of European religion. To varying degrees the two Reformations promoted a rational ethic of "brotherly love" instead of the earlier equity-conscious popular ethic of reciprocity that had governed both interpersonal relationships and those between human beings and the spirit world. In economic terms the new ethic privileged the expression of capitalistic forces of world mastery. However, the disenchantment fostered by the Reformations was far from complete. Schneider points to marginal areas where equity-conscious religion and spirit beliefs remained vibrant. Even in less marginal areas the triumph of reform was often superficial, as Schmitt's (1983) study documenting the persistence to the World War I era of rites associated with Saint Guinefort, the Holy Greyhound, suggests. Likewise, many of the papers in the present volume attest to the continuing expression of the style of religion opposed by the Tridentine church.

This is particularly clear in Brettell's analysis of the dialectical tension between official and unofficial religion in Portugal. In Chapter 3 Brettell outlines four main areas of conflict between these traditions. First, she points to the opposition between individual salvation and community solidarity that Bossy (1970) has identified as central to the program of the Counter-Reformation church. Brettell then deals with the differing definitions held by priests and parishioners of appropriate behavior in sacred contexts such as *festas*. While official policy often condemns such profane activities as dancing, feasting, and courtship in conjunction with religious holidays, the lay participant does not necessarily view these as contradicting or defiling the sacred experience. Clearly, the recreative significance of religious festivals is not a uniquely Portuguese phenomenon. In Chapter 5 Dubisch underscores the point that vacation activities are fully compatible with the fulfillment of religious vows on Greek Orthodox pilgrimages, and dancing remains a central feature of *pardons* or patron saints' festivals in Brittany despite three hundred years of clerical opposition.

The third theme discussed by Brettell is that of anticlericalism. In Portugal, as in the Spanish and Breton contexts described in Chapter 4 and Chapter 6 by Behar and Badone, anticlericalism amounts to a religious system of its own. Joyce Riegelhaupt was among the first anthropologists to point out that criticism of priests and the church as an institution does not necessarily imply a rejection of religion (Riegelhaupt 1984). The villagers of São Miguel, where Riegelhaupt worked, considered themselves better Christians than their priests, a sentiment echoed in Freeman's Valdemora as well as in the Portuguese communities studied by Pina-Cabral (1986) and Cutileiro (1971). The same holds true in Brittany and the León region of Spain, as the papers by Badone and Behar indicate. Behar presents particularly revealing comments from men in Santa María del Monte, who argue that "priests" have always been enemies of the true Christian message—after all, was it not the Jewish priesthood that rejected Christ? From the perspective of these Santa María men it remains the case now, as at the beginning of the Christian era, that representatives of institutionalized religion pervert the faith that ordinary people uphold, even in their rejection and criticism of formal church practices. If, following Schneider's example, we look at such anticlerical sentiments in the light of Weberian theory, they can be interpreted as a rejection of the "routinization of charisma," or the process whereby religious leadership and expression become rationalized and embedded in a bureaucratic structure (Weber 1958b:297).

Closely linked to the theme of anticlericalism is Brettell's fourth area of concern: that of the class-based opposition between priest and parishioners. Writing of Andalusia, Driessen (1984) interprets religious brotherhoods or *cofradías* as vehicles for the expression of class divisions and conflict over ritual style between priests and working-class *cofradía* members. Similarly, Gilmore (1984) sees the "erotic" anticlerical discourse in Andalusia as a form of protest against the perceived alliance of clergy and social elite against less politically and economically powerful segments of society. Breton anticlericalism also has much to do with class-based resentment against the social power of the priest. In the Monts d'Arrée area of interior Brittany this resentment is fuelled by the fact that the majority of priests come from another Breton subregion that is renowned both for its piety and its wealth. Even when the priest is a "local boy," however, as in the cases documented by Behar for the León, his education and lack of participation in the manual agricultural labor that forms the backbone of the peasant economy and life style have, until recently, set the priest off from the majority of his parishioners and marked him as a member of the elite classes.

In Salazarist Portugal and Franco's Spain anticlerical sentiments developed in reaction to the intimate symbiosis between church and state, which enhanced the secular authority of parish priests and increased their ties to the social establishment. Writing of Portugal, Cutileiro (1971:265–268) notes that prior to the Salazar regime, during the Republican period, a form of ideologically motivated anticlericalism developed among urban intellectuals who challenged the legitimacy of religion and criticized the church as an institution. Cutileiro contrasts this "elite" anticlericalism with the nonideological anticlericalism he observed in rural Portugal during the 1960s. Such popular or "peasant" anticlericalism included "pious" criticism of individual priests that did not challenge religious doctrines or question the validity of the church as an institution. Cutileiro associates this "pious" anticlericalism with women, claiming that male popular anticlericalism tends to be more secular or antireligious in character. It is probably unwise to regard Cutileiro's categories as rigidly distinct. As Riegelhaupt (1984:97, 110) observes, in the Portuguese Estremadura differences between men's and women's anticlericalism are less pronounced than in the Alentejo of southern Portugal where Cutileiro worked. Likewise, the dichotomy between elite and popular anticlericalism may not exist in all parts of Europe and may assume different modalities in different historical periods. For example, Brandes (1980), Gilmore (1984), and in the present volume, Behar and Badone, describe situations in which popular anticlericalism is just as politically conscious as that of urban intellectuals. Moreover, in formulating a category of popular anticlericalism we re-create the distinction between the elite as spiritual or intellectual "thinkers" and the folk as practically oriented "doers" that has already proved problematic in the concept of popular religion.

The relationship between gender and religious practice is another key area of concern in anthropological writing on European Catholicism and Orthodoxy. In the present volume these issues are raised in the chapters by Dubisch and Badone. Elsewhere Brandes has proposed a psychoanalytic account of male alienation from the church, suggesting that while Catholicism provides support for Mediterranean cultural norms regarding female sexual purity, the church's stance on sexuality radically conflicts with the local construction of male gender, which prescribes the unrestricted expression of sexual passion (Brandes 1980:179–185). In a similar vein Christian (1972) has argued that Catholic imagery simultaneously reinforces women's preoccupation with sin and purification, while bolstering a male-dominated pattern of gender relations and providing consolation for women within that system.

Ireland presents a marked contrast with southern Europe in terms of male support for the church. Likewise, the kind of class-based anticlericalism that exists both in the Mediterranean and in Brittany is conspicuous by its absence in Ireland. Here, as Taylor points out in Chapter 7, the social dynamic is different. Where the holders of political power and economic privilege are members of a different ethnic and religious group—Anglo-Protestants—the priest's interests are likely to be identified with those of his parishioners by virtue of their common Catholicism. In an earlier paper Taylor (1985) has shown how in Irish folklore the supernatural powers of priests are used to champion the cause of the poor against the large Protestant landowners seeking to introduce a rationalized, capitalistic pattern of economic production. Somewhat paradoxically, given the rationalizing impetus of the Counter-Reformation, these "heroic" Irish priests are depicted as upholding the equity-conscious reciprocal ethic of the "folk" against the rational ethic of accumulation held by Protestant outsiders.

For Schneider the basic contrast between popular and learned religion is precisely that between the ethical presuppositions of the two systems. Like Di Tota (1981), Schneider sees popular religion as embedded in an economic pattern and set of values that emphasizes reciprocal exchange rather than capitalist accumulation. To some extent the battles for ritual control described by Brettell in this volume and by Riegelhaupt (1973, 1984), Freeman (1968), Pina-Cabral (1986:131), and others for different European contexts revolve around this opposition between ethics of reciprocity or redistribution and accumulation. Recall the critical comments that Riegelhaupt heard in São Miguel, and that are also voiced elsewhere, to the effect that priests treat religion as a "business" (Riegelhaupt 1984:100). As Brettell points out, villagers in the Lanheses region of Portugal fight with the priest over the issue of who will control the funds raised through *festas*.

The same kind of conflict between equity-based and rationalizing ethics, focussing on money as a symbol, is apparent with respect to sacrifice. Citing Sanchis (1983), Brettell notes that the modernizing clergy in Portugal discourage *promessas* or vows involving physical mortification in favor of monetary donations. Likewise, in Lanheses the priest encourages Easter donations of cash rather than the traditional *folar* or offering of eggs to the church. As Schneider points out, the concern of the church is to promote a spiritualized conception of the divine-human relationship instead of one based on reciprocal social ties. In giving a cash donation to the church one sacrifices the possibility of using that cash to purchase pleasurable goods, thus "spiritualiz[ing] the self in the name of world rejection" (Schneider, Chapter 2). No reciprocal social contract is implied in this type of relationship with a God who is far removed from the human domain. In contrast, the older form of *promessa* derives its logic from the "tit-for-tat" ethic: one gives in the expectation of, or with thanks for, a counterprestation.

The idea that one contracts social relationships based on reciprocity with humanlike divine personages is central to religion in Santa María del Monte, as Behar's subtle analysis in Chapter 4 shows. Here the concept of individual salvation, promoted by the church since Trent, is less important than " 'recompensation,' a notion of exchange or reciprocity." One will be recompensated in the afterlife for regular attendance at mass during one's earthly existence, for example. Likewise, blasphemy and profanation reap their recompensation of divine punishment. The consciousness of equity that underlies this notion of recompensation is abundantly clear.

Throughout Catholic Europe and Latin America the vow or promise is the primary means whereby individuals can establish a reciprocal relationship with divine figures (Christian 1972). Through vows individuals bind themselves to particular personal patron saints, whose aid is invoked during times of need and with whom a special spiritual relationship is maintained (Christian 1972). Analyzing this phenomenon of supernatural patronage, Boissevain (1977) has linked it to social-structural conditions favoring the development of patron-client relationships in the natural domain of this-worldly social interaction. Di Tota (1981) takes a slightly different position, arguing that supernatural patronage should be viewed as a metaphor for the patron-client system rather than as a simple reflection of it. Interaction with both human and saintly patrons is predicated on expectations of reciprocity, but the character of the two kinds of relationship differs (Di Tota 1981:328).

The vow also plays a central part in Greek Orthodoxy, as Dubisch's paper demonstrates. In the specific case that she describes, the act of pilgrimage serves in itself as the fulfillment of a vow. One presents oneself as an offering to a divine figure—in this case, the *Panayía*, or Madonna—to obtain aid or a cure from physical or spiritual disabilities. The act of pilgrimage can be supplemented by physical mortification, such as walking barefoot or crawling to the shrine on one's knees. Here the penitential or purificatory aspect of the vow that Christian has identified is apparent. Describing vows undertaken in the Nansa valley of Spain, he concludes:

> At first glance it might seem that promises were strictly instrumental, but from
> my experience and observation it has often seemed that they partook in their

most public manifestations of a sense of guilt: the self-imposed obligations were undertaken not merely to repay God for some favor he had granted, but also because either the person was unworthy of having the favor granted in the first place or the unhappy situation that called forth the promise might itself have been a punishment from God that one was called upon to suffer. In the latter case the mortification involved in the promise could be seen as a suggested substitution for a divinely ordained misfortune (Christian 1972:166).

Popular religion in the Greek Orthodox context clearly shares many of the concerns of popular Catholicism, including the importance accorded to pilgrimage and vows. However, it is highly significant that the Reformation and Counter-Reformation made little impact on Greece, and the Greek Orthodox church never developed an equivalent reform movement of its own.[7] Religion in Greece thus escaped the rationalizing impetus that affected Catholicism from the sixteenth century. For this reason, as one observer of Greek religion has noted, the fusion of official and popular religion in Greece is much more complete than in Catholic Europe. Beliefs and practices that would be considered "superstitious" in a more disenchanted Catholic context are easily integrated into the formal structure of the Greek Orthodox church (Kokosalakis 1987; see also Ware 1963:275–279).

The complementary synthesis that arises from the dialectical interplay between popular and official devotions, aptly delineated in Dubisch's analysis, may be even more evident in Greece than in Catholic Europe because of the absence of the Counter-Reformation tradition. As Dubisch notes, the shrine on Tinos she describes is neither identified exclusively with the official nor with the popular religious system. Rather, it pertains to both. The official sacred site serves as a focus for individual religious expression, which takes place independently of official direction or control.

At the shrine individual actors creatively manipulate the symbols and ritual practices of an official setting to achieve meaningful solutions to their particular spiritual dilemmas. This style of religious expression, while certainly not absent in Catholic Europe, is perhaps more characteristic of Greek Orthodoxy, where the relationship between the believer and the church has always been a flexible one. Lacking the legalistic approach to religious practice and belief epitomized in Catholic doctrine and canon law, the Greek Orthodox church allows lay persons a wide margin of autonomy with respect to requirements for participation in formal church ritual. Morality is considered to be the personal responsibility of each individual and while "the reciprocal relationship between the individual and the institution takes place in the context of a framework of rules and principles, . . . it is up to the individual to follow them" (Kokosalakis 1987:42; see also Ware 1963:275–276). This relative fluidity provides scope for the individual Greek Orthodox believer to define and control his or her particular religious experience, as do the pilgrims on Tinos.

In Dubisch's paper the emergent quality of popular religion is emphasized. Rather than something static, locked in a dichotomous relationship with the formal church, popular religion is negotiated anew by each pilgrim in the official context of the shrine. Dubisch's analysis thus complements Behar's emphasis on the circular quality of the relationship between official and informal religion. Church and people need not be viewed as two homogeneous and isolated bodies, one of which "asserts" while the other "resists."[8]

In Chapter 6 and Chapter 7 the focus of the collection moves from southern to northern Europe. The Monts d'Arrée region of interior Brittany shares certain features in common with the popular Catholicism of the Mediterranean, such as its anticlericalism and male antipathy to the church. However, most other parts of Brittany, especially the Léon region to the north of the Monts d'Arrée, resemble more closely Taylor's Irish case, especially in terms of high levels of regular religious practice by both men and women.

The Irish and Breton churches have close historical links and followed similar patterns of development during the formative era of the sixth century. Important contacts were maintained between monastic institutions in Brittany and the British Isles. A number of the saints credited with the widespread propagation of Christianity in Brittany emigrated to Brittany from the British Isles. Some of these saints had Irish connections, and several local saints from Ireland are venerated in Brittany (Chadwick 1969:238–291, see especially pp. 251, 259, 263, 267). Catholicism in both regions has integrated elements of pre-Christian, possibly Celtic, religious traditions (Croix 1981; MacNeill 1962; Melia 1978). Despite their local distinctiveness, however, both Brittany and Ireland share with the Mediterranean the veneration for natural features of the landscape associated with the sacred, such as springs or holy wells and mountain or hilltop pilgrimage sites.

As Taylor points out, following Larkin (1972), the devotional revolution of the mid-nineteenth century fundamentally transformed the character of Irish Catholicism, entrenching the hegemony of the church and contributing to the rationalization of religion. Likewise, since the devotional revolution the church in Ireland has followed a "civilizing" agenda, campaigning to suppress uncontrolled drunkenness, violence, and sexuality. Integrating Freudian and Weberian perspectives, Taylor's paper focusses on the metaphor of control in Irish legends about drunken priests. Whereas priests and parishioners vie for control of rituals in southern Europe, in the Irish context the issue of control is most prominent in the

psychological realm. From one perspective the drunken priests who figure in the legends Taylor recounts can be interpreted as metaphors for
the libido when it escapes from the internalized moral dictums of the
church. Yet the drunken priest has special supernatural powers both to
bless and to curse precisely because he has been "silenced" or barred
from performing his sacerdotal functions within the official church structure. Clearly, institutionalized religion does not have a monopoly on
grace, but it is just such claims for the possibility of achieving grace outside the official sacramental channels that contribute to the tension between orthodoxy and popular faith.[9]

In Ireland the unorthodox supernatural powers of drunken priests are
used primarily for the benefit of ordinary people, except when they
thwart the priests' quests for intoxicating liquor. Like these Irish clerics
and the *bruxo* priests of northwestern Portugal described by Pina-Cabral
(1986:201–202), Breton priests can also serve on occasion as *guérisseurs*,
healers and unwitchers. Most frequently, however, at least in folk narratives from the Monts d'Arrée, the magical abilities of the priest are
directed against his parishioners, especially the anticlerical or those too
poor to contribute financially to the church. In the Monts d'Arrée, rather
than deriving supernatural power from their own drunkenness, priests
have the reputation of working harmful magic to punish others who drink
to excess.

Since the 1960s the traditionalist character of popular religion in Catholic Europe has opposed it to the reform movement instituted by the
Second Vatican Council. Outlined in detail in Behar's chapter, the Vatican II reforms have attempted to promote a style of religious expression
in which ritual and mystery are deemphasized in favor of an ethically
oriented, human-centered, and spiritualized type of faith. However, as
in the Port Marly case there have been many popular demands throughout Europe for a return to the older ritual forms (see Brandes 1976). In
the present volume Behar and Brettell record expressions of dismay and
discontent about the post-Vatican II liturgy from Spanish and Portuguese
contexts. Likewise, in Catholic Dutch Brabant, Bax (1983, 1985b, 1987,
1988) shows how the popular desire for traditional ceremonies has intensified competition between religious regimes, with the monastic clergy
responding to local needs by providing a traditional style of ritual that the
reformist parish clergy disparage. Bax's work is particularly helpful in
highlighting the fact that the church establishment is not a monolithic
entity presenting a united front to the laity.

The kinds of divisions within the ecclesiastical domain that Bax describes are not restricted to Holland. In Switzerland and France, as well
as in other countries outside of Europe, the Integrist movement led by
Archbishop Marcel Lefebvre has challenged both the changes set in motion by Vatican II and papal authority to implement these reforms. Le-

febvre and his followers refuse to accept the liturgical innovations of Vatican II, including the substitution of vernacular languages for Latin in the mass. Lefebvre also rejects the doctrinal reforms adopted by the church after Vatican II, particularly those concerning ecumenism, the right to religious liberty, and collegiality, or the concept that the church is not directed uniquely by the Pope but by all of its bishops under his leadership. Lefebvre castigates these developments as compromises with modernism and the false teachings of other faiths. Although prohibited since 1976 from performing mass or administering the sacraments, Lefebvre has attracted a worldwide following among conservative Catholics. However, his movement is strongest in his native France, where it appeals to parishioners like those in Port Marly and where it is also frequently linked with an extreme right-wing political stance. In June 1988 Lefebvre was excommunicated by the Vatican, after he defied Pope John Paul II's authority and ordained four new traditionalist bishops to provide ongoing leadership for the Integrist movement. A formal schism has thus taken place between Lefebvre and the Vatican. Along with his new bishops he is no longer considered part of the Roman Catholic church. Although such schisms have occurred previously in the history of Catholicism, the most notable being the separation of the Eastern Orthodox church, Lefebvre's schism is the first to develop since 1870 (Greenhouse 1988; Grelot 1988; Steinfels 1988).

As Lefebvre's break with the Vatican indicates, division and conflict exist within the ecclesiastical hierarchy as well as between the hierarchy and lay persons. Attitudes toward social policy as well as questions of ritual can also provoke dissension among clerics, as the contemporary debate within the church over liberation theology illustrates. Developed in Latin America and influenced by Marxism, liberation theology contests the established social order and seeks to free the poor from economic and spiritual oppression. In contrast to Lefebvre, proponents of liberation theology are more, instead of less, radically reform-minded than the Vatican, and aspects of liberation theology have been severely criticized by Vatican officials.[10] In the anthropological literature on Europe Kertzer's (1980) study of a Bolognese parish depicts a conflict similar to the controversy surrounding liberation theology. Here both an activist Catholic youth group and a socially radical young "storefront priest" seeking to ameliorate living conditions among the poor found themselves ostracized by the more conservative parish clergy (Kertzer 1980:186–210).

AREAS FOR FURTHER RESEARCH

Kertzer's study, which juxtaposes and contrasts the Catholic and Communist world views in Bologna, is virtually unique in its urban focus.

While stressing the continuing need to understand the religious life of rural European communities, the authors of the present volume recognize the importance of future fieldwork on religion in urban contexts. Pina-Cabral (1986:191–192, 212–213) has started to fill in the gaps in our knowledge of popular religion in urban Europe with his work on herbalism, parapsychology, and "white witches" in the towns and cities of northwestern Portugal. More research is needed, however, on urban phenomena such as charismatic cults in Italian cities, urban Catholic "base communities" promoting social reform, and the relationship between Catholicism and non-Catholic belief systems concerning the occult (Lanternari 1982:126, 131–132).

Most of the work by anthropologists on popular religion in Europe has focussed on Catholicism and Eastern Orthodoxy rather than Protestantism. The more highly developed processes of rationalization and disenchantment in Protestant contexts have narrowed the gap between official and popular styles of religious expression. Conflict between Protestant ministers and their congregations is less pronounced than in Catholic settings, although Verrips (1973) has examined a case of this kind of tension in rural Holland. One of the few studies of Protestant popular belief is Clark's (1982) *Between Pulpit and Pew*, which explores Methodist folk religion in a Yorkshire fishing village. In southwestern Germany the relationships among religion, socioeconomic change, and attitudes toward agricultural modernization have been compared in neighboring Protestant and Catholic communities by Golde (1975). Gaines' (1985) research on contrasting aesthetic styles and patterns of family organization among Protestants and Catholics in Strasbourg is motivated by a similar concern to elucidate the connections between religious beliefs and social action. Focussing on the Scottish border region, Neville has examined the ongoing significance of Catholic symbols transferred from the religious domain to that of secular ritual in a region that has been nominally Protestant for over four hundred years (Neville 1987; see also Neville 1979, 1980). Other research on Protestant groups in Scotland has been carried out by Borker (1978, 1986), Maltz (1978, 1985), and Nadel (1986). Stromberg (1981, 1986) has examined religious symbols, individualism, and notions of community among Swedish Protestants. In urban Sicily Cucchiari (1987, 1988) has studied non-Catholic Pentecostalists, giving special attention to gender relationships and the conversion experience. Additionally, a number of works, notably those of Obelkevich (1976) and Moore (1974), have focussed on British Protestantism in historical contexts.

Despite the clear parallels between the Protestant Reformation and the Catholic Counter-Reformation, the Protestant world represents a different religious field with its own set of problems. By focussing exclusively on Catholic and Orthodox Christianity in Europe, the authors of this volume have sought to emphasize the common threads uniting these religious traditions. Clearly, in a single collection of essays it is impossible to do justice to the complexity of regional differences in religious expression, and particularly for Eastern Orthodoxy, our book must be read in the context of other important studies on Greece by Campbell (1964, 1966), Danforth and Tsiaras (1982) and du Boulay (1974, 1982, 1984), and by Kligman (1988) on Romania. It is to be hoped that others will be inspired by the present work to publish comparable volumes on other aspects of European popular religion, especially in Protestant cultures. In addition, much interesting work remains to be done on popular Judaism in Europe, building on research by Kokosalakis (1982), Moore (1976), Trachtenberg (1977), and Weissler (1987a, 1987b).

In Catholic Europe, despite the diversity of regional religious styles and the existence of conflicts that divide members of the church hierarchy from one another and oppose clerics to lay parishioners, the church represents a common bond of unity. Whatever their disagreements, Catholics in both rural and urban Europe continue to see themselves as part of a single, overarching religious tradition. The work of Joyce Riegelhaupt has made it abundantly clear that even those who challenge the church do so in terms of its own moral discourse. Riegelhaupt focussed on a specific Portuguese context, but as the papers by Behar, Brettell, and Badone in this volume suggest, such attitudes are widespread. Catholics in rural Europe may criticize the church, they may refrain from participation in regular religious observances, but they remain Catholics in essence. Newer evangelizing religions such as the Jehovah's Witnesses have discovered that, at least in many parts of rural Europe, to be religious is synonymous with being Catholic. In fact, it might be said that at least until recently to be fully human has also meant being Catholic (see Brandes 1975:159).[11] In the face of local religious variation the Catholic church acts as a potent symbol of order and unity. Ecumenical efforts inspired by Vatican II indicate that even the historical schism between Roman Catholicism and Eastern Orthodoxy does not preclude the possibility of a *rapprochement* (Kilmartin 1979; Ware 1963:321–324). Together the two churches represent the longest-lasting institutions of European society. For nearly two thousand years they have served to convey, not without some reshaping, a particular cultural system and world view. Over the centuries their ability to integrate local models and symbols of "religion as practiced" into the larger structures of "religion as prescribed" has surely been a key to their coherence, durability, and power.

Notes to Chapter 1

I am indebted to all the participants in this volume for helpful comments during preparation of this Introduction. Special thanks are extented to Ruth Behar and Caroline Brettell as well as to Gérard Vallée of the Department of Religious Studies at McMaster University, all of whom offered detailed and stimulating suggestions on earlier versions of this chapter. I am also grateful to Stephen Jones for his clear judgment, sound advice, and technical expertise with word-processing. A grant from the Arts Research Board at McMaster University helped to cover research costs associated with this project.

1. See Ortner (1973).

2. To note but a few; it is impossible in the present context to survey the vast quantity of valuable historical research on popular religion undertaken in France during the twentieth century.

3. The similarities and differences between ethnographic research and historical studies based on Inquisitorial sources are discussed by Carlo Ginzburg (1989).

4. See Devlin (1987:6–21) for an example of this approach.

5. For discussions of witchcraft, evil eye beliefs, and supernatural curing see Christian (1972:191–194), Cutileiro (1971), Pina-Cabral (1986:174–213), and Pitt-Rivers (1954). Omens of death are described by Danforth and Tsiaras (1982:15), Douglass (1969:19–20), Pina-Cabral (1986:217–218), and Badone (1989).

6. Geertz (1975:72).

7. More generally, the historical development of Eastern Orthodoxy as a whole differs markedly from that of Western Christianity because of the absence in the East of movements comparable to the Reformation and Counter-Reformation (Ware 1963:9; see also Benz 1963:53).

8. Dubisch suggests that the close association of the Greek Orthodox church with Greek national identity in a patriotic sense has also contributed to the close interpenetration of official and popular religion in Greece (personal communication, April 4, 1988).

9. In this connection see Christian (1984, 1987a), Kselman (1983), and Brettell (this volume).

10. For an overview of liberation theology and its relationship to the Vatican see the works of Boff (1985), Gutiérrez (1973), and Segundo (1976, 1985), among others.

11. Likewise, as Dubisch points out, to be truly Greek is to be Greek Orthodox (personal communication, April 4, 1988).

CHAPTER 2

Spirits and the Spirit of Capitalism

Jane Schneider

THROUGH a succession of reform movements, of which the Protestant Reformation was but the most thorough, literate clerics and preachers of Western Christianity progressively demonized European peasant animism, assimilating beliefs in earth spirits and spirits of the dead to a concept of ontological evil and then, after the Enlightenment, denying the existence of these spirits altogether. Western social scientists, themselves a product of this centuries-long process of disenchantment, give us two competing accounts of the peasant culture that fell victim to the trend. On one side is a romantic folk model that emphasizes homogeneity, an ahistorical traditionalism, the permeation of everyday life by the sacred, and the subordination of individuals to the community. Negative images stress superstition and idolatry—the "idiocy" of rural life.

Both views of generic peasantry, the romantic and the ridiculous, attribute fundamentally different modes of thought to folk and official religion. In both, peasants are held to dwell on magical solutions to the practical problems of health and good fortune, whereas religious officials engage in theological and philosophical reflection. These caricatures, as pervasive as they are inaccurate, distort our ability to think clearly about the relationship of reformist Christianity to the rise of capitalism—a big question, given their coincidence in time and space, yet one that is often reduced to a trivial debate over which came first, religion or economy. Arguing for an alternative understanding of animistic religion, this essay asks how its marginalization at the hands of Christian reformers interacted with the breakthrough to capitalist forces and relations of production.

The understanding of animism that I propose depicts peasants as no less reflective than the learned religious specialists who tried to reform them. The point is to appreciate what they were reflective about. Ethnographic studies of small-scale societies provide a clue: beliefs in earth spirits and spirits of the dead betray a philosophical concern with the cosmos—its forces for good and evil—and with equity—the reciprocity of give and take in spiritual as well as actual social relations. I have, quite frankly, used this clue to imagine a past for European peasants, much as the early evolutionists used ethnographic knowledge of the Iroquois to imagine ancient society. Like Henry Maine, however, I distrust ideas of a first "stage" or "primordial base line" and attempt to ascertain historical developments—"verifiable . . . sequences of cause and effect"—where possible (see Stocking 1987:167–185; Schmitt 1983:8).

Fortunately, a growing band of anthropologically minded historians has generated a body of case material on the interactions between learned and popular religion in Europe from the thirteenth through the eighteenth centuries. Scholars of the *Annales* school in France such as Jacques Le Goff and Jean-Claude Schmitt are important contributors, as are participants in the school of *microstoria* in Italy, for example Carlo Ginzburg and Giovanni Levi. At university centers in Scandinavia and Eastern Europe there are such historians of folklore as Gustav Henningsen and Gabor Klaniczay. A historical anthropologist, Thomas Hauschild, is rethinking popular religion in West Germany as are the historians Peter Burke and John Bossy in England and Natalie Davis in the United States. These scholars depart from Keith Thomas, whose earlier portrait of "the decline of magic" in Europe neglected to consider the simultaneous emergence of magical beliefs as a stigmatized, hence distorted, category (see Geertz 1975:76; Davis 1974). They have also produced evidence that peasants thought reflectively about cosmic meanings and the ethics of their relationships with spirits.

It is my thesis that the peasants' world view made them cautious about the exploitation of both natural and human resources, whereas the Christian reformers, committed to an ethic of brotherly love and a belief in providence, de-emphasized personal accountability in these regards. To the extent that lay populations internalized the reformers' outlook, the moral climate for the expansion of capitalism improved. This is not to imply a foundation for capitalism in religious reform. That foundation lay in the explosive urban and commercial development of the corridors linking the Mediterranean to the Low Countries and southeastern England beginning in the Middle Ages. Significantly, the dynamism of these corridors also underlay wave after wave of religious reform, from the medieval "heresies" of the Albigensians, Waldensians, and so on, through the coopted mendicant orders of the Dominicans and Franciscans, to the various strains of Protestantism and the Counter-Reformation. Like capitalism, these movements all gained their momentum from this urbanizing, commercializing source.

But if the prophets of reform shared a historical trajectory with capitalism, they were rarely themselves motivated by economic "interests." On the contrary, reformers characteristically decried accumulations of wealth in the hands of princes, aristocrats, bishops, and monks. Most of them voluntarily embraced the poverty of Jesus as indicative of a higher spiritual state. Most were also preoccupied with demonstrating their faith in a world-rejecting, providential deity through various forms of frugality and restraint. Nevertheless, the reformers' particular solution to the moral dilemmas arising from social differentiation, rootlessness, the corrosiveness of money, and the growth of cities differed from solutions implied by animism, and differed in ways that—I argue—favored capitalist expansion. Propelling religious specialists into the surrounding countryside, the urban-based reform movements exposed Western Europe's rural populations to a strong pulse of transformative energy at the same time that commodity markets and a tempting new materialism penetrated their villages. The question of which came first, economic or religious change, is obviated by a centuries-long interaction between urbanism, markets, and religious reform.

Obviously, this effort to relate the decline of magic to the rise of capitalism owes much to Max Weber, who compared religions in terms of precisely their ethical systems and the associated psychological sanctions that shape moral behavior and social action. Weber also emphasized the autonomy of religious reformers from economic motivation while at the same time attributing to their dogmas certain inexorable (if unintended) consequences for the accumulation of wealth and the division of labor. Best known for tracing this paradox in relation to the Calvinist and Puritan work ethic, he showed how believers, in their restless search for religious justification, committed themselves to a "this-worldly" asceticism that made them rich and acquisitive almost in spite of themselves. Here I concentrate on another of his concerns, the rationalizing "disenchantment" of the world whereby people presumably stopped acting on beliefs in earth spirits and ghosts.

Spirits and ghosts are not necessarily incompatible with capitalism. On the contrary, capitalist expansion in the nineteenth and twentieth centuries has in some instances intensified animistic practice, multiplying the resources available for spirit cults. On the eve of capitalism in the sixteenth and seventeenth centuries, however, reformist attempts to suppress spirits, their human interlocutors and devotees, took the form of a great witch-hunt that was sometimes unrelenting in its violence. I fall short of proposing an impact of witch-hunting on peasant consciousness that was independent of an already unfolding transformation of village life by processes of commoditization, and I fully acknowledge the conclusion of many historians that the overall results were superficial. Yet I also suggest that in villages that were proximal to the corridors of commercial expansion the extirpation of witches was morally propitious for the subsequent massive accumulation of capital in private, entrepreneurial hands, the enclosure movements that excluded multiple users from property, and the legislative unfettering of the forces and relations of production. In retrospect one wonders if the pioneers of these changes could have cultivated their self-confident "spirit of capitalism" had an ethical system based on equitable exchanges with nature, the dead, and fellow humans remained institutionalized on the local level, not experiencing the vigorous competition of the reformers' alternative guidelines for moral practice.

In *The Protestant Ethic and the Spirit of Capitalism* Weber cynically queried whether the "tremendous development" of rational capitalism, by then an "iron cage" devoid of religious meaning, would eventually run its course, giving rise to new prophets or a "great rebirth of old ideas and ideals" (1958a:181–182). My account is shaped by less pessimistic anthropological sources: Mart Bax's (1987) description of Christianity as a "regime" with competing centers of economic and political power, and ethnographic research on local religion—especially the work of William Christian (1972, 1984, 1987a), Joyce Riegelhaupt (1973, 1984), and the contributors to this volume. These sources show that, contrary to Weber, the pulse of reform was neither unidirectional nor all that efficacious. Indeed, some of the most interesting questions in Europe's religious history concern the syncretic transformations of offical doctrine by local belief and practice, the inconsistent hegemonies of mystical and scholastic Catholicism, and the continued appearance, even within Protestantism, of renewed projects of disenchantment because older projects had failed. Cognizant of the reverse flows of energy from "periphery" to core, and of the contradictions within the core, I make my case for genuine culture change relevant to the rise of capitalism only in relation to circumscribed times and places, and only with the caveat that the change could be resisted and undermined.

THE ETHICS OF ANIMISM

Following anthropologists' usage, I think of animism as a set of beliefs and associated rituals according to which the world is permeated by the ghosts and ancestors of humans and animals and by humanlike spirits that dwell in the objects and forces of the earth. Considered real, these spiritual essences interact and communicate with each other and with humans (see Guthrie 1980). Not relegated to a transcendental, "supernatural" order, they participate in the daily life of kinship groups and small communities. Weber argued that a social ethic of reciprocity governs relations within such units, promoting the behavioral characteristics of support in distress, generous hospitality, loans without interest, fulfillment of obligations, and an "in-group, out-group morality" (1958b:329–330). At stake is the "very general need" that "the fortunate is seldom satisfied with the fact of being fortunate [but] needs to know that he has a *right* to his good fortune. He wants to be convinced that he 'deserves' it, and above all that he deserves it in comparison with others. . . . Good fortune . . . wants to be 'legitimate' " (Weber 1958b:271). Bound by this ethic, the members of small communities anticipate spiritual danger from "overstepping" their legitimate bounds, the more so when they entertain the existence of a world animated by spirits.

Various anthropologists have addressed the social psychology of overstepping. Hauschild reminds us of Freud's dictum that possession of something precious means fearing the envy of others. Following Freud and Schoeck, he locates the roots of envy in the childhood rivalry of siblings or agemates for the affections and goods of adults, the fundamental narcissism of each developing into an intense concern with equity as they mature. The result is a universal psychological " 'wish' for regulated anarchy that, unless modified by competing ideas, makes humans both jealous of what they have and expectant of envy in others" (1982:81). Tracing suspicion of evil eye in an Indian village, Pocock discovered it to be most intense among near equals (that is within, but not across, castes) and in people whose greed, vanity, or stingy feelings prevented them from enjoying good fortune without anxiety (1973:25–41).

In his study of the Sidamo of Ethiopia Jan Brögger relies on the term "hubris" to capture "the suspicion that we really have received more than our fair share" and cognitively appreciate "the transactional nature of our relationships both to each other and to nature" (1986:16–17). According to Beidelman, the East African Kaguru believe that "the public iteration of adversity [is] a way to avert it. Conversely, mentioning good fortune is often a sure way of losing it" (1986:97). Evan Zuesse, a scholar of African religions, proposes that empathy leads humans not only to consider others' suffering but to fear "their necessarily mysterious power to endure and assert their own independent existence. . . ." Both resentment and bad conscience or "attributed resentment" have spiritual implications (1985:227–231).

I would like to suggest that animism encourages an exaggerated sensitivity to the predicament of anyone, human or spirit, who is pushed aside or marginalized by productive and reproductive activity. This does not mean that believers would, out of empathy, refrain from getting ahead in the world, even at the expense of others. To the degree that they worry about equity, however, we see them looking over their shoulders as they seek health and good fortune, honor and possessions, for themselves and their families. For it is important to conciliate those who are left behind. Indicative of this realization is the practice of wearing amulets against "evil eye" and the staging of threshold rituals in which moments of advancement such as the opening of a business or the celebration of a marriage are marked by expansive distributions to spirits, neighbors, and kin.

Regarding spirits, two categories—those of the earth and those of the dead—seem consistently enmeshed in the animistic politics of sensitivity to grievance. Significantly, both kinds of spirit have a claim to being "prior inhabitants" who perhaps were pushed aside. My evidence with regard to earth spirits consists in the humble or cautious pose that so many peoples adopt vis-à-vis the natural resources of their environment. It is not that they hold back from harnessing these resources, even on an expanding scale. Reflective about what they are doing, however, they may ask the permission of a tree before felling it, or perform a small ritual of propitiation and respect lest its justly offended spirit come back to haunt them. Hallowell's famous interpretation of Chippewa bear cere-monialism illustrates the same ethic in relation to animals: bears are ob-jects of worshipful respect precisely because they are prey. Bear hunters, he records, apologized to these "other-than-human 'persons' " as they coaxed them out of their dens in the spring to kill them (1960:35; see also Eliade 1964).

Just as rituals of propitiation and the observance of respectful taboos kept the spirits of bears at bay for the Chippewa, cultivators of rice offer food to field spirits at the time of sowing to neutralize the spirits' displea-sure at having to make room for the crop. Again, believers acknowledge prior habitation. According to the "colonization" myth of Javanese peas-ants, the carriers of rice cultivation into Southeast Asia flushed numerous spirits out of the landscape as they deforested it. Some of these spirits were banished to volcanic craters or the floor of the Indian Ocean, but others, presumably more tractable, remained to perpetuate a claim. "The picture," suggests Geertz, "is one of an incoming flow of migrants push-ing back the harmful spirits, . . . all the while adopting some of the more helpful ones as protectors of themselves and their new settlements." En-gaged in a reciprocal exchange with the latter, peasants offer them the aroma of desired foods on ritual occasions (1960:16–29).

I am reluctant to cite Frazer because he so radically separated the en-lightened thought of elites from the superstitions of the folk. Yet *The Golden Bough* relates magic to the ethical dilemmas of the "savage" who, believing himself "exposed," does not hunt prey without "making excuses to it and begging that the animals would not take it ill" (1963:600–603). The same ethic applies to "the vermin that infest his crops and his cattle." Estonian peasants, Frazer tells us, "stand in great awe of the weevil . . . even put [it] under a stone in the field and offer corn to it. They think that thus it is appeased and does less harm" (Frazer 1963:614). Lynn White, the historian of Western technology, once saw Asian road builders leave cones of earth undisturbed "until the snakes that inhabited them went away of their own accord" (Spring and Spring 1974:4). The experience prompted his 1974 essay, "The Roots of our Ecological Crisis," in which he laments the Christian idea that "the Lord gave man control over the beasts of the field" (White 1974).

Ideas about snakes and serpents seem to me especially diagnostic of an ethical outlook in relation to the earth and its spirits. The Dinka ethnographer Francis Mading Deng notes that among his people snakes "often symbolize clan spirits to be respected and protected as relatives." His grandfather rescued dangerous snakes from the clumsy feet of grazing cattle, patting them as he released them into the wilderness. Deng's Christianized brothers had a different outlook, one that vilified snakes. When one of these brothers killed a puff adder near their mother's house and several sisters fell ill, a diviner attributed the misfortune to the curse of the murdered snake (1972:124–125; see also van Velzen and van Wetering 1982:48–49). Weston La Barre's (1969) ethnography of a southern United States snake handling cult points to a similar contrast. Although the members of this cult fondled poisonous snakes, it was to prove that through faith one can overcome evil. In their Christianized interpretation of the ritual, the writhing creatures were thoroughly demonic. In contrast, in the snake cults of Asia and Africa, catalogued by La Barre, serpents are propitiated and encouraged to grow.

From La Barre's survey we discover that cattle-keeping peoples frequently offer milk, the product of cows, to snakes notwithstanding that, by zoologists' reckoning, snakes refuse this beverage even when deprived of water (La Barre 1969:94–96, 186, 193n). In Deng's ethnography not only did the grandfather protect adders from being crushed by cattle; he gave them butter to lick (1972:124–125). A belief system that characterizes snakes as prior inhabitants, victimized by grazing bovines and deserving of their output, can coexist, and has for centuries, with the incremental expansion of humans, their crops, and livestock. But it stands in the way of ranching and other large-scale enterprises on private land. Consistent with a respectful stance toward nonhuman life forms, Asian mythology fuses the water-giving serpent with the life-giving bird, producing a beneficent winged, reptilian dragon, the guardian of emperors and kings. To Europeans the same creature spelled destruction and evil, the chaos of untamed nature, such that their heroes, saints, and conquerors gained mystical power by slaying it.

Seeking reciprocity from displaced serpents is not qualitatively different from maintaining ongoing social relations with dead kin and neighbors. Ritual acts of propitiation, conciliation, and communication acknowledge the past contributions of the dead and assuage their longing, their wish to remain engaged. Such acts also show concern that the dead might resent the living, particularly those who died before their time. To take but one of many revealing examples, Cantonese ghosts return in seances at which mediums interpret their demands. Potter (1974:208–

210) describes the returning ghost of a girl who believed she died because her parents were late in calling a doctor. Angry as well because she was buried in a grave so shallow that dogs got at her body, she harbored the kind of "understandable grievance against the living" that villagers greatly feared. According to Potter, her parents burned silver paper for her twice a month and considered becoming the clients of an especially expensive medium—these being two ways to deflect the ghost's designs on her surviving siblings and the family's financial reserves. Such costly and mentally exhausting acts of ritual contrition cannot help but slow, or episodically deflect, the future-looking projects of the still-alive.

THE ELABORATION AND SUPPRESSION OF EQUITY-CONSCIOUSNESS

The preceding examples of equity-conscious belief and action were drawn from societies as diverse as the Chippewa and Chinese, illustrating the universality of a norm of distributive justice. But the related capacity to sense suffering and attribute resentment gains its fullest religious expression in small-scale, classless societies where spirits are constantly marshalled in support of "fair play." Here, as Collier and Rosaldo (1981) emphasized in their useful overview, people put forth an enormous effort to achieve not dominance but parity and are reluctant to abuse or alienate each other for fear of retaliation or loss of future support. Although inequities exist, not least in the control of spiritual knowledge, it is important to mask them, be generous with goods, avoid the provocation of undue assertion, and conceal any undue wealth. As Zuesse notes, skillful shamans apply the same logic to spirits, respecting their prior autonomy and their claims to a share of human productivity in order to win their support (1985:185).

It is an assumption of this essay that the development of stratified out of classless societies, of states out of "acephalous" polities, was linked to the transformation of this religious modality so that people would spend less energy in anxious prophylaxis, having more left over to organize their existence and exploit their environment on a wider and less equitable scale. In the following paragraphs I briefly compare two paths of transformation: systems like ancestor worship that modify animism, together with its ethic of equity, through an internal elaboration, and the "salvationist" religions that, in theory at least, shatter equity-consciousness from without. Christianity falls into the latter category, but to highlight its radicality I will first sketch the outlines of internal elaboration.

How people think about the spiritual domain, how they conceptualize its powers and processes, is influenced by the world in which they live, even though modern scholarship refutes the early evolutionist schemes that matched social structures to pantheons. Events that intensify suffering in particular encourage philosophical speculation on two cosmic principles broadly associated with bad and good. On the bad side is a set of ideas about mystical and contagious pollution for which humans are not to blame but which they can try to contain through avoidances, precisely executed purification rituals, or sacrifices of expiation upon defilement. Bordering on a notion of evil that transcends moral responsibility, these ideas evoke, as Pocock puts it quoting Hume, the ontological weight of "disinterested malice" (1985:44–46). The converse principle contains ideas about grace, blessing, or "mana"—an equally cosmic flow of force that may, but need not, emanate from a high god (see Durkheim 1965:309–333; Keesing 1982:46–49; Parkin 1985). Belief in cosmic forces outside the universe of human morality raises the possibility of differentiating spirits into some that are primarily protective and caring of the human community and a standard for its improvement and others that, if they do not wish it harm, are at least an untrustworthy and capricious source of chaos (Durkheim 1965:309–333, 455–461; Horton 1962).

In animistic belief systems spirits are humanlike, which is to say ambivalent with regard to good and bad or orderly and disorderly conduct, and this encourages equitable interactions with them. In contrast, the differentiation of benevolent from malevolent spirits—or spirit principles, as when a single essence encompasses both poles—calls equity into question. Each pole at one remove from a balanced reciprocity with humans, the good spirits selflessly promote the prosperity and morality of the people they protect to the neglect of their own well-being, whereas the bad ones are gratuitously unpredictable or mean, hence unworthy of a relationship. Either way, believers are relieved of the obligation of a continuous give and take and can feel justified in the development of a more aggressive stance toward both spirits and each other.

Hence, perhaps, the association of bifurcated spirits with hierarchically organized chiefdoms and kingdoms. Here guardian spirits in the form of ancestors, mythologized heroes, or such forces of nature as the sun and rain, legitimate social ranks, even deifying the rulers, and bless endeavors like cattle keeping and the taking of slaves that have an irreversible impact on "prior inhabitants." To the extent that they approve of human activity ancestors and heroes control capricious earth spirits and may well uphold the male elders of their protectorates in manipulations of these spirits that are aimed at maintaining dominance over women and juniors (e.g., Fortes 1965; Keesing 1982; van Binsbergen 1976; Zuesse 1985). Women and low status men, meanwhile, seem especially vulnerable to possession by demanding spirits who, unlike the autonomous essences of shamanistic practice, can realize themselves only by inhabiting human bodies whose egos they selfishly eclipse (Zuesse 1985:187–191).

Yet, although the differentiated (and often possessing) spirits of hierarchical chiefdoms and kingdoms seem a step removed, in various ways, from humanlike norms of reciprocity, they remain grounded in this world, having evolved from death and from nature. As such they frequently intervene with humanlike demands. So, for example, although the Kuranko call their bad spirits Djinn as if they were truly evil, cordoning them off and dealing with them through avoidances, they also believe that these "spirits of the wild" inhabited their territory before them and have a prior claim. Hence, suggests Jackson (1977), the Kuranko not only avoid but simultaneously propitiate the Djinn, and they do so with the valuable, not the trivial, products of their land and labor. Typically such spirits up the ante in times of crisis, soliciting unprecedented offerings from their collective protectorate or inducing individuals whom they possess to become almost antisocial in fulfilment of their demands. Hard times sharpen feelings of anxiety over neglected obligations, the more so when they follow on expansion and prosperity, juxtaposing boom with bust, intensified production with ecological collapse, military victory with defeat. Indicative are the Yoruba who, in sacrificing to their Orixa, can choose between merely smearing a shrine with the blood and entrails of the offered beast and eating the meat themselves or burying or burning all of it. Diviners point the way, recommending the more costly rite when large groups of people are at risk (Idowu 1962).

In other words, spirit bifurcation and the cultural recognition of spirit possession represent a compromise, but not a break, with the ethic of equity as applied to spirits and humans. Imagining spirits or spirit principles that are, morally speaking, "better" or "worse" than themselves, actors mitigate the inhibiting reciprocities of "purely" animistic interactions, but the parameters of equity-consciousness are not necessarily broken, only stretched. Myths still link spirits to source points in the world, ensuring their fundamentally humanlike potentialities, so that it remains crucial to divine their wishes for remembrance and respect, discover the sources of their displeasure, anticipate and deflect their understandable if terrifying exactions, at least in moments of distress.

I emphasize these elaborations of animism in order to dramatize a contrast with the salvationist religions that charismatic prophets enunciated in the explosively urbanizing Near East of the first millennium B.C. Having as their central characteristic the project of individual redemption in another or afterlife, these religions charted a departure from (not merely an internal modification of) earlier spirit beliefs (see Bellah 1964; Weber 1958b:267–329; Weber 1963:118–137). Good spirits, synthesized as an omniscient and omnipotent supernatural deity or as a pure spirit, were in varying degrees detached from the world, rejecting it as steeped in sin or completely bereft of meaning. In the monotheistic variants of salvationism—Judaism after the prophets (see Donald Taylor 1985), Christianity, and Islam—bad spirits were assimilated to Satan, a distillation of evil. In practice these religions show considerable variation over time and place in their tolerance for human interactions with "prior inhabitants"—a point I explore for Christianity below—but all propose (in contrast to the competing "dualist" theology of the Zoroastrians and "monist" religions of Asia) that God has the upper hand over Satan and should, therefore, be the arbiter of spirit demands (Parkin 1985).

According to Weber, the conceptualization of a supernatural deity encouraged the substitution of a "religious" for a "social" relationship with the spirit domain (1958b:327–330; Parsons 1963). Whereas the social relationship hinges on reciprocal exchanges with humanlike entities, the religious one promotes worship of a distant and less knowable power. The goal of equity gives way to the goal of the religious state of the individual soul, salvation depending not upon giving things to world-derived, world-seeking spirits—meat, prestige crops, money—but upon giving up "things" in order to spiritualize the self in the name of world rejection. Deprivation becomes a "gift of righteousness" in the apt phrase of Raymond Firth (1963), who drew attention to the immaterial characteristic of prayer and good behavior as compared with the materiality of animistic sacrifice. But refraining from delicious pleasures—from the "naive enjoyment of the goods of this earth"—was not for everyone (as Weber emphasized), and the salvationist religions readily spawned spiritual elites of ascetically devoted "virtuosi" (1958b:275, 287).

The distinction between a "social" and a "religious" interaction with the spiritual domain is easily exaggerated, with the result that the terms become proxies for the misleading opposition of (practical) magic to (reflective) religion. Rites of propitiation, expiation, abstention, and communion in fact coexist in all religions (Horton 1960). More significant, I think, is Weber's identification of a larger ethical transformation in which the animistic preoccupation with equity lost ground to ideas of a generalized, abstract love for everyone in the widening community of the faith. Such abstract love was supposed, as in Buddhism, to embrace all living things including the most microscopic insects or, as in Christianity, to suffuse even one's relationship with one's enemies. "Forgive us our trespasses," says the New Testament prayer, "as we forgive those who trespass against us." So generalized a moral sentiment obviates dwelling on the consequences of one's acts or venting outrage at local-level injustices and encroachments (Parsons 1963:lv–lvi; Weber 1963:221–242).

Significantly, salvationist religion emphasizes the needs of whole categories in distress, above all widows and orphans, but interprets their circumstances as the outgrowth of generalized worldly depravity rather than of victimization by particular, and responsible, others (Weber 1963:221–242; 1958b:329–330). With salvationism, moreover, misfortune and illness are no longer understood to flow from lapses of social obligation toward specific neighbors, kin, or spirits but constitute an aspect of the vast orchestration of sin and divine forgiveness that is, at least in part, beyond comprehension. In animistic relationships with spirits, restitution follows encroachment and resentment is forever feared. If it is true that this engenders recurrent second thoughts in the exploitation of natural and human resources, then the salvationist prophesies, although in tension with worldly affairs, were at least potentially liberating. Not inclined to attribute resentment or acknowledge its legitimacy, they do not dwell on the problem of just compensation for the spirits or humans whom intensified production pushes aside.

CHRISTIAN SALVATIONISM AND WESTERN CHRISTIAN REFORMS

Of all the salvationist religions to emerge in the Old World's urban revolution, Christianity departed most decisively from the animistic conception of spirits and its corresponding social ethic. In a well-known essay Hubert and Mauss underscored the extent of the departure by showing that, despite its "astounding likeness" to earlier forms, Christian sacrifice turned these forms on their heads. No longer did the offering consist of goats, cattle, or humans; in the Christian transformation it had become the god itself. Divinity sacrificed his own son in order to save humans from inevitable, original sin (Hubert and Mauss 1964:80–81, 93–94).

Original sin was also a radical concept. According to Abraham Heschel, the Hebrew prophets imagined their God to experience a profound pathos. Forgiving the contrite, he remained involved in his peoples' community or nation (Heschel 1975:8–9). In contrast, the Christian God forgave all in exchange for the penitent's faith. Original sin, suggests Heschel, implies a "blindly working guilt" in which humans are begotten but for which they cannot be held individually accountable. It is not "something that happens, but . . . something that is and obtains regardless of man's relationships to the gods. The condition leads to despair that contrition can never bridge the opposition of divinity and humanity" (Heschel 1975:8–9). Just as original sin transcends the moral responsibility of humans, Divinity's categorical sacrifice is something they can never repay.

Underlying the Christian position on sacrifice and sin is the core doctrine of love, which is also diagnostic of Christianity's break with animism. Transforming the righteous but involved God of the Old Testament into the categorically forgiving deity of the new one, Christians propagated a message that as God redeems the faithful, so humans should forgive each other, unconditionally. Indeed, the New Testament holds up as models the meek, the merciful, the peacemakers who, like

Jesus, ask expiation for their persecutors. "You have learned," says the Savior in the Sermon on the Mount, " 'Eye for eye, tooth for tooth.' But what I tell you is this: Do not set yourself against the man who wrongs you. If someone slaps you on the right cheek, turn and offer him your left. If a man wants to sue you for your shirt, let him have your coat as well. . . . You have learned . . . 'Love your neighbor, hate your enemy.' But what I tell you is this: Love your enemies and pray for your persecutors; only so can you be children of your heavenly Father, who makes the sun rise on good and bad alike" (Matt. 5:38–46).

From the beginning Christians harnessed God's love through the rituals of baptism and the Eucharist that united participants with each other and all believers in the comforting body of the sacrificed Jesus. As Wayne Meeks explains, the resulting community, or *communitas*, solidified the small urban bands that under Pauline leadership dedicated themselves to Christian love in the arc of towns and cities of the northeastern Mediterranean—the expanding Roman Empire's commercial and military highway. Although drawing heavily from the middle strata of freed slaves, artisans, and tradesmen, many of them geographically mobile, these little congregations were not internally homogeneous but "generally reflected a fair cross-section of urban society" (Meeks 1983:73). Paul, following Jesus, encouraged the use of familial terms like brotherly love and children of God to describe congregational life and admonished believers to come to the Lord's table full of forgiveness and love for each other, despite their differences of status. According to Meeks, Paul preached that the ritual meal could sicken people who violated the "norms appropriate to the sacred occasion." The violations, he explains, were not "ritual errors, in the narrow sense, but offenses against the social cohesion of the group caused by tensions between people of higher and lower social and economic positions" (Meeks 1983:86–87, 103, 159; also 1 Cor. 10–16 *passim*).

For the early centuries of the Western church, Jack Goody's provocative book traces how the papacy pursued and acted upon Jesus' command in the Sermon on the Mount that the obligations of kinship be subordinated to Christian love. In contrast to Eastern Orthodoxy, which left this problematic unrealized, authorities of the West challenged the integrity of kin groups, legislating prohibitions against cousin marriage, divorce, concubinage, adoption, and widow remarriage. Whether or not one accepts Goody's thesis that the goal of this legislation was the interception of "strategies of heirship" so that ecclesiastical institutions could accumulate donated properties, his reconstruction of the ascendancy of "brotherly love" over kinship loyalties well explains how Christianity could nurture the formation of a new, more stratified and developed social order (1983). In a reformulation of Goody's thesis Verdery proposes that as the invasions of Western Europe in the early Middle Ages has-tened the creation of the feudal system out of petty chiefdoms, Christi-anity gave "would-be warriors . . . a supernaturally sanctioned motive for rejecting their obligations to kinsmen so as to interact" in a wider and more potent world (1988:268).

Meeks' and Goody's interpretations of early Christian history suggest to me a fundamental contradiction in doctrine. The concept of brotherly love, and the voluntary poverty of Jesus, easily reinforce ideologies of social and economic equality. Both have conferred legitimacy on egalitar-ian, or equalizing, social movements up to the present day. Since the Middle Ages, moreover, Christian doctrine has also lent support to the manumission of slaves and the abolition of slavery: in the eyes of God all persons are equal. Yet as a set of beliefs and behaviors, brotherly love and voluntary poverty constitute powerful solvents of the tit-for-tat ethic of equity—the mutuality of obligation among kin and neighbors—with the opposite consequence of facilitating processes of differentiation within small communities. While I recognize the potentially egalitarian and abolitionist messages of Christian love and poverty, it is rather their potential compatibility with local-level class formation that concerns me here. Excusing injustice, radically abstracting action from history, and trivializing its consequences because all is forgiven indicate "ways of han-dling the problem of evil that are easier to stand than the traditional ways" (Hauschild, personal communication; see also van Velzen and van Wetering 1982). These ways, I think, helped steel the nerve and enhance the legitimacy of protocapitalists.

Given that the ethic of equity extends to earth spirits in animist belief, its dissolution also encouraged the progressive and unencumbered ex-ploitation of nature—forests, game, water, and soils—on which capital-ism depends. In Lynn White's words, by opposing pagan animism Chris-tianity made possible a "mood of indifference to the feelings of natural objects" (1974:14–28; see also van Binsbergen 1976).

To say that Christian doctrine gave an opening to new relationships among humans, and between them and their environment, is not to con-clude that the opening was automatically seized upon and used. It is my argument that a centuries-long series of reform movements, themselves outgrowths of urban and commercial expansion, promoted the suppres-sion of equity-consciousness in favor of brotherly love. Marked by syn-cretisms and apostasy, these movements were far from lineal, yet cumu-latively and in certain times and places they produced manifestations of culture change. In the following sections I examine a series of case stud-ies that illustrate this tendency, its moments of compromise as well as its peaks of violence. As a prelude to that discussion this section concludes with a brief overview of the major reforms. Targeting first and foremost the wealth and power of the institutional church—the "regime" of Christianity (see Bax 1987)—reformers were "egalitarian" in many ways. It is only by uncovering their role in the attack on animistic beliefs and practices that one appreciates the contribution they made—and then not only as Protestants—to the rise of capitalism.

Following the Crusades, Europe's center of urban and commercial dynamism shifted from Byzantium to the West and with it shifted the conditions that appear, historically, to have generated waves of enthusiasm for religious reform. From the twelfth century the regions of greatest urban growth in northern Italy and the Low Countries, and the corridors of trade that connected them, spawned numerous prophets and mystics who synthesized the religious and moral needs of mobile traders, artisans, patricians, and soldiers, troubled by the "gross materialism" of the new age (Ozment 1980:94–95). Embracing poverty, the prophets spread their insights through itinerant preaching and the creation of new communities, for example the Albigensians or Cathars, the Waldensians, the Beguines and Beghards, the followers of Saint Francis and later the Franciscan Spirituals (Cohn 1961:21–22; Leff 1967:33–34; Ozment 1980; Thomas 1971:663–668).

Although it is important to acknowledge variation, the reform movements of the twelfth through fifteenth centuries had in common a deep distrust of the ecclesiastical hierarchy and religious orders whose virtuosi received or extorted—depending on the viewpoint—unconscionable donations of wealth and property in exchange for saving souls. Against the clerical and monastic elites of medieval Catholicism, the new sects—labeled and persecuted as heretical—advocated ritual and behavioral avenues through which lay people could apprehend, without mediation, the poverty, chastity, simplicity, and suffering of Jesus and the apostles. Spiritualizing their lives accordingly, the laity could thus pursue their own salvation, independent of the good offices of such intercessors as the cloistered Benedictines. In this understanding of salvation, as well as in their largely urban provenience, the various heretical, reformist movements presaged the Protestant Reformation.

Recent interpretations of Christianity emphasize the continuities between the late medieval and early modern movements for religious reform, drawing attention to the powerful reformist currents that in each instance entered the established church as it met its critics. After an initial attempt at the violent suppression of heretical movements, the thirteenth-century papacy initiated a policy of cooptation through which it absorbed and legitimated certain heresies as a bulwark against the rest. The compromise yielded vibrant institutions in the form of the mendicant Dominican and Franciscan preaching orders and the papally dominated Inquisitorial courts. Seen as bastions of corrupt wealth and power by subsequent "heresies" and Protestant reformers, the mendicant orders were in their own time carriers of the reformist ideal that lay populations should not have to depend for their salvation on a restricted elite of monks and clergy but could seek it on their own (Kieckhefer 1979).

Just as the heresies of the late Middle Ages forced the established church to incorporate reformist programs, the Protestant Reformation provoked a regrouping at the Council of Trent (1545–1563). Parallel to the mendicant preaching orders and to the Inquisition as institutional responses to religious revolt were the Jesuit Order and a vastly expanded network of parochial churches and schools. Earlier scholars, convinced that "the" Reformation of the Protestants was an isolated revolution, declined to see continuities between the Jesuitical and parochial structures of Counter-Reformation Catholicism and the institutions that the Protestants were building at the same time. Delumeau (1977), the *Annales* school historian, and Bossy (1970), his English promoter and translator, write convincingly of the Counter-Reformation as only moderately less reformist than Luther and Calvin (see also Burke 1978:207–244; Klaits 1985; Weber 1958a:118–124, 158, 175). All construed salvation as more difficult than the late medieval system of merit and indulgences had allowed, while at the same time insisting that lay populations could lead "religious" lives. All had as their central goal the evangelization of these lay populations not only along an urbanized trajectory but in the countryside as well, and all funneled human and material resources into parish-level religious instruction as the most effective way to achieve this end (Bossy 1970).

In a recent synthesis of historical writing on early modern religious change Klaits proposes that the Protestant Reformation and the Catholic Counter-Reformation were "twin movements" that can be "referred to collectively, for convenience, as the Reformation" (1985:59–60). Something of an exaggeration, this formulation makes light of the Protestant break with God's immanence and church-mediated salvation—Catholic doctrines not too far removed from ideas of mystical contagion and *mana* (Donald Taylor 1985). Whereas Counter-Reformation Catholicism still permitted humans to redeem themselves through "works," penances, confessions, and saints, Calvinists entertained the impossible idea that God's grace is discretionary and predestined. As Cucchiari has put it (personal communication), "different understandings about the church's authority in the enterprise of . . . salvation have led Catholic and Protestant movements and churches into quite different long-term relationships with folk-religion. . . . Protestant soteriology allows less flexibility and is driven to unrelenting attacks on religious consciousness itself."

In the following sections we will see that, among Western Europe's rural populations, mendicant preachers of the later Middle Ages had little impact on equity-consciousness, if anything facilitating its syncretism with official religion. Subsequently, ideologues of both Reformations— but the Protestant more than the Catholic—attempted a much more thorough disenchantment.

REFORMERS AND RURAL EUROPEANS

While Christian doctrine everywhere rejected religious ideas of equity among humans and between them and the "prior inhabitants" of their communities and land, Western Christianity, with its succession of powerful reformist movements, institutionalized that rejection. The process, however, was neither simple nor linear. Each wave of reform or coopted reform pressed for doctrinal purification in its own particular way, the carriers being in varying degrees and to varying ends intolerant of local religion. Moreover, peasants, and the artisans in their midst, were hardly isolated from the urban and commercial development of the late medieval and early modern periods and must be assumed to have generated new religious ideas, including salvationist ideas, on their own. Carlo Ginzburg's noteworthy history of a simple miller in the sixteenth-century artisan network of the Friulian villages near Venice is a fitting reminder that innovations could emerge from popular culture. The formulator of a cosmology that likened the creation of the earth to cheese making, the miller also held ideas in common with Anabaptists and Lutherans. These included "an implicit denial of Purgatory and thus of the utility of Masses for the dead; condemnation of the use of Latin by priests and monks; rejection of 'sumptuous churches'; limitations on the cult of saints" (Ginzburg 1980:18–20, 26). Through skillful detection, Ginzburg shows that the miller, Menocchio, generated his critique of the established church from village experience and oral tradition as well as from the books that, being literate, he subversively read and discussed with his friends.

Using histories of interaction between learned and popular religion that, like Ginzburg's study of Menocchio, build on contributions from "below," I explore three domains of equity on which the reformers operated: how people related 1) to the dead, 2) to earth spirits, and 3) to manifestations of resentment and envy among themselves. Regarding the dead, the research of Jacques Le Goff on the concept of Purgatory in the late Middle Ages is suggestive. Understood since Classical times to be an intermediate place of burning and purification between Heaven and Hell, this life and the next, the concept was elaborated after the twelfth century as a cornerstone of the Roman Catholic system of merit which held that acts of suffrage could be performed by the living on behalf of the dead. Specific acts, such as giving alms to mendicant preachers, undertaking crusades and pilgrimages, doing charitable "works," saying prayers and participating in the miracle of the Eucharist, were, according to this system, especially efficacious ways to hasten expiation for the "deadly sins" of pride, avarice, envy, melancholy, anger, gluttony, sloth, and lust. In performing these acts living persons helped particular dead kin and friends cleanse themselves of sinful deeds unpunished during their lifetime (Le Goff 1984).

Most of the heretical sects and all of the Protestants joined Eastern Orthodox Christians in rejecting the doctrine of Purgatory which, they claimed, only led to the corruption of ecclesiastics who deceived penitents with the false promise of salvation in order to collect fees (Le Goff 1984:168–173, 278–280). So vehement was the Protestant critique that it has obscured the extent to which the doctrine of Purgatory initially advanced the disenchanting cause of reform. First of all, the coopted but reformist mendicants popularized it, their sermons replete with didactic examples of particular souls for whom the suffrages of others had "paid off." Second, the elaboration of Purgatory distanced the church from animistic beliefs. As Salomon Reinach wrote in 1900, "Pagans prayed to the dead, Christians prayed for the dead" (quoted in Le Goff 1984:45).

The contrast suggests a differential need for vigilance against the demands of "prior inhabitants" and ghosts. According to the doctrine of Purgatory, ghosts are prisoners, allowed to escape and return to the living only at the instigation of God, and then not to agitate for redress but simply to bear witness to the ordeals of expiation. Rather than interpret their visitations as quests for food and human company, Christians should heed their descriptions of purgation and their pleas for additional suffrages on their behalf. In other words, the Purgatory concept upset the balance between the living and the dead in favor of the living, relieving them of the inhibiting thought that their aggrandizing actions in the world, if not their very existence, might be resented by their predecessors, the more so those who had prematurely died (Le Goff 1984:269–270, 277; Davis 1974:327–328).

If the living were anxious that their aggrandizing projects could, potentially, provoke retribution, then perhaps they found comfort in the examples with which the propagandists for Purgatory illustrated their sermons. In reviewing these Le Goff notes how many *exempla* concerned the souls of men in precocious but stigmatized professions and occupations, including the practice of usury. To medieval Christians, lending money at interest was a sinful activity that should be left to Jews and others of the unredeemed. Purgatory, however, made it possible for a usurer's wife or kin to atone for this sin once he died. In Buddhist doctrine usury is not condemned, but as it is rooted in worldly affairs, it cannot be articulated with salvation. Western Christian reforms of the late Middle Ages pointed in a different direction, the direction that would eventually render profit making entirely compatible with religious justification even as it engendered indebtedness and dislocation. Hence Le Goff's remark that "Purgatory, by making the salvation of the usurer possible, contributed to the birth of capitalism" (1984:305).

The mendicant orders of the late Middle Ages could only go so far in promoting the idea of Purgatory. According to Le Goff, their audiences rejected an "infernalized" image in favor of the benign afterlife of Celtic or Germanic folklore, thereby taking less seriously the notion that ghosts had been removed from human society (1984:110, 289, 314). Consistent with this skeptical outlook are the many surviving syncretisms of the Purgatory concept, for example among Breton peasants. Badone writes (personal communication) that until recently people in Brittany believed that the dead, once released to heaven, interceded for the living who had prayed for them, even shortening *their* stay in Purgatory when it came their turn to die (see also Ariès 1982:466; Davis 1977:94; Rothkrug 1979:33, 51–52). We have to remember, too, that until the age of the twin Reformations sermons did not penetrate much beyond the commercial corridor that was the friars' itinerary. In many respects the Protestants and the Jesuits of the sixteenth century picked up where the earlier reformers left off, distancing still further the fate of the dead and pushing the message aggressively in rural areas.

One thinks immediately of the Calvinist doctrine of predestination that disallowed all communication between the living and their predecessors, but Jesuit priests also set about building churches in the outskirts of villages to calm peasants' fear of ghosts. Delumeau, the forceful observer of continuities between Protestantism and the Counter-Reformation, describes the effort of the Counter-Reformers at the fires of Saint John. Lit each June in public squares to honor the Christian martyr, the bonfires (from "bone" fires) were locally believed to have great significance for spirits of the dead. Villagers might place stones around the fire's perimeter for their returning dead to sit and warm themselves on, or believe that the flames warded off the justifiably aggrieved yet menacing "tombless dead"—those whose lives had been robbed "before their time." At the conclusion of the ceremonies people took home burning grasses and embers to protect their respective households until the following year. According to Delumeau, sixteenth- and seventeenth-century priests, newly emboldened by Jesuit hegemony, stood beside the fires of Saint John with buckets of water, poised to douse the grasses and coals before they could be removed. Thanks to such examples of reformist energy during and after the religious wars between Catholics and Protestants, skepticism of ghosts gained ground in Europe, undermining peoples' responsiveness "to the presumed wishes of past generations" (Thomas 1971:587–606; see also Davis 1974:328–330; Davis 1977:92–96). (In the eighteenth and nineteenth centuries, however, ghosts returned as dis-embodied spirits, above all in Protestant Europe, giving rise to the new religion of Spiritualism [Ariès 1982:454–468].)

The responsiveness of Europeans to earth spirits, a second diagnostic arena for the exploration of interactions between learned and popular religion, was also undermined. In folklore these spirits—the fairies, dwarfs, green men, and trolls who now populate children's literature—are occasionally linked to ancient ancestors buried near the rural communities of their descendants (e.g., Christiansen 1964:xxxvi–xxxix). More commonly they appear as "prior inhabitants" who yielded turf to settle, however unwillingly, in rocks and caves, woods and springs, as human populations and agricultural activities expanded. Thus deprived of space, their personalities reveal a capricious indulgence in mildly vengeful acts: urinating in humans' wine, washing in their beer, stealing milk from their cows or grain from their fields, and keeping their butter from forming in the churn. Ritual offerings of cooked food or a portion of the harvest, and deferential shows of respect, can mitigate such acts, however, even winning fairy support for certain endeavors. Fairy reprisals in the domain of reproduction are less easy to control in a perfunctory way, although subject to the same reciprocities. According to animistic belief, the "little people" lost so much ground as a consequence of human expansion that they cannot perpetuate themselves without assistance. Whether offered or extorted, assistance means appropriating women's wombs to gestate fairy children and human midwives to deliver them. Especially wide-spread is the idea that fairies rob human cradles of healthy offspring, leaving behind weak and sickly changelings, forever crying and hungry, in their place (Thomas 1971:607–614).

The belief that fairies were "prior inhabitants" and the commitment to appease them in equitable ways did not strike medieval European peasants as incompatible with established religion. On the contrary, rural populations welcomed, indeed passionately sought, as much Christian grace as could be directed their way through the cult of saints, the sacraments, and the priestly blessing of candles, herbs, water, and salt. Seizing upon such objects, they placed them in their households and stalls as protection against the caprices or malefices of disgruntled spirits. According to Scribner, peasants expected to be healed by the Eucharist, had their priests carry it in processions to ensure rainfall, even scattered it on their fields to make them fertile (1984; see also Rothkrug 1979). In addition, they propitiated Christian saints as if the saints themselves were prior inhabitants, hoping that gifts of food and clothes, money and treasure, would ensure good health and harvests in return. In the words of Klaniczay, the legends of saints "were capable of reconciling Christian morality with pagan myth," while the festivals in the saints' honor "offered the Church the possibility of controlling fertility rites and rites of passage of peasants" (1983:57).

But if belief in fairies, with its underlying equity-consciousness in relation to nature, was easily syncretized with the flow of grace that characterized medieval evangelizing, these manifestations of peasant animism clashed with the reformist movements, especially as improved means of transportation and communication allowed reformers to scrutinize more carefully the "enchantment" or "paganization" of Christian forms. Already cognizant of the tension, the mid-thirteenth-century papacy took control of the beatification and canonization of saints, applying the rigorous criterion that the candidate's life must resemble the life of Jesus and the apostles. Continued gatherings at the departed's tomb, invocations to intercede in obtaining divine favor, and claims of miraculous cures no longer served to establish sainthood unless this condition of biography were met. Consistent with the trajectory of reformism in Western Christianity, the hardened Reformations of the sixteenth century advocated additional constraints: Catholics further restricted the legitimation of saints while Protestants dismantled their cults altogether. Counter-Reformation Catholicism also purged particular saints of animistic elements—for example removing the dragon from the hagiography of Saint George (Burke 1978:211–217).

In his remarkable "micro" history of a greyhound saint, Jean-Claude Schmitt (1983), a student of Le Goff, focusses on the late medieval interaction of a Dominican Inquisitor and the peasants of the Dombes region, north of the Dominican's seat in Lyons. Committed to the identification and persecution of heretics, the friar became simultaneously interested in peasant "superstitions"—their casting of lots, divination practices, propitiation of "demons," and improper "demonized" worship of the true God. The Dombes region provided him with an instructive example that he wove into his sermons. Here peasant women sought cures for their children at the tomb of Saint Guinefort, whom they believed to have been a dog. According to legend, a manor house had once stood on the tomb site, its lord and lady being the authors of a heinous deed. Leaving their infant in the care of a trusty greyhound, they had, upon returning, hastily murdered this noble animal, mistakenly thinking that it had allowed a snake to kill the child. In fact, the dog had saved the baby by killing the snake. The lord and lady, full of remorse, buried the martyred creature, which became the focus of a peasant cult, their manor reverting to a barren and wooded wilderness. It was not a righteous cult, however, in the eyes of the Dominican Inquisitor, who had the dog's bones dug up and burned, together with the trees that marked the grave site.

Given that the peasant actors were caught up in a web of equity-conscious relationships with spirits, why was the snake an aggressor in this legend rather than a "prior inhabitant" worthy of propitiation in its own right? According to Schmitt, the motif of a noble baby being left alone with an animal has a wide Indo-European distribution. In one version, at least, recorded in Greece about A.D. 160–180, the child's protector is a snake and not a dog. By what combination of influences did the peasants of the Dombes come to demonize reptiles? Were they pulled in this direction by the medieval bishops who "savagely" destroyed sacred trees and groves, replacing them with basilicas, and by the many Christian martyrs and saints who faced off with serpents and dragons? Or did they arrive at the characterization on their own? Whatever the mix of elite demonology and popular creativity, snakes apparently were, at the time of Schmitt's story, demons to avoid and not to mollify (Schmitt 1983:21–23; 60–61).

Yet the propitiation of earth spirits lived on. According to the record left by the friar, the women who visited the tomb of Saint Guinefort believed that the sick and hungry children in their tow were changelings. On the advice of a female diviner from a neighboring town, they offered salt and other things to the fauns (woodland spirits) of the surrounding forest. Since the time of Saint Augustine theologians conflated fauns with incubi—the male protégés of the devil—but to the peasants of the Dombes they were fairies, amenable to returning the healthy children they had kidnapped if granted due respect (Schmitt 1983:19–21, 69–82).

The peasant women's belief in fairies, as recorded by the Dominican Inquisitor, is consistent with their mythic attention to the destruction of the lord's manor and its replacement by the tomb and trees. In their view this constituted evidence for divine retribution against the lord for having overstepped certain limits. Thanks to Schmitt's imaginative probing, we learn that in the friar's time lords were constructing artificial ponds on the natural depressions of their estates so as to raise fish for an expanding market in Lyons. Dislocated by vanishing fields and commons, undermined by the spread of malaria and malnutrition, peasants perhaps saw in this commercialization of property an analogous "overstepping." In Schmitt's words their "narrative . . . was formed in a climate [of] opposition" to baronial power (1983:165–166). Both the Guinefort legend and the fish ponds persisted until after the French Revolution when the latter were drained and the land restored for use by local peasants.

A final arena in which microhistorians have traced the interaction of official and popular religion in Europe is the arena of imagined spiritual danger among the living. Reformers of the late medieval and early modern period believed that to participate in the church's central ritual—the Eucharistic mass—with hatred in one's heart was a sin of such gravity that in committing it one polluted the entire congregation. For as it commemorated the sacrifice of Jesus, the mass created unity in his love. According to Bossy, late medieval clerics were distressed that their parishioners, partaking of the body and blood of Jesus, prayed to God to deliver the souls of the dead from sin and give them the gift of charity but made a distinction between their friends and their enemies. The same distinction applied to the living, reflected in prayers that sought deliverance from an enemy's machinations. Indeed, evading such machinations was thought crucial to salvation, so much so that one might even pray for an enemy's downfall (if rarely for his death). In other words, concludes Bossy, the late medieval mass was as easily a vehicle for the pursuit of interpersonal hostility as for the consolidation of Christian love and peace, leading to renewed pressure for reform (1983:42–49).

Under the two reformations, with their territorial expansion of religious institutions, the pressure began to bear fruit. In a sensitive study of church visitation records for Protestant Swabia in the 1580s David Sabean found local pastors making "massive inroads" into peasant consciousness as they imposed the reformed religion on a social field where rules of equity were still salient (1984). For example they intervened in the custom of bell ringing, by which the local sacristan alerted the community that a dying person was about to receive Communion at home. Although intended to encourage overall reflection on the cosmic battle between God and the Devil, and thus on personal salvation, villagers interpreted this practice as an opportunity for "fair exchange." The better-off should demonstrate their good will by sending food and drink to the sickbed, while anyone harboring a secret grudge had best visit or accept mystical responsibility for the crisis. Promoting the competing theory that God, not humans, caused illness, and then only as a punishment for sins or a test of faith, several pastors outlawed the ringing of the bell (Sabean 1984:52–59).

In addition, they reported on particular "agitated" parishioners for whom the words of the Lord's Prayer, "forgive us our trespasses as we forgive those who trespass against us," stuck in the throat. Unable to submerge their feelings of envy and malice, these people could take the Sacrament only at the risk of ritually endangering others. According to Sabean, pastors and local magistrates pressured such parishioners to repent, considering them to be stubborn, quarrelsome, and blasphemous when they refused. Significantly, socioeconomic change intensified the clash of ethical systems, Swabia being on the threshold of enclosing common land and adopting new, less equitable forms of inheritance. Recalcitrant parishioners were frequently involved in litigation related to these developments such that stigmatizing their resentment was an early example of the now familiar Western cultural pattern of blaming the victim (Sabean 1984:47–52).

In his survey of records from a parish in Essex between 1380 and 1750

Alan Macfarlane found the word "evil" to be little used except for "people who broke into other people's property and were termed 'evil doers' " and for debtors fleeing their debts (1985). Hobart (1985) describes the opposite for Bali, where the word for evil evokes greed. Similarly, among the Kaguru, as possibly in most of the non-Christian world, greed is more readily placed outside of moral bounds than envy. Kaguru with prosperous gardens, much livestock, fine clothes, and a pattern of neglecting obligations to kin, are often accused of witchcraft, while hoarding food is the ultimate heinous crime (Beidelman 1986:140–147). We will see that in Western Europe's witch-hunt the accused were feared more for their envy than for their greed.

By focussing on the ethics of animist belief I have tried to characterize European peasants as reflectively attentive to equitable relationships among themselves and with spirits, as well as practically concerned with the goals of prosperity and health. This being the case, the most fundamental contrast between their world view and that of the friars and preachers who sought to reform them was a contrast of ethics. Of the two sets of ethical concerns the Christian concept of brotherly love is the more "egalitarian," yet this concept has a malignant other side: it can smooth over and even delegitimize the sharpened ethical dilemmas that accompany monetization, commercialization, and capitalist development, leaving the victims of these processes open to the contempt of those who gain.

THE GREAT WITCH-HUNT

Contrary to an earlier view that European witch-hunting was the last gasp of the Dark Ages, the phenomenon is now widely attributed to religious reform. In 1486, well before the Reformation, two Dominican Inquisitors in Cologne, Heinrich Kramer and Jacob Sprenger, produced an encyclopaedia on peasant witchcraft (the *Malleus Maleficarum*, or *Witch's Hammer*) that, with papal sanction, initiated "learned" strategies for detecting, convicting, and executing witches. The Inquisition, moreover, constituted a critical prosecutorial apparatus, particularly after the Protestant breakthrough rendered less relevant its investment in routing out heretics (Kieckhefer 1979). Most important, Protestant as well as Catholic reformers committed themselves to the "extirpation" of witches, the former at times spreading the panic more forcefully than the latter, and both making use of Europe's emerging absolutist states as well as the ecclesiastical authorities (Anderson and Zinsser 1988:164; Klaits 1985; Kors and Peters 1972:193–212; Larner 1981:157–174; Midelfort 1972:36–66; Thomas 1971:493–501).

That the early modern witch-hunt of Western Europe, reaching its

peak from the mid-sixteenth to the mid-seventeenth centuries, was a social movement for religious reform is also suggested by its continuities
with the Enlightenment. For although on the surface embracing world
views of opposite dimension, so much so that the Enlightenment put the
last of the witch-hunting demonologists out of business, both of these
intellectual currents were hostile to rural animism—its rituals, beliefs,
and ethics. Whereas the enlightened philosophers pictured themselves
sending "shafts of light" into the terrain of fairies and ghosts, witch-hunt-
ers used fire without metaphor, burning peasant animists at the stake.
Arguing that the two movements were connected by their common enemy, Hauschild quotes a Protestant pastor of the witch-hunting era who
wrote of the "vast waters of superstition, which, flooding everything,
hardly recognize a difference of the estates. One burns it finally," he pronounced, "with all its changelings in the fire of the sacred love which
Jesus Christ has ignited as the most magnificent witch's stake for all quar-
rels, all envy, all strife, malice, and evil on earth" (quoted in 1982:76).

To me, as to Norman Cohn (1975), the witch-hunt constituted an attempted "final solution" to animism on the part of religious reformers,
but this is not to say that the demonization process was entirely of their
own creation. Folkloric studies from the least-developed peripheries of
Europe show that, at the very least, peasants had their own, richly em-
broidered mythology of evil forces, having already dreamed of or imagined flying cannibal witches, covens, and "shaman-like" mediation with
nasty spirits (see Cohn 1975; Henningsen 1984; Klaniczay 1984; Larner
1981:23–24). Ginzburg's microhistory *The Night Battles* is in part a brief
for peasant contributions to the maligning of animistic phenomena as ac-
couterments of the Christian devil. Like his account of Menocchio, the
miller, *The Night Battles* is set in Friuli which, in the latter half of the
sixteenth century, was becoming a Venetian breadbasket. Again Inquisition records supply the evidence, this time documenting the existence of
a network of young, mainly male, curers who over several decades from
1575 to 1648 were brought before the court. Initially these animistic specialists claimed to be *benandanti*, or "good walkers," who protected the
harvests through ritual combat with spirit-witches whom they encountered outside their villages after a disembodied, nocturnal flight. Subsequent defendants attributed the names of fellow villagers, often older
women, to these witches. And, finally, toward the end of the sequence
young male curers called themselves witches, too.

But was the transformation of the *benandanti* from curers to witches a
change that came mainly from "below?" According to Ginzburg, it reflected exposure to the church's teachings and Inquisitorial manipulation.
For even though the Inquisitors of Friuli did not use torture to extort
confessions, the menace of torture and the weight of the trials shaped the
peasant response (see Ginzburg 1983). Nor is the *benandanti* case among

the worst. In several analyses of trial testimony historians have been able to demonstrate a contrast in language between accusers and accused and, among the accused, a shift from their initial statements to the confessions they eventually uttered under torture. The shift was one from a language of "simple sorcery," or *maleficium*, to a language of devil worship or apostasy (Kieckhefer 1976; Larner 1981; Muchembled 1979:231–232).

In effect the "diabolizing process of popular idea complexes" began with Kramer and Sprenger (Henningsen 1984:19). Approved by the papacy, their witch-hunting manual, the *Malleus Maleficarum*, was translated from Latin into German and French, the vernaculars of the absolutist states. Benefiting as did the Bible from the new printing technology, its words were in sixteen editions by 1520, thirty-two by 1660. State builders and intellectuals such as Jean Bodin, James I, and several Jesuits and Protestants were inspired to produce additional demonologies with an eye to secular as well as ecclesiastical courts (Anderson and Zinsser 1988:166; Kors and Peters 1972; Thomas 1971:440–441).

The demonologies began with the premise that the devil was on the move again, recruiting village women as his allies. In contrast to the earlier medieval period, he could not be managed through "holy water, the sign of the cross, holy candles, church bells, consecrated herbs, sacred words," or priestly exorcisms (Thomas 1971:493). By the same token, village relationships with spirits, earlier tolerated as superstition or magic, were now said to reveal a devil pact. To make their point, the demonologists resurrected Satan as the champion of necromancy and other monstrous perversions that peasants themselves thought evil and assimilated to him all manner of spirit, above all the tombless or unbaptized dead and such "prior inhabitants" as snakes, vermin, toads, insects, lizards, and the once propitiated but more recently vilified goat.

Formerly an ambivalent figure, the devil further became, in the demonologists' rhetoric, a slick and over-sexed extortionist who offered money and lustful copulation in exchange for the performance of antisocial deeds against others of the human community. His gifts, metamorphosing into grotesque substitutions, included ointments and potions that empowered the recipients to fly at night and induce impotence, miscarriages, infant death, livestock disease, and hailstorms (Cohn 1975:35; Midelfort 1972:73–140; Monter 1976; Seligman 1948:150–164). Where diviners and curers imagined sharing ritual meals and dances with spirits, or staving off witches in battle, demonologists saw orgiastic sabbats in which "all the elements . . . acquired opposite values": fairies became devils, food a stinking brew, and dance the foreplay of rape by the devil (see Henningsen 1984:22; Klaits 1985:48–86; Larner 1981:145–156; Muchembled 1979).

Among those accused of witchcraft were the practitioners of animistic rituals—the diviners, healers, and "cunning folk" who, like the instructor of Saint Guinefort's devotees, knew what it took to invoke fairies on behalf of health and good fortune or, like the *benandanti*, to keep "witches" at bay (Anderson and Zinsser 1988:162–163; Horsley 1979; Klaits 1985:94–103; Larner 1981:94, 142–143). In Sicily, to take one example, the Inquisitors tried women who cured illnesses and found lost objects by divining offenses to fairies and recommending compensatory offerings. Among the defendants was a nun who had interpreted a client's illness "as a punishment for having thrown a stone at a snake who was in reality a 'woman of the company' " (Henningsen 1984:13).

The demonological propaganda for a complete rupture of social relations between humans and spirits was paralleled sociologically by propaganda for rupturing analogous human ties. Several monographs present evidence that as itinerant Inquisitors and professional witch-finders pressed rural communities to identify their witches, accusations flowed toward people who were already reputed to be disgruntled—often because the productive and reproductive activities of others had marginalized them in some way. It is probably premature to make a general statement, and interesting variations exist. For example, South German accusers targeted both older women of low status and local powerholders: merchants, innkeepers, and notables (Midelfort 1972:187–188). Yet the greedy miser, the person who would hoard and not share, was less likely to be prosecuted than the marginal older woman. Demographic and economic upheavals associated with the penetration of villages by commodity markets were implicated in the tensions that led to accusation, while in most of the analyzed cases, accusers were better off than those they accused (e.g., Larner 1981; Macfarlane 1970; Muchembled 1979).

Perhaps two-thirds of the victims of accusation were women—especially spinsters, widows, and other women beyond their childbearing years. Midelfort has proposed a connection between this fact and the parallel development of a marriage pattern and inheritance rules intended to retard the fragmentation of (increasingly commoditized) land. The resulting practices of late marriage, nonmarriage, and single-heir inheritance created a stressful environment for women, especially when considered in relation to the church's taboo on sex outside of marriage (Midelfort 1972:183–185). Perhaps for related reasons women were the main subjects of the demonological tracts, which characterized them as more "animistic" or superstitious than men, more open to sexual temptation, "intellectually like children," and inclined to harbor exaggerated sentiments of envy (Kors and Peters 1972:120–123). Conceptualized as weak, women further attracted the kind of contempt that masks fear of a weak person's resentment. In a pornographic rhetoric the demonologists associated them with "mockery of the mass, desecration of the host, orgies on a Witches' Sabbath, cannibalism of newborns, drunkenness, gluttony, lewd dancing, intercourse with every variety of creature in every possible position" (Anderson and Zinsser 1988:166; see also Klaits 1985:48–86; Larner 1981:89–97; Zuesse 1985:231).

Historians debate whether ordinary but quarrelsome women with a grudge or cunning folk, who were also for the most part female, were the prototypical victims of witch-hunting. The understanding of animism proposed in this essay explains how both humans who felt aggrieved and the diviners of spirit grievances might be demonized as witches by the same intellectual movement (see Muchembled 1979:252–255). Whoever the prototypical victims, the witch-hunt was awesome in its violence and had a wide distribution. Based on the research conducted so far—and much remains to be uncovered—there was a noteworthy surge of witch-craft trials in the Basque provinces in 1507, 1512, the 1520s, and again in 1610; in southern Germany, eastern France, lowland Switzerland, and the southeastern counties of England after 1560; in Wurzburg, Bamberg, Franche-Comté, Alsace, and the Scottish lowlands in the 1620s; in south-eastern England again in 1645, Franche Comté in 1657, and in the areas around Stockholm and Paisley in the late seventeenth century. Northern Italy, Denmark, and the Low Countries were also loci of witch-hunting, as was New England and, in the early eighteenth century, Hungary and Poland (Anderson and Zinsser 1988:167–168; Henningsen 1980:22; Larner 1981:18–19).

Taken as a whole, the witch-hunt was perhaps superficial: peasants re-turned to their old ways once the prosecutory apparatus was withdrawn. I suggest, however, that in the more urbanized regions where commod-ity forms already existed the trials helped break up the integument of reciprocity associated with peasant animism, publically "extirpating" or burning the carriers of equity-conscious beliefs. In so doing they sup-pressed at least some peasants' ways of respecting the "interconnected sanctity of a living and fragile cosmos" (Cucchiari, personal communica-tion) and called into question their fear of spiritual danger from class for-mation processes in their own midst. Thus enlarging the opening whereby arrogance replaced reticence, witch-hunting intensified the contribution of reformist Christianity to capitalism that was (and not by coincidence) emerging at about the same time. As Muchembled con-cludes for his case studies of the Catholic Low Countries, "the war against witchcraft can be seen as the result of a marked change in reli-gious thinking occurring within the context of an evolving economy" (1979:225–226).

CONCLUSION

In this essay I have reviewed some recent microhistories of the interac-tion of popular and official religion in Europe, emphasizing for popular religion the ethical problem of equity. My purpose has been to extend

Weber's discussion of the relationship of Christianity to capitalism in terms that transcend *The Protestant Ethic*, taking into account the centuries-long effort of Christian reformers to "disenchant" the countryside. I have suggested that an ethical system in which equity is paramount induces caution in the exploitation of natural resources and makes it difficult to conceptualize labor (except the labor of outsiders or slaves) as "free" of all constraints against dislocation. By contrast, the ethical systems of the salvationist religions allow for circumventing these constraints, the Christian doctrine of brotherly love constituting an especially liberating example. Among Christians the Western variant, fed by the succession of reform movements that accompanied urbanism and commercialism, imposed the ethic of love with special vigor on rural as well as urban populations.

In other words, Western Europe's rural populations were uniquely subjected to the transformative energy of religious reformers, just as this part of the world experienced a precocious mercantilism, independent of political control (see Wolf 1982:267–268). No other of the salvationist religions went so far as to stage a massive witch-hunt against animistic practice and belief. On the contrary, rural Asia and Africa are replete with examples of the peaceful coexistence of literate and popular religious traditions, in which their respective ethical systems are not only richly syncretized but share in a ritual calendar that acknowledges the value of both (e.g., Tambiah 1970). In some European regions, generally the most peripheral, the exposure to reform only papered over the peasant world view which, retaining its vitality, continued to shape at least some branches of the official regime. In other regions, however, a new culture, more compatible with the capitalist exploitation of both nature and labor, did, in fact, emerge. Having first demonized peasant animism, carriers of the new pattern went on to ridicule it in the eighteenth century and then, a century later, to paint it in romantic terms. Clues from the ethnography of small-scale societies, and evidence from the new microhistories of Europe, hold out the possibility of recovering not only quaint magical practices but their associated ethical concerns, buried as these have been under increasing layers of misunderstanding. As Henningsen (1984:22) suggests, scholars now have a "big fish on the hook way below in the ocean of history" and can start to pull it up for examination.

As capitalism spread from its heartland in Western Europe to acquire a global presence, it revealed ever more what Wolf considers a defining characteristic: "an extraordinarily destabilizing power in its continuous search for higher profits and sustained . . . accumulation." Capital, he writes, "forever abandons older sectors of the economy and relocates in new and more promising industries and areas." In doing so it continuously alters people's "social and cultural arrangements," not to mention the environment in which they live, subjecting them (and nature) to constant tremors and at times to "major quakes" (1987:147–148). Is it not fascinating that America, the "richest country in the world," is also the most opposed to disciplining capital, the most ideologically committed to its incredible dynamism and associated political freedoms, and the source of Christianity's most fundamental, which is to say radical, movements for reform? According to fundamentalist ethics, human accountability for historical action pales before faith in the love of Jesus—a position that makes it both logically and psychologically possible to justify extremes of dislocation, up to and including nuclear war, giving them an apocalyptic rather than a moral dimension.

But what about the discipline of capital by socialists? Products of the Enlightenment, and more broadly of a Christianized Western culture (even when atheists or believing Jews), they too have suppressed manifestations of equity-consciousness, their ideological egalitarianism being ethically different from, as well as reminiscent of, the leveling implications of animism. One need only think of the many European socialists who mistrusted agricultural laborers and newly urbanized workers for their "personalistic" or "wildcat" way of expressing indignation or grievance. Labeling them "immature," socialist intellectuals also shunned folklorists of the Left—the Italian de Martino, for example—perceiving their interest in peasant rites to be a flirtation with "the irrational" (Cases 1973:xxxviii–xxxix; Gallini 1977:lxxii–lxxvii). Nor have socialists been quicker than capitalists to comprehend that environments violated by arrogant investment will return to traumatize humanity with depredation and disease. No more respectful of nature than capitalists overall, they too participated in history's deep and suicidal break with the logic of equity in relation to the earth.

Today, of course, "green" movements are spreading in both capitalist and socialist contexts and are working their way back to a humbled sense of the place of humans in the cosmos. It is misleading for these movements to idealize animistic religion, whose ethic of equity has the potential to intensify interpersonal rivalry and hostility, often at a psychic and organizational cost. Yet one can draw from the animistic world view a key lesson for our time: ecological and social justice are interconnected human concerns such that the struggle for one need not preclude a commitment to the other and vice versa.

Notes to Chapter 2

This essay owes much to several cohorts of graduate students in my European Ethnography and Ethnology course who pushed me to develop a framework in which to present "Christianity." Eager to introduce them to the contributions of historians as well as anthropologists, I found myself overwhelmed. The questions and observations of listeners whom I both confused and provoked helped me to develop what I hope is a more coherent result. Three students, John Burdick, Frances Junghams, and Elanah Sherman, criticized an earlier draft of the manuscript from the perspective of their own studies of Christianity, giving me many useful insights to consider. Ms. Sherman also made trenchant editorial suggestions as did the editor at Princeton University Press.

The following anthropologists offered lengthy evaluations of my central thesis, often adding bibliographic suggestions: Ellen Badone, Fredrik Barth, John Comaroff, James Fernandez, Stewart Guthrie, Thomas Hauschild, William Roseberry, Wilhelmina van Wetering, Peter van der Veer, and Brackette Williams. Unable to follow all of their good advice, I have tried to come to grips with some of it, and I extend my thanks. I am especially grateful to Salvatore Cucchiari, who wrote his review in the form of a five-page letter that deserves publication in its own right, and to Carlo Ginzburg who, notwithstanding his historian's skepticism of the scope of my undertaking, kindly drew my attention to some mistakes of fact and problems of interpretation. I am, of course, responsible for any remaining mistakes and problems. Vincent Crapanzano, knowing of my project, introduced me to Gustav Henningsen's article on the witch-hunt in Sicily, a source I might otherwise have missed. And as always Peter Schneider mercilessly questioned my assumptions and mercifully improved my prose.

CHAPTER 3

The Priest and His People: The Contractual Basis for Religious Practice in Rural Portugal

Caroline B. Brettell

IN THE opening pages of his novel *Catholics* Brian Moore (1972) introduces us to Father Kinsella, a liberal papal emissary who has been sent to western Ireland to confront a traditionalist abbot who continues to cater to popular demand in the celebration of a pilgrimage banned by the Catholic church. Kinsella represents a church where priestly garb is no longer worn, where private confessions are no longer given, and where miracles are looked on with skepticism. As the situation of conflict develops, a friend tells Kinsella, "People are sheep. They have not changed. They want those old parish priests. . . . They don't want this ecumenical tolerance" (p. 17).

While Moore's fictional rendition of a confrontation between people's religion and institutional religion is set at some point in the future, it evokes a structural opposition that is centuries old and that forms the basis for definitions of popular or folk religion. Popular religion, according to the Italian historian Gabriele De Rosa (1977), applies to any social situation where a conflict or dialectic emerges between official religious models proposed by the ecclesiastical hierarchy and "unofficial" forms. "Folk religion," argues Peter Williams (1980:60), "involves an implicit tension and may be viewed as a dialectic between two opposed forces which those who are caught between them attempt to reconcile into an uneasy equilibrium."

This chapter employs this dialectical framework as the basis for a discussion of Catholicism in rural Portugal. My purpose is not to consider doctrine or belief per se but to explore the way in which priest and parishioners negotiate the practice of religion in their communities. Therefore I will have no direct concern with agricultural rites that may or may not date to "pagan" times; nor will I treat in any great detail beliefs about the healing powers of saints, the magic of witches, or the power of the evil eye. Rather, I am interested in the contractual relationship between the doctrinal definition of religion adhered to by the parish priest and other church officials and the ideas about religion and community behavior that are the will of the people. Folk Catholicism is rooted in this contract such that manifestations of religious practice (embodying both belief and behavior) are neither totally of the orthodox institution (represented by its priests) nor totally of the people. They are, more often than not, an accommodation between the two.

The data for this analysis are drawn from my own field research, as well as from other ethnographic and historical data assembled by scholars of Portuguese culture and society. In reviewing this material I have identified four structural oppositions that are important facets of contractual religiosity in the Portuguese context. While not mutually exclusive, I treat them separately because they permit me to emphasize different issues. The first opposition focusses attention on the tension between individual faith and community solidarity. Here I deal with quite distinct religious models that occasionally come into conflict depending on how rigorously the priest upholds the tenets of post-Tridentine Catholicism. The second opposition emphasizes the uneasy balance between the sacred and the profane. These are not separate realms but instead complexly intertwined aspects of Portuguese Catholicism. The third opposition is rooted in the notion of anticlericalism as religious belief. The parish priest must carry out his orthodox functions in cooperation with his people and in face of their censure and criticism. The final structural opposition emerges from the class-based relationship between the priest and his parishioners. There is a significant regional difference in this relationship within Portugal that has affected religious practice.

While I feel that these four oppositions cover the significant and identifiable tensions in Portuguese religious practice, in different cultural contexts others may emerge. Conversely, although I have neither the space nor the breadth of knowledge to treat it in depth here, all of these oppositions have cross-cultural manifestations. I have attempted to indicate this by briefly introducing appropriate comparative material in the text and notes.

Individual Faith or Community Religion

During fieldwork conducted more than a decade ago in a Portuguese immigrant community in Toronto I interviewed a young Portuguese priest who was ministering to his countrymen—most of them from the Azorean archipelago. In a few weeks he was to be faced with the task of celebrating the Feast of Espírito Santo in his parish. He talked about the personal spiritual problem that this task posed to him. As far as he was concerned, this particular feast, and others like it, were an unfortunate aspect of Portuguese religiosity but one that the people—like the Catholics in Brian Moore's novel—demanded. He then talked about the emphasis in seminary training upon an individual's relationship to his God and his church.

This was the kind of religion that he wanted to foster—not the communal and public celebration that the Feast of Espírito Santo represented. Yet, as the Portuguese ethnographer Jorge Dias has pointed out, it is the latter that is at the very heart of Portuguese Catholicism. Of the people of the communitarian village of Rio de Onor, Dias wrote: "Their exuberant and extroverted temperament is directed more to the exterior manifestations of religion than to silent prayer or exalted mysticism" (1981:159).[1]

In a study of São Miguel, a parish made up of thirty-four villages and hamlets and located in the province of Estremadura northwest of Lisbon, Riegelhaupt (1973) has explored this conflict between interior individual faith and exterior communal religion. She delineates a grid of *festa* celebrations according to the degree of church involvement and the social/ territorial units involved. Over time there has been a decline in the number of *festas* approved of by the church. Conversely, and in response, the number of festivals organized at the village level rather than in the parish seat has increased. Riegelhaupt argues that local differences and local rivalries, and therefore communal solidarity, are manifested in these *festa* celebrations. They are expressions of group membership.[2] In São Miguel even life cycle events are turned into communal "rites of intensification" that involve the entire village (Riegelhaupt 1973:851). Pina-Cabral (1986) makes a similar point for the two villages in northwestern Portugal that he has studied. In addition, he describes the *compasso*, an Easter ritual that takes the priest and processional cross on an ordered (always to the right) visit to each household, thereby binding parishioners together into a community of *vizinhos* (neighbors).

These life cycle and annual rituals are both officiated over and tolerated by local clerics because they are accompanied by quite orthodox behavior. Saint processions, on the other hand, are another matter. These are the traditional rites that the priest of São Miguel adamantly refuses to sanction. His objections, as described by Riegelhaupt, are similar to those I had heard from the Portuguese priest in Toronto. In Portugal "modern Catholicism . . . is designed for individual salvation and it does not see itself as the institution through which communal identity should be expressed and celebrated" (1973:849). According to the priest in São Miguel, only activities that take place physically in the church constitute religious behavior. The opposition to processions voiced by the priest of São Miguel is similar to that reported for other regions of western Europe. A priest in the Dutch Brabant, for example, told the ethnographer Mart Bax (1983:170), "never in my life a procession in this parish!" Like the Portuguese priest I interviewed in Toronto, the Dutch cleric wanted, at least ideally, to guide his parishioners "as well-equipped Catholics into modern society." In a slightly different vein the priest in the northwestern Portuguese village studied by Pina-Cabral (1986:131) favors the *festa* of St. Sebastian (his chosen saint) and opposes all others—a hypocritical stance from the perspective of his parishioners. When he attempted to assume greater control of this *festa*, he was opposed by his parishioners, who refused to attend. This, in Pina-Cabral's view, illustrates the dilemma of priests who are "torn between the religious beliefs of the church hierarchy and those of 'popular religion.' "

The conflict between a religion stressing local community experience that often occurs beyond the physical boundaries of the church and one centered on individual salvation has a long history in Portugal. For example, a 1477 synodal charter for the city of Braga, the seat of the Catholic church in the north of the country, prohibited masses at the foot of trees, in fields or village squares, processions to the mountains or simply to open fields (Sanchis 1983:133). If attempts to rein religion into the confines of the institutional church are pre-Tridentine, the reforms emerging from the Council of Trent were aimed specifically to turn "collective Christians into individual ones" (Bossy 1970:62). Yet, local historical documents, in addition to ethnographic accounts, repeatedly yield descriptions of the survival of collective religious traditions despite the Tridentine reforms. Some priests clearly continued, and continue, to accommodate themselves to the will of parishioners who prefer the exterior and communitywide expression of religion.[3]

In the parish of Santa Maria de Alvarenga in northwestern Portugal the *Usos e Costumbres* (Practices and Customs) of the early eighteenth century recorded a tension between "a popular religion of shoutings [*clamores*] that emphasized community identity and the individual, family-centered, religion of the priest" (Johnson 1983:191). *Clamores* were short pilgrimages around the village or within the region to specific sanctuaries or localities. Very often they united priest and parishioners in penitential processions to ward off or give thanks for relief from prolonged dry spells, damaging rains, famines, and plagues.[4] In the village of Arca, in the district of Ponte de Lima, at the end of the eighteenth century the priest led a *clamor* every Friday during Lent, and on each occasion the penitents raised an offering of 600 *reis* (Soares 1977:140).

The twentieth century counterparts to these eighteenth-century *clamores* are the *romarias* to local and regional shrines that occur throughout northern Portugal during the summer months. Sometimes local clerics are present; other times they are not. For example, in the region of Portugal where I carried out fieldwork there is an annual pilgrimage in early June to the shrine of Santa Luzia located at the top of the hill that overlooks the provincial town and county seat of Viana do Castelo. This pilgrimage dates back to 1918 when the Spanish flu devastated the population of this region. It was initiated in the form of a collective vow or promise (*promessa*) by all the villages in the region to give thanks for the disappearance of this disasterous epidemic. At its inception it was approved by the church hierarchy. Under the anticlerical First Republic, this was, after all, a period of great difficulty for the Catholic church in Portugal. And yet a year earlier the miracles at Fátima had enthralled the population of the nation, giving evidence to the force of public and mass religious expression.

While the parishioners of villages in the District of Viana do Castelo have continued to observe the pilgrimage to Santa Luzia, local clerics have occasionally become lax in their involvement. One year, according to several informants, few priests showed up and the people became extremely angry. During the summer of 1978 when I participated in this pilgrimage a group arrived in the town for the early mass only to find the doors of the church locked. The assembled pilgrims joked about lazy priests who were still in bed and commented that they did not seem to take the occasion as seriously as their parishioners. However, later in the morning parish priests were in full force, organizing the procession into alphabetical order by village for the penitential march up the hill to the sanctuary. They led the parishioners in song and prayer during the procession and participated in the outdoor mass at the shrine. People made comments about the relative strengths of representation of one village as opposed to another and therein demonstrated the *bairrismo* (parochialism) that is manifested in both local and regional *festas* and pilgrimages.

A few weeks later during the same summer, on the occasion of the annual *romaria* to a shrine of Our Lady of Minho high in the mountain range that overlooks the Lima River valley in northern Portugal, the new bishop of the recently formed diocese of Viana do Castelo passed through the village of Santa Eulália de Lanheses where I conducted fieldwork. The priest encouraged his parishioners to extend him a hearty welcome, and local pride was gratified when, on the succeeding weekend, the priest read a letter from the bishop thanking Lanhesans for their warm reception and their expression of faith. Indeed, it is probably safe to conclude that the naming of a new bishop reinvigorated communal and public religious practices like the *romarias* to Santa Luzia and Our Lady of Minho. Like the 1910s, the late 1970s was a period of difficulty for the Catholic church in Portugal as it attempted to define its position in the young democracy of the post-Salazar era. Exterior manifestations of support communicated louder messages than interior and individual expressions of faith.

The *clamores* of old, the numerous summer-month *romarias* of today, and the range of local village *festas* serve to define and reinforce community identity. They extend, at least in the minds of believers, sacred space into secular space (Christian [1981a] uses the expression "God-in-Landscape") and very often provide the basis for an expansion of mar-

Welcoming the image of Nossa Senhora do Minho in Santa Eulália de Lanheses, Portugal.

riage networks. While some priests vocalize objections to these public and communal manifestations of Catholic faith, others participate fully, recognizing not only their importance to parishioners but also the occasional benefits that they provide in terms of continued mass support for the institutional church. But because such communal forms of religious expression serve equally as opportunities for diversion and entertainment, they aggravate a confrontation not only between individual faith and communal solidarity but also between the sacred and the secular.

THE SACRED AND THE SECULAR

In what should be considered a classic article on folk Catholicism Freeman (1978:102) distinguishes "faith" (what she calls religion) from a number of other elements that are "often bound up with its expression: habit, or tradition; display, or ostentation; and the pursuit of leisure." The latter two elements often fall into a category that some label "profane," and yet they are fundamentally linked to the notion of "faith." Thus, a nineteenth-century traveler to Portugal described a *romaria* that he had witnessed in the following way:

> The *romarias* are more serious affairs, and occupy a large place in the social life of the peasantry. . . . At these gatherings there are sermons to be heard,

religious exercises to be performed and, as the occasion has some of the characteristics of a country fair, there is an immense deal of laughing, gossiping, dancing and singing (Latoche 1875:96–97).[5]

The recreational aspect of religious festivals has been noted by a number of anthropologists of European society (cf. Boissevain 1984; Dubisch this volume), but the response on the part of the church hierarchy, whether in the past or at present, has been explored less systematically.[6] In the Portuguese context the clerical attitude is apparent in a widely circulated "Pastoral Letter on *Festas*" of 1943 written by a northern Portuguese bishop, D. Agostinho de Jesus e Sousa. Sousa wrote of the "abuses and disrespect for the church and the damage to souls" that *festas* manifested. His goal was to "restore the *festa* to its essentially religious character." "As it is not legitimate," he stated, "to mix sacred things with profane things, every effort should be made to eradicate, during religious *festas*, profane diversions, above all nocturnal carnivals [*arraial*] that frequently become an affront to God and the ruin of good habits. The Council prohibits, on the occasion of *festas*, dances and spectacles in the courtyard or near the church" (Sousa 1943). D. Agostinho asked his priests to avoid hiring musical bands, to abandon the custom of auctions (*leilão*) or raffles (*rifas*). He reminded his clerics of the aims of *festas*—to honor God and the saints, to attend to the divinity of Christ and the worship that he requires, to attain pardon and mercy for the sins of humanity, and to give thanks for the numerous benefits that God constantly concedes.

In 1979 the bishop of the newly formed diocese of Viana do Castelo disseminated a similar pastoral urging his priests to discourage the more profane aspects of *festas*. The major objections in both these pastoral letters was not, therefore, to the *festa* per se but to that part of it that involved dancing, music, fireworks, and other forms of public entertainment—the *arraial*. Similar objections were directed by the Portuguese Catholic hierarchy toward *romarias*. Thus, a priest writing about the parish of Vieira do Minho in 1923 observed: "When the Church *festa* has finished, the people exit and the *festa* becomes almost sensual and completely pagan. Already no one remembers Our Lady nor the saints. It is the sad side of *romarias*" (Vieira 1923:221; my emphasis). Since *romarias* are often cited as examples of the gaiety of the Minhotan peasants of northern Portugal, this priest's choice of the word "sad" is both ironic and significant.

The conflict between *festa* and *arraial* became an intense matter of debate in the parish of Lanheses. Briefly, the annual *festa* of Senhor do Cruzeiro received new vigor during the late 1960s and 1970s as a result of contributions made by emigrants to France (Brettell 1983). It was organized and controlled by the parish priest who disapproved of the peo-

Senhor do Cruzeiro, Santa
Eulália de Lanheses, Portugal.

ple's desire for a musical band to play on Saturday night, although he
conceded each year in hiring a band to play in the Sunday procession and
in the courtyard in front of the church after the procession. In general,
parishioners felt that the *festa* without its Saturday evening *arraial* and
dancing was no *festa* at all, and they wanted the band to play on the
village square (*feira*) (the secular center) and not in the courtyard of the
church (the sacred center). More particularly, young people claimed that
the band hired by the priest from year to year "não presta para nada" (is
worth nothing) and accused him of being tightfisted with the money that
was given for the celebration of the *festa*. In fact, few parishioners, young
or old, remained by the church to listen after the procession. Instead,
they went off to eat and drink with family and friends.

Disagreements over control (to which I will return) and organization
became so intense by the mid 1970s that several villagers were motivated
to launch their own laically organized and laically controlled *festa* two
weekends later. This *festa* had no religious procession and no saint's image associated with it. It had all the attributes of a carnival, with live
entertainment and dancing on the village square on Saturday night. It
was held for three successive summers, but pretty soon villagers became
tired of contributing money to two *festas* and began to claim that the

second was "not a real *festa* because it had no saint's image." Curiously, emigrants expressed this sentiment most strongly. Their ties to their native village are closely allied with the annual saint's *festa*, and they time their summer vacations in conjunction with its celebration. The saint, in short, is a symbolic representation of their identity.

Support for the laically organized *festa* declined, and it eventually ceased. But the *festa* of Senhor do Cruzeiro continues, celebrated as the priest wants it to be. Yet the tensions have not been eliminated: just as the attempt at the laity-organized *festa* was considered incomplete without its saint's image, so too the priest-organized *festa* remains incomplete without an *arraial*.[7]

The central importance of the saint in Portuguese *festas* and *romarias* is also described by Sanchis (1983:90). What celebrants want to hear in the homilies delivered on these occasions are details of the lives of the saints, "especially miraculous episodes that manifest their power." Any other theme, particularly one of a more secular nature, will not do. Sanchis records, for example, the dissatisfaction that the people in the parish of Tinalhas expressed when the guest preacher tried to generalize from the life of the Virgin to a discussion of the Christian woman in Portugal today affected by war and the emigration of men. Yet Sanchis equally recognizes the significance of the *arraial*. Band and preacher (*pregador*), procession and fireworks, each is evaluated with equal interest by those

Bearing the Holy Sacrament, *Festa* of Senhor do Cruzeiro, Santa Eulália de Lanheses, Portugal.

attending local *festas* or regional *romarias*. Only with *all* these elements is a *festa* a true *festa*.

PIETY OR PRELACY: ANTICLERICALISM AS RELIGIOUS BELIEF

While Riegelhaupt touched upon the issue of anticlericalism in her analysis of the *festa* cycle in São Miguel, it was in later papers (1982, 1984) that she focussed on it more forthrightly, defining it as a fundamental part of the system of belief in Portuguese society. Anticlericalism, she claimed, may have little to do with irreligiosity. Rather, it is generally directed toward the priest as an individual and the church as an institution. As one Lanhesan informant phrased it, "I like the mass, I like religion, but I do not like priests." In Salazarist Portugal the priest was an effective agent of the state at the local level. Added to this political role has been, at least in some cases, an entrepreneurial tendency to make religion into a lucrative "business." Together these have been sufficient to feed a resentment that generated anticlerical sentiments that were either "pious" (criticisms of the way the priest conducts the religious life of the parish) or "secular" (criticism of the worldly activities of priests) (Cutileiro 1971; Riegelhaupt 1984:97).

Anticlericalism is often couched in gossip about the inability of priests to keep their vows of celibacy—they are, after all, "just like any other man." In Lanheses I heard as many allusions to the lovers (*amantes*) of priests as I think Riegelhaupt (1982, 1984) heard in São Miguel and Pina-Cabral (1981, 1986) heard in his Minhotan villages. In fact, anticlericalism, particularly its "eroticized" form, is something that most ethnographers of European peasant society have confronted and recorded in their field notes.[8] Certainly historical records kept by the church mention behavioral problems within the priesthood. For example, an 1845 report from the parish of Aboím da Chocas, in the district of Arcos de Valdevez, reported the concubinage of a forty-two-year-old priest with a neighbor (Soares 1975:18). In the parish of Aguia the sixty-two-year-old prelate was supposedly living "more cautiously and with less scandal" today than in the past (Soares 1975:26); and in the parish of Cardiellos (district of Viana do Castelo) the local priest "did not enjoy the good opinion of his parishioners because of a sister-in-law who has lived with him for many years and, in the opinion of many, her husband had died full of disgust" (Soares 1980:130).

In a preliminary analysis of the data from periodic inquiries into the moral behavior of parish priests, Soares (1982) calculates that 25 percent had "censurable" conduct, though censurable did not always refer to sexual behavior. In fact, Pina-Cabral (1986) has suggested that greed, egoism, and incompetence are perhaps more deeply resented than the lack of chastity. Goldey (1983:8) cites an eighteenth-century tussle between a local parish priest and the villagers over a piece of common land that he was using for his own purposes. Accusations "of the priest's failure to provide the last sacrament to the dying, and his demanding more money from tithes to cover church expenses" were also brought before the tribunal.

The greed of the parish priest was repeatedly an issue raised by parishioners in Lanheses. After the procession in honor of Senhor do Cruzeiro there is an auction of the tiered trays laden with food and wine (*tabuleiras*) that the patrons (*mordomas*) of different saints' images carry on their heads during the procession. It is interesting that the priest concedes to this activity. Such auctions, it will be recalled, were also considered objectionable and profane by D. Agostinho in his 1940s pastoral letter. The concession is made because the auctions raise significant sums of money. While villagers enjoy the sparring that bidding entails (Brettell 1983), after the fact complaints about accountability arise. The priest is accused of hoarding the funds, of spending it on himself when he should be spending it on a better procession, band, or firework display.

Such head-on battles between priest and parishioners over funds raised by the patron saint during the annual *festa* have been described for other regions of Portugal (Riegelhaupt 1973) and elsewhere in southern Europe (Schneider and Schneider 1984). In her analysis of the exploitation of both the economic and political potential of saint feasts by priests and political parties in southern Italy, Di Tota (1981:322) concludes "that a distinction must be drawn between what the saint cults actually represent for their supporters and the outside speculations made on behalf of the saint cults."[9]

In São Miguel parishioners began to accuse the priest of "running a business" rather than observing a religion (Riegelhaupt 1973). In Lanheses this accusation is most strongly manifested in complaints that emerge about the discouragement (by the church hierarchy) of religious vows that involve physical sacrifice (walking barefoot during the procession, for example) in favor of monetary vows. Village emigrants are most able to make substantial monetary contributions, a fact that "buys" them prestige (one villager referred to it as "holy vanity") since the donated sums are published in the village newspaper. Nonemigrants, whose contributions are also published, feel they look cheap by comparison.

Sanchis' (1983) more widespread study of *festas* in Portugal indicates how generalized the preference for money is within the church hierarchy. He describes locales where the "price" to support the sermon at the *festa* (a form of vow) is three times as costly as that for a regular sermon and suggests that the efforts to discourage theatrical promises in favor of more discrete donations represents a vying for control. When people are

Three young boys dressed as *anjinhos* to fulfill a religious promise (*promessa*), Santa Eulália de Lanheses, Portugal.

fulfilling sacrificial promises, he observes (1983:51), they rarely consult the priest and even if they do his words hardly have authority.

Money has become an issue in discussions of many of the other annual religious or life cycle rituals that are celebrated and that have always involved a contribution to the church or the priest. In Lanheses angry words were exchanged when the priest tried to charge three times as much for a wedding mass once he heard that several of the bride's cousins who were members of the local choral group had offered to sing at the service. Those who spoke of the conflict saw no authority for the priest in setting a new price; the parents, some claimed, were not rich, and the gesture was a family affair not a church affair. They viewed the adjustment of fees by the priest as an opportunistic attempt to coopt the new prosperity of the village, much of it the result of emigration to France in the 1960s and 1970s. By contrast, several villagers commented that the parish priest who served between 1927 and 1967 often charged nothing for baptisms, marriages, and funerals, especially if he saw that a family had few resources.

It has also become common practice for the priest to send envelopes around at Easter. Donations of *escudos* are supposed to replace the traditional offering of eggs (the *folar*). Criticism emerges not only from discontent over the greater amount that is required but also over the loss of symbolism associated with the *folar* and the increasing impersonality of vows. Yet as Goldey (1983:11) has so eloquently written in her study of aspects of folk religion and death in another community in northwestern Portugal, the modern clergy "discount the fact that [these symbols] are ultimately both ideologically and ritually within the tradition of Catholicism, and are contained within the same belief system." Underlying all these censures of either the pious or secular behavior and practice of priests are, as Riegelhaupt (1982) recognizes, native notions about what religion *should be.* Thus, residents of São Miguel, particularly the women, had their own expectations for the appropriate form and timing of particular aspects of worship and complained vocally when the priest introduced changes. One Lanhesan woman strongly criticized the priest for using the pulpit as a vehicle for political statements.[10] Another complained of the priest's decision to move the celebration of the feast of Santo Antão (an occasion in the past when farm animals were blessed) from a Thursday to a Sunday against the desires of the parishioners. During the Easter *compasso* of 1988 the priest in Lanheses sent two laymen in his place around the village with the cross and holy water. Many parishioners were outraged, and in one hamlet alone only one of the twenty households opened its doors in welcome. "This ceremony needs to have a priest," commented one villager. "If he could not go, he should have arranged to have a priest from another village. But he wanted to save money." "Our priest was censured by the priests of neighboring parishes," added a second villager. "They felt sorry for the people of Lanheses."

In the villages of Paço and Couto studied by Pina-Cabral (1986:211), the priest was described as lazy for his reluctance to bless water; his refusal to exorcize people possessed by the soul of dead relatives was attributed to cowardice. In Pina-Cabral's view such comments are facets of personalized anticlericalism. However, they also indicate precisely where the parish priest draws the line in what he considers to be appropriate religious (as opposed to superstitious) practice.

Riegelhaupt (1982:1226) has argued that underlying the complaints and accusations is a fundamental "questioning of the privileged position of the priest to mediate between man and God, to have exclusive responsibility for ritual performance, exclusive control of sacramental graces, and to be responsible to the upper hierarchy rather than the local congregation." In Lanheses such objections were rather curiously manifested in debates about the pros and cons of the vow of priestly celibacy. Given the fact that priests are "men like other men," there was a general feeling that permitting them to marry would be a good thing. However, reservations arose when villagers began to consider how the wife of the priest might view herself. She would, they thought, set herself up as the mistress (*dona*) of the parish and feel superior to everyone. This was unacceptable.

In the final analysis it was very difficult for the Lanhesans with whom I raised the question to decide definitively whether priestly celibacy was a good idea or not. But in their discussions of this issue they raised complexities that the ambiguous position of the parish priest generates—particularly the contradiction between social normality and local power and control. Freeman (1970), for example, compares shepherds in Valdemora to priests. Both are seen as celibates, but celibacy is unnatural. Both are vulnerable to, and suspected of, illicit liasons. Such doubts about sexuality, she argues, arise for people who are occupationally marginal, isolated from the social control that characterizes life in a small village community. Yet for Portuguese villagers the ability to criticize the priest, to comment about his behavior, is a means of having some sort of control over an individual who, through both his education and his position, can exercise significant power over them. Gossip helps to neutralize this power.

Many Portuguese villagers are now beginning to reject the priest as a superordinate mediator altogether. Indeed, in the post-Salazar period Lanhesans, particularly the men, are characterizing the local priest as the "servant" of the village, subject to their will rather than the reverse. In the past rejection of the priest by the male segment of the population more often took the form of nonparticipation. However, nonparticipation should not be considered equivalent to secularization. Low church attendance may have little to do with the strength of religious beliefs, or may measure something completely different from what it is presumed to be measuring. Riegelhaupt (1982) suggests that nonattendance is a form of protest against a religion that is not practiced the way people want it to be and against a clergy that abuses its privileges. Embedded in this perception of abuse is, at least for some, an element of class conflict.

FOLK VERSUS ELITE: RELIGIOSITY AND CLASS CONFLICT

Taking their lead from Gramsci, several recent scholars view the dimension of class as crucial to an understanding of popular religion or folk Catholicism. Saint cults are seen as the religion of the socially and economically marginalized within Catholic societies. Popular religiosity represents an affirmation by lower classes (both urban and rural) of their culture (Appel 1982; Di Tota 1981; Pace 1979; Prandi 1977).

Some of these writers, notably the historian De Rosa (1977), prefer to conceptualize a complex intertwining of the religion of the marginalized with that of the dominant—the relationship is not always adversarial. Others disagree, arguing that where the dichotomy has emerged, it is linked to the institutionalization of a class of priests or to churches allied with economic and political powers (Lanternari 1982; see also Badone this volume). Through popular religion lower social strata respond to dominant classes, or a whole society responds to outside forces, as in the case of nativist movements.[11]

In Portugal the relationship between class antagonism and folk Catholicism is at the root of a fundamental regional difference between the north (and to a lesser extent the center) of the country—peasant Portugal—and the south—rural proletarian Portugal. In the south, since at least the early 1830s when the church backed the reactionary regency of Dom Miguel in the short-lived Civil War, Catholicism has been viewed by many as the religion of the elite and land-owning classes. In rejecting what is the national religion landless laborers were (in pre-1974 terms) rejecting the economic and political "powers-that-be" who were more closely allied to the institutional church. In addition, the clerics who ministered to the population of the south were more commonly associated with religious orders and were weakened during periods of history when their properties were seized (in the 1830s and again under the First Portuguese Republic between 1910 and 1926). They have traditionally been outsiders rather than natives of the parishes to which they minister.

Several aspects of the character of religion and the role of the church in southern Portugal are well-documented by Cutileiro (1971) in his study of Vila Velha. Priests who have served the village have commonly been landowners, "exacting regular payments and showing little understanding for the difficulties of their tenants or sharecroppers" (Cutileiro 1971:262). Cutileiro describes one incident where the local priest asked a wealthy landowner what time he would prefer the mass to be held on a succeeding Sunday before announcing the time to the rest of the parish. When another wealthy nonresident decided to build a house in the village, he placed the priest in charge of payments to local workers. Although the owner agreed to pay urban rates, the priest decided that these sums were too high and instead paid at the local rate. This action, according to Cutileiro, was interpreted by villagers as an alliance between the local priest and a wealthy outsider of the community, and ultimately as a manifestation of the gulf between rich and poor.

Vila Velha had no resident priest between 1911 and 1945. Although a priest took up residence in 1945, attendance at church ceremonies has remained low. At the time of Cutileiro's research a number of the local chapels were in ruins. While their number may be evidence of a stronger religiosity in the past, Cutileiro demonstrates that support for the church was weak well before the introduction of the First Republic. The permanent presence of a priest since 1945 has not, in his view, reinvigorated the part played by the church in the life of Vila Velhans. At most the local population pays attention to life cycle events, though even in this regard the intervention of the church varies depending on prevailing political, ideological, and administrative conditions (Cutileiro 1971:256). Popular festivals are observed but with an evident independence of tradition and liturgy (Cutileiro 1971:254).[12] Serrador's (1983) observations of the *festa* of the "Senhora da Boa Nova" in a town east of Evora in southern Portugal led her to focus more on the responsibilities of and conflicts within the lay commission of *festas* than on the role of the priest or the nature of religious devotion.

Sanchis (1983:103) illuminates the connection between religion and class confrontation in southern Portugal in a discussion of the formation of the League of Catholic Agriculturalists of the Alentejo by the bishop of Evora in 1923. The aims of this league, he argues, were to defend the interests of the church and of *latifundia* agriculture in the region. "In order to restore religious spirit, two means were particularly emphasized in the statutes: the celebration of religious rites of an agricultural nature [the *festas*] and Christian moralization, the true remedy against social revolution." A little more than a decade later, and faced with the Civil War in Spain, a pastoral issued by the bishop of Portalegre tried to bring rich and poor together and show each their obligations. To the first the bishop preached the necessity of just salaries; to the second the dangers of revolution. And yet he concluded that the poor should be more reasonable in their demands, conquer the heart of the landowners ("whose cross to bear is sometimes heavier than yours") with their zeal and love of work. "The *patrão*," he admonished, "ought not to be viewed as a tyrant, because he almost never is" (quoted in Sanchis 1983:103). Such cooptation, Sanchis argues, has weakened adherence to both orthodox religious forms as well as to some more popular manifestations in southern Portugal.

By contrast to the southern half of the nation, the north of Portugal, where gaps in wealth are much less pronounced, is labelled the most Catholic region. The people of this region stood behind the Catholic church after 1974, responding to sermons delivered from the pulpit which suggested that a Communist Portugal would deprive them of the properties that had been in their hands for generations.[13] Into the present the ratio of priests to population has been much higher, and parish priests have been integral to the life of their local communities. Many, as Pina-Cabral (1986) points out, have been serving the same parish for more than twenty-five years. In Lanheses the current priest and two of his recent predecessors have been local sons. The penultimate priest served the parish for almost as long as Salazar ruled the country, from 1927 to 1967. The priest who ministered to the parish in the late nineteenth and early twentieth centuries is remembered particularly as a *lavrador* (peasant) who shooed away the *beatas* (overly devout women) on any other day but Sunday. Though he does not work the land himself, the current priest (in office since 1967) takes an interest in the property that he inherited, and his family is classified among the more substantial peasant households in recent times. In the summer of 1984 an elaborate ceremony celebrated the ordination of the son of a respected peasant family. The pride in such an achievement is felt by the community as a whole. In other words, local priests in northern Portugal are commonly insiders rather than outsiders. While their profession sets them apart, they nevertheless share interests and very often ties of kinship with their parishioners. It is precisely the complexity of priestly involvement that makes northern anticlericalism different from that in the south.

Although they were instrumental to the Salazar regime to monitor behavior and relay official propaganda (Gallaghar 1987), northern parish priests equally kept alive some of the religious traditions to which the orthodox hierarchy was itself sometimes opposed. Pina-Cabral (1981) draws, I think, a very important distinction between types of priests: old-fashioned, *bruxo* (white witch), and modern. Old-fashioned priests still wear robes, and their churches are often unmodernized. Although they do not claim to believe in superstitions themselves, they do not wholly condemn such beliefs among their parishioners. *Bruxo* priests are closely involved in miraculous and symbolic religious behavior for which they may accept payments in kind or in cash. They are more often found in remote, out-of-the-way parishes.

Modern priests make up the majority of Portuguese priests today. They have, in Pina-Cabral's view, been most influenced by Vatican II, though he rightly cautions the extent to which changes were made in Portugal by comparison with other Catholic Western European countries. Many of these modern priests, including the priest in Lanheses, combine their religious duties with educational responsibilities in local high schools. Their functions are, in short, secular as well as sacred. Needless to say there are Lanhesans who strongly object to the amount of time that the local priest spends on secular matters associated with the school. Moving *festas* from mid-week to Sunday is done to accommodate these secular activities, but the parishioners feel that a priest's major responsibilities lie in the sacred realm.

The significant implication of the differences among priests is that in order to fully understand the nature of rural Catholicism it has to be examined at the local level as it revolves around the character, social interactions, and outlook of particular parish clerics. Do they view themselves, as most do in southern Portugal, as members of the bourgeois elite; or do they aim to be "popular" in the Portuguese sense—that is, a man of the people? Is their world view consistent with that of the people, or is it something different? It is these distinctions that help to explain local variations in anticlericalism and in the relationship between the religion of the people and that of the priest. As Almeida (1986:329) has so bluntly put it, "to feel good or bad about religion, to demonstrate conformism, indifference or revolt depends many times, for the *vizinhos* [neighbors], on the way in which they evaluate the behavior of the priest who at that moment has befallen them."

CONCLUSION

In his study of miracles and prophecies in nineteenth-century France Thomas Kselman (1983:10) concludes that the ambivalent attitude of Catholicism toward popular religion "results from its suspicion of supernatural graces obtained outside the sacramental system and its simultaneous realization of the importance of such graces in the religious life of the ordinary believer." This ambivalence, and the process of accommodation that is associated with it, are the basis for an ongoing contractual relationship between the orthodox religion espoused by the church hierarchy and its representatives and the folk religion of local parishioners. Though I have treated it here with respect to Portugal, this contractual relationship has obviously characterized the practice of Catholicism throughout western Europe from the beginning of the Christian era. Even the generosity with which marital dispensations were granted can be taken as further evidence of the process of accommodation. The church could make it difficult to marry a first cousin, but it could not totally prevent it.

Just as the abbot on the fictional Irish island locale of Brian Moore's novel could not ignore the pressures of a populace that demanded the continued celebration of outdoor masses at a holy site, so too have local Portuguese clerics catered to popular desires for pilgrimages to holy shrines, public observances of saint feasts, and myriad other forms of religious practice that the hierarchy does not always deem appropriate. Occasionally there are struggles within the hierarchy itself, a point made forcefully clear by Bax (1985a) in a discussion of religious infighting between secular and regular clergy in the Dutch Brabant. Bax is in fact responsible for what is one of the most curious descriptions of accommodation and negotiation in the ethnographic literature on western Europe. He traces the expansion (1490–1876), waning (1876–1965), and revival (1965–) of the devotion to St. Gerlach among the population of the rural town of Roersel. Although Rome was questioning the saintly status of Gerlach by the mid 1970s, the fathers of a local monastery that was struggling to survive catered to popular demand in keeping the devotion alive through support of a public procession. However, they went further, introducing a new public ceremony.

Every second Saturday in June, large numbers of motorists from the town and the district have their cars blessed. The ceremony provides special protection against increasingly dangerous traffic but also encourages careful and responsible driving. Some 200 persons, united in the Confraternity of the Blessed Gerlach, meet several times a year for instruction, devotion, and retreat with special masses. (The rear windows of cars bear a small protection sticker—an example to others) (Bax 1985b:221).

The power of accommodating to the way in which the people want religion to be practiced has been recognized by both sacred and secular institutions. In Portugal the Catholic church quickly recognized the political significance of Fátima. Salazar made a very conscious decision when he promoted a tour of her image throughout the country in the early 1950s. And today, regional government funds are available to support local religious *festas*. They are good for tourism. Not only do they bring the emigrants back, they bring their remittances back. Bax (1985a:71) is right to call for more studies by ethnographers of European society of the conditions and forces that not only generate but also perpetuate popular religious practices and folk belief.

Notes to Chapter 3

I am grateful to a number of foundations that have supported my work in Portugal over the years. Among these are the Social Science Research Council, the Gulbenkian Foundation, the Wenner-Gren Foundation for Anthropological Research, the Institute of Emigration in Lisbon, and the National Institute of Child Health and Human Development.

1. Vasconcellos (1958) and Unamuno (1911) have made similar observations and on this basis outline important differences between Spanish and Portuguese religiosity.

2. The role of religious festivals either in enhancing or neutralizing political divisions has been widely discussed. In Europe it is treated by Boissevain (1965, 1984), Di Tota (1981), Freeman (1968), Rapp (1986), and Silverman (1976, 1981). The body of literature that is building on ethnic festivals in the United States certainly indicates their importance as mechanisms for the expression of community identity and a sense of belonging (see, for examples, Orsi 1985 and Swiderski 1986).

3. Devlin (1987:6) describes a similar preference among the rural folk of nineteenth-century France. The people "knew little of elementary doctrine and preferred self-interested supplication and festive celebration to introspective piety and devotion."

4. Christian (1981a) views the sense of defenselessness in the face of epidemics, blights, drought, et cetera to be at the root of the devotional acts associated with local (folk, popular) religion. Further discussion of *clamores* can be found in Braga (1943). Larkin (1972) cites the devotional revolution of mid-nineteenth century Ireland as the mechanism that brought people into the church. In prefamine Ireland, according to Connolly (1982), pilgrimage shrines and holy wells (originally magical springs) rather than the church were more common foci of group religious behavior.

5. A similar assessment was made about the Neapolitan Festa of the Madonna dell'Arco by a mid-nineteenth century traveler to Italy: "While in the church and the presence of the unveiled miraculous effigies of the Virgin, the people are devout, silent, reverential, and very commonly in tears, in tears of adoration and tenderness; but as soon as the service is over and the images have been worshipped, they bound from the church door to an open level space and begin dancing and singing, feasting and drinking as if their salvation depended on it" (MacFarlane 1846:79).

For a good discussion of a variety of Portuguese *romarias* see Ernesto Veiga de Oliveira (1984) and for a discussion of sacred and profane aspects of medieval pilgrimages see Brooke and Brooke (1984).

6. One exception is Sperber's (1984) remarkable study of popular Catholicism in nineteenth-century Germany. See also Larkin (1972) and Tackett (1977).

7. Kertzer (1974) reports on a curious accommodation between sacred imagery

and secular practice in Italy. The festival cycle supports the established values and institutions of the Catholic church, but in some parts of Italy a competing cycle is staged by the Communist party as a deliberate counter to the political activities of a Catholic-dominated Christian Democratic party. Communist *feste* have a similar format and decor, they are better attended than the religious *feste*, and within their context political party values are ritually expressed.

8. See Brandes (1980) and Gilmore (1984) for a discussion of "eroticized anticlericalism" in Andalusia. The nineteenth-century Portuguese writer Eça de Queiroz fictionalizes the problem in his novel *O Crime de Padre Amaro* (The Sin of Father Amaro). Further discussions of anticlericalism can be found in Badone and Behar in this volume.

9. The business of saint making and the conflict that is therein generated between religious belief and economic profit reaches its greatest heights in association with centers of mass pilgrimage such as Fátima in Portugal or Lourdes in France. See Kselman (1983).

10. Nevertheless it was the church that was largely responsible for rallying an anti-Communist backlash in northern Portugal during the summer of 1975.

11. Outside the European context the work of Pedro A. Ribeiro de Oliveira (1979) on Brazil is enlightening in this regard. In this country, he argues, popular Catholicism became a controversial force against capitalism, emerging in response to modernism rather than surviving as a legacy of tradition. The escape into saints was an escape from proletarianization. It should be noted that this class-based interpretation does not necessarily contradict the view that in earlier centuries both folk and elite participated equally in forms of popular piety (Christian 1981a; Brown 1981). Monter (1983:20) dates a growing separation to the eighteenth century when "a learned elite (with clerics at the forefront) reclassified witchcraft as a form of superstition."

12. Cutileiro's description of religious attitudes in the southern Portuguese town of Vila Velha is similar to Henk Driessen's (1984) discussion of the role of religion as a dimension for the expression of class antagonism in the town of Mirabuenos in Andalusia. In Mirabuenos competition between classes takes on a ritualized form in the rivalry between seven different brotherhoods, each of which is associated with different elements of the class structure.

13. The Maria da Fonte incident of 1846 provides a historical precedent for the political cooperation between clerics and peasants in northern Portugal (see Pinto 1979 and Riegelhaupt 1981). Pina-Cabral and Feijó (1983) describe a confrontation in 1976 when a pro-Communist was attacked and killed by a mob in a conservative region of northern Portugal. Under orders from the archbishop the priest refused to bury the dead man if Communist flags were flown at the funeral. When one appeared, the priest departed. The association between the Portuguese church and anticommunism has of course been explored in discussions of the apparitions at Fátima in 1917 and the cult that stems from it. Christian (1984) develops a more general discussion. Despite all these incidents Gallaghar (1987) raises an extremely interesting point. A mass Catholic political party like those that emerged in Germany, Italy, and Spain failed to materialize in Portugal during the First Republic. Nor has such a party emerged since 1974, a fact that some contemporary observers of Portuguese society and politics find quite significant.

CHAPTER 4

The Struggle for the Church: Popular Anticlericalism and Religiosity in Post-Franco Spain

Ruth Behar

IN THE summer of 1987 the priest of Santa María del Monte, a village in the Cantabrian foothills of Spain, told me the following story:

> I remember I once scandalized a man, scared him. I was in charge of a village in the mountains, very far from here. And there was a saint, the work of a popular saint-carver, and it was very badly made; it was horrible. It was made of wood, but just because it was made of wood doesn't mean it had any art to it. Because it didn't have any. It was horrible. So we ordered another one, of plaster. Now I don't like images made of plaster, because artistically they have no value, but at least they look more normal. So we ordered another one. Someone agreed to donate it. What were we going to do with the other one? I said, this is so ugly that it's a degradation, and what we need to do is burn it. Because it's not good enough to take to a museum or anything. It has to be destroyed. So I burned it. I burned it one day. I went to the cemetery and I made a bonfire there and burned it. The president of the village saw a fire in the cemetery . . . and rushed over . . . and found me there, burning Saint Tirso. He turned white. He froze. And he said, "If they gave me two million I wouldn't do it." "Well, look, I'm doing it and it's nothing. Don't worry. We have another, better one. Don't worry." But the man was left dry. And maybe the thing was that he was attached to that saint and his faith did not go beyond the image. . . . It was hard on him, seeing Saint Tirso there, burning, it was hard. But it had to be done.

I begin with this story because it provides, quite literally, a revealing set of images with which to embark on an analysis of the changing relationship between the institutional church and popular religion in Spain since the reforms of the Second Vatican Council in the early 1960s and the death of General Franco in 1975. This changing relationship, as viewed from the perspective of both local priests and peasant villagers in and around the community of Santa María del Monte, will be the subject of my paper.

Santa María, today a village of just over one hundred people at or near retirement age, forms part of the constellation of small farming and cattle-raising villages clustered near one another in the central valleys of León (cf. Behar 1986). In these villages, ranging in size from fifty to four hundred people, the land, traditionally fragmented into minute fields, has been owned and worked by peasant proprietors, communal institutions of reciprocity and work exchange have been strong, and every community has, until recently, been considered a parish with its own priest. Santa María is located in the most Catholic and rural region of Spain, today known as the autonomous region of Castile-León, where anarchist ideas never took root, large landowners are scarce, and where, despite pious anticlericalism, there is the highest rate of church attendance in Spain.[1] Today in Spain only about 15 percent of the population still works on the land, a significant drop from 1950, when nearly half the population was employed in farm work (Tezanos 1986:52–53).[2] Thus in this paper I offer an analysis of the religious beliefs and practices of a very small minority of rural people, most of them "on their way to their tombs," as they themselves say, whose views are of interest to few in modern, urban Spain.[3]

To understand the meaning, impact, and implications of the religious changes occurring in places like Santa María—to understand, in other words, why that villager turned white at seeing the priest burn a saint's image—we need to view these changes from a historical perspective, taking a look at the rhetoric and reforms of the new "young church" (la iglesia joven) which has developed in contrast and opposition to the religious ideology and style of religiosity of the Franco period. This history, in turn, forms part of the larger history of Spanish Catholicism, which has played a central role in the formation of the Spanish state and Spanish national consciousness.

The point I want to argue here, following Joyce Riegelhaupt (1984), is that the relationship between the priest and his parishioners, especially in the village setting, is one rooted in struggle, a struggle for the church, for the "ownership" of the church. Since the struggle for the church is a struggle for power, I will focus this interpretation on the relationship between religion and power. With its hierarchy, priestly domination, and long history of disciplining the people about their faith, Catholicism seems to lend itself especially well to the perspective that religion needs to be studied not only as an expressive system but, in the words of Talal Asad, as "forms of thought and action that are taught and learnt" (1983:251). In particular, one needs to ask "what are the historical conditions (movements, classes, institutions, ideologies) necessary for the existence of particular religious discourses and practices? How does power create religion?" (1983:252).

While I am in basic agreement with this perspective, I also think we have to be cautious about attributing too much power to the church, making our model of power relations between official religion and popular religion too top-heavy. Village people not only unlearn and reinterpret what they are taught by the church; they have, for centuries, found ways of resisting clerical control over religious belief and practice. Thus popular religious traditions, which the clergy devalue by terming them "superstitions," have often been maintained long after the church presumed them "extirpated" (cf. Schmitt 1983; Riegelhaupt 1985). And the church has long had to struggle with the "magic" of its own practices (cf. Thomas 1971:25–50; O'Neil 1984). On the other hand, it is unquestionable that in the dialogue between a clergy ever bent on reform and village practitioners bent on maintaining continuity with the past the clergy has frequently succeeded in producing drastic changes in the discourse of popular religious cultures (cf. Ginzburg 1983). My aim here, therefore, will be twofold: while considering the particular ways in which power has created, and continues to create, religion in a local Spanish setting, I also want to pay close attention to the ways in which this power is subverted and destabilized by villagers through a complex discourse of pious anticlericalism rooted in the idea that the people themselves, and not the priests, are the bearers of the true faith.

The kind of anticlericalism I will describe here is not new nor unique to rural Spain. The reader who is familiar with Carlo Ginzburg's *The Cheese and the Worms* will see parallels between the critique of priests made by people in Santa María today and the critique of Menocchio, the sixteenth-century Italian miller who was not afraid to tell the Inquisition that the Pope "is a man like us," that the priests work at a "business," and that the sacraments of the church are so much "merchandise" created for the profit of the priests. "Against this enormous edifice built on the exploitation of the poor," Ginzburg remarks, "Menocchio set forth a very different religion, where all members were equal because the spirit of God was in all of them" (1980:17; cf. Davis 1982:326). This same notion of clergy and laity being equal before God—with the clergy actually faring worse for their hypocrisy—likewise animates religious thought in Santa María, as does a deep-rooted resistance against the hierarchical structure of the church.

While we can draw out such parallels, religious cultures are obviously not static and need to be seen in a contextual, comparative, and relational light, set squarely and fully within the milieu of a particular time and place. In particular, as Natalie Zemon Davis points out, "a religious culture should be seen in a two-way communication with the structures of authority around it" (1982:324). It is this two-way communication I hope to get at here. In the first part of the paper I focus on the discourses of the new "young church" and the Francoist church that preceded it, looking at the ways priests trained in each of these religious ideologies have interacted with village people. Then, in the second part of the paper I turn to the village discourses of anticlerical critique and religious practice, letting many different informants speak so as to create a multivocal text. Finally, in a brief conclusion I set forth some theoretical statements for understanding the meaning of this two-way communication in the rural Spain of the recent past and the emerging present.

POST-CHRISTIAN PAGANISM AND THE YOUNG CHURCH

Let us return now to the burning of Saint Tirso by Don Laurentino, the priest of Santa María. Don Laurentino told me this story in the context of a discussion about the difference between internal and external images. He feels that village people grab hold too much of external images; their religiosity is based on the "fixed image," the "petrified sacredness" of their patron saints and their processions and not enough on internal images based in deep faith in and knowledge of the Gospels. Don Javier, a Franciscan monk who used to lead the Holy Week missions to the villages, expressed much the same view, saying that village people believe fervently in the rites of Catholicism, but they don't know why they be-

An ex-voto painting in the sacristy of the parish church of Barrillos. The text reads: "Angel Mirantes, resident of this place, without hope of living, being sick with dropsy, by the mercy of this miraculous Holy Virgin of the Assumption, may I regain my health. Year 1793."

lieve. The faith of the peasant, in their view, is a mechanical, hollow faith, tied to forms rather than profounder realities. It is the task of the priest, in Don Laurentino's view, to help people go beyond the forms to those profounder realities: "The saint of wood is nothing more than a form. If we get stuck on it, we can get stuck on an idol, a fetish, an empty figure. This is what we have to combat."

While the Catholic church, both in Europe and in missionary outposts, has for centuries fought battles against forms of popular religion that it defined as "idolatry," Don Laurentino is here speaking very much as a post-Vatican II priest. The concern to separate religion from what is viewed as a magical view of the world in order to purify the faith is evident in the various changes introduced by the Second Vatican Council. These included the switch from the Latin to the vernacular mass, which the priest now celebrated facing the congregation rather than the altar; the new ruling reducing the fast before Communion from midnight the night before to a single hour previous to attending mass; and, finally, the major transformation in the appearance of the priests themselves, who were no longer marked by the tonsure (a shaved spot on the back of the head) nor required to wear the soutane except when performing religious obligations. These rationalizing reforms were, from the point of view of the Vatican, an effort "to divest Catholicism of much of its mystery and mysticism" (Brandes 1976:25), thereby stripping away the ritualistic accretions concealing the pure faith.

Holy Mother Church thereby hoped to make the religion more relevant to a modern, urban world turned critical of the faith by the advances of science, technology, and industrialism and turned both richer and poorer by the contradictions of late capitalism (cf. Second Vatican Council 1966). But what she did not envision, nor perhaps even think to take into account, was the reaction of the few remaining pockets of peasants. In the small agricultural communities of central and northern Iberia peasants greeted the work of reforming priests schooled in Vatican II ideas with resistance, shock, and resentment, accusing them of taking away their religion (Brandes 1976:23; cf. Christian 1972; Riegelhaupt 1973, 1984). These reforms have served to further thicken the peasant discourse of pious anticlericalism.

Don Laurentino's disposal of the Saint Tirso image—which he describes as too repulsive to engender any sort of devotion, so repulsive that it is not an image but an idol—is in keeping with a ruling of the Second Vatican Council calling for the careful but insistent removal of those images "which offend true religious sense either by depraved forms or by lack of artistic worth, mediocrity, and pretense" (Second Vatican Council 1966:57). The notion that images can be judged for their "artistic" value, and destroyed if not found up to par, is certainly foreign to the village setting; it calls for a radical departure from the traditional view of images as repositories of, and intercessors with, the holy. And, further, in allowing for desacralizations of things once holy it smudges the line separating the sacred and the profane.

Don Laurentino feels that village people are ignorant about the artistic value of the images in their parish churches. Like other priests, he has taken it upon himself to bring any images he considers worthwhile to the recently created Diocesan Museum of León; in general, for these priests popular religion is more palatable if turned into an object that one can admire from a distance, as a spectator.[4] In one village where Don Laurentino discovered what he described as fair but not outstanding images that, if taken to León, would have ended up in the basement of the Diocesan Museum, he created a parish museum and gave the village elderly a series of lectures about art history. He culminated these lectures with a tour of the village museum as well as a visit to the museums of religious art in León. For Don Laurentino, as for other priests trained since Vatican II, the priest is, above all, a teacher; he, in fact, also teaches school in addition to being parish priest of Santa María and three other villages. Don Laurentino extends his mission to teach the flock to the wider world beyond the parish, acting as a kind of tour guide on the excursions he is constantly arranging to Barcelona, to Cuenca, to Fatima, to Lourdes. He takes pride in the fact that he was the one who showed many of the retired villagers the sea, which not even their own children had done.

Village people are aware that they are at a comparative disadvantage to the priest with respect to education, and they are his eager students on excursions. While they may also accept his opinions about the artistic value of the images in their churches, they still object to the loss of the images. Frequently it is suspected that priests steal the images in order to sell them. Villagers believe that the images belong to the community. They are part of the history of the community, and priests are seen as overstepping their authority in removing them from the church. Villagers object, too, when priests change the arrangement of the images in the church, as when the former priest of Santa María, Don Efigenio, moved the image of Saint Roch, protector against the plague, from the main altar to a side altar in order to make more room for images of Mary and Jesus, which the post-Vatican II church would like to see supplant the pantheon of the saints. This action was particularly resented by the brotherhood of Saint Roch, which had helped to pay for the renovation of the main altar and expected their saint's image to be placed above it. The rulings of Vatican II caution priests against allowing an excess of statues and pictures to remain in local churches and state that "their relative positions should exemplify right order. For otherwise they might provoke astonishment among the people and foster devotions of doubtful orthodoxy" (Second Vatican Council 1966:57). The images of saints, like the cults of saints, have historically been major points of contention between village people and their priests (cf. Christian 1981a), and it is part of the struggle for the church that rural people continue to wage in Spain, though the church is clearly gaining the upper hand.[5]

Lauded for, among other things, expressing the kind of social consciousness that made liberation theology possible, Vatican II is still symbolic of the church's power to create religion, in this case to change the meaning of religion; it is in this sense a worthy successor to the Council of Trent. Don Laurentino felt no need to consult with villagers before burning the image of Saint Tirso, as though burning it had been a moral imperative, something, as he says, that had to be done. He took it upon himself to desacralize the holy, shocking the villager who said he wouldn't do it for any amount of money and taking on powers that, from the village perspective, only God, and not humans, should have.[6] The church as a whole has likewise carried out, or in the village setting imposed, the major reforms of Vatican II, radically redefining the meaning of the holy and the practice of religion in accordance with its current vision of what constitutes the true faith.

It is significant that Don Laurentino destroyed the image of Saint Tirso in the village cemetery. As he explained to me, burning it in a sacred place was a dignified way of destroying it; had he whacked the image to pieces and used it for firewood, that would have been a profanation. The death of the image in the cemetery, in the company of the souls of the village dead, can be taken as a metaphor for the mission of the Vatican II church to put popular rural religion to rest, tactfully and with dignity if possible, or otherwise enshrined in a museum case, but to rest nonetheless.

The Spanish church has responded actively to this mission, as can be seen in the proceedings of the national conference held in Madrid in 1985 bearing the title "Evangelization and Man Today" (Congreso de Evangelización 1985). The new Spanish church presents itself as a youthful church, a church full of optimism, energy, and courage; a church that is opening up its shutters and letting in the fresh and revitalizing air of change, which, in the words of the bishop of León, "we old communities need to be cured of our myopia" (Angel 1985:271). Among the programmatic changes suggested at the conference were the need to reevaluate and change religious practice when necessary in order to keep the faith in Christ alive and grounded in the realities of our historical epoch; the notion of faith as a personal choice rather than a taken-for-granted part of the world of established ideas; and, finally, the idea that, with democratization, authority is no longer conceived of as absolute and that, therefore, "the faith must no longer be imposed but proposed." While seeking to disentangle itself from the discourse of power and domination, the new church continues to call for evangelization or, more exactly, reevangelization, since secular trends have created indifference and incredulity and brought into being a strange kind of phenomenon: namely, what the bishop of León has called "post-Christian paganism."

Most Spaniards, notes the bishop, continue to consider themselves Catholic, whether practicing or not, almost as a matter of identity; many participate in the sacraments and rites of the church but do so "with a pagan spirit," remaining untransformed by the Christian message (Angel 1987:29). These nominal Christians, like those who have been totally dechristianized, need to be reevangelized, led by their local priests toward a more "adult faith" than that based on a catechism that ended with their First Communions. In all this there is an implicit rejection of what is perceived as the old, "myopic" popular Catholicism of the villages, based on historical traditions and social conventions.

There is, too, an explicit rejection of the outmoded orthodoxy of the National Catholicism of the Franco period. The image of the young church is being forged in dialectical opposition to the religiosity of Francoism and its particular model of the relationship between religion and power. Thus Don Laurentino, for example, blames the legacy of National Catholicism, with its "theology of fear," for instilling in people an adherence to external religious forms. From the modern church, then, let us turn back now to the church that preceded it, using once again a local perspective. Here I want to consider the conflicts that emerged in a very different historical moment between the people of Santa María and the priest who ministered to them during the later part of the Franco period.

NATIONAL CATHOLICISM

Don Efigenio was parish priest of Santa María for twenty-five years, from 1956 until 1981, in the very years when the "economic miracle" catapulted Spain, a nation where nearly half the population still lived and worked on the land in 1950, into the world of late capitalism. For Don Efigenio the public expression of religious unity and orthodoxy mattered above all else, and in particular he viewed attendance at mass as the crux of Catholicism. This attitude contrasts sharply with that of Don Laurentino, who even tells his parishioners in mass that going to mass is not the crucial thing but rather living the Gospels: "We can't go around thinking, I'm a very good Christian because I go to mass on Sundays. That's not enough. We shouldn't be content just with forms." But Don Efigenio, schooled in the enforced Catholicism of the Franco period, demanded 100 percent attendance at mass. He would often ring the bells for mass

Former parish priest of Santa María and his sister posing with a late medieval Virgin and Child in the church of Barillos.

and then, to the irritation of everyone, force people to wait in silence until he felt that a large enough group had shown up to begin. At mass he would announce how many people had been missing the previous week, and his sermons, harshly critical of the villagers' neglect toward the concerns of the spirit, went on sometimes for as long as two hours; then, during the offertory he would ask God to forgive the young for their "excesses."

Wanting his parishioners to go to Sunday mass at all costs, even if by force, Don Efigenio precipitated a major conflict between himself and the people of Santa María in the early 1970s. At that time many people were beginning to make their living from selling milk to the growing urban market in León. The problem was that the self-employed milkman arrived to collect the milk on Sundays at the very hour of the mass. To Don Efigenio's irritation a number of people would stay home waiting for the milkman rather than go to mass. He wanted the milkman to change his schedule, and the people wanted Don Efigenio to change his. When Don Efigenio learned that the milkman did not have the proper license to drive a truck, he promptly denounced him to the civil guards, who came to arrest him one Sunday. By a ruse the milkman slipped into the church, where he remained until the mass was over. When he came out, the guards were waiting for him, surrounded by the people of Santa María. The guards announced that they had come to arrest the milkman.

People immediately responded that the milkman wasn't going anywhere. Then the president of the village, in Venerable Prieto's version of the story, spoke up, saying: " 'The *pueblo* will take responsibility for him. If it's anything to do with the priest, take the priest before anyone. We will take responsibility for this man.' And then the priest came out. And the people surrounded him. He [the president] said, 'Let's see if you tie up your shoelaces and get moving, because the one who gives us our bread is this man. Not you.' "

While such defiance would not have been possible in the early years of the Franco regime, by the 1970s the village could defy both the priest and the civil guards, both of whom, in their respective uniforms, had represented the oppressiveness of that social order. The village, in this case, allowed neither priest nor civil guards to exercise their power, making it clear that when it came to defending their daily bread—in fact, the only steady flow of cash sustaining village families—they stood united. In their defense of the milkman they showed that when it came to a choice between religion and bread, they would choose bread. As the popular saying puts it, "Mass, sermon, and pepper are of very little sustenance" (*La misa, el sermon, y el pimiento son de muy poco alimento*). On the less triumphant side we can say that this defiance showed just how dependent people had become on the expanding capitalist market that had undermined the logic of their peasant economy (cf. Behar 1986:38–40).

Don Efigenio had a penchant for comparing his parishioners to animals—a use of primordial metaphors to make comment on their moral qualities (cf. Fernandez 1986:3–14) that revealed his proximity to the peasant world of his parishioners. (In fact, he is a native of the neighboring village of Barrillos, where he is now parish priest.) In his sermons Don Efigenio frequently compared villagers to pigs and calves, criticizing them, in an era of newfound prosperity, for being "fattened up with too much of the material and too little of the spiritual." When, at one particular sermon, he went so far as to compare the villagers to burros, a riot nearly broke out in the church. On that occasion one of the men, among the most devout in the village, shouted back to Don Efigenio that he should be quiet and go on with the mass. Angered in turn, Don Efigenio pulled off his soutane, stepped down from the altar, and would have headed for the choir had he not been stopped in his tracks by two women sitting near the altar. A number of people walked out of the church on this occasion. After the mass many of them were waiting to confront him, but he ran off in the other direction. In the street Don Efigenio was mild-mannered and incapable of arguing; it was only in church that his desire for religious orthodoxy would get the better of him and make his tongue fly in wild insults that he always regretted afterwards.

Don Efigenio, it is true, was fanatical to the point of neurosis, having suffered from "nerves," as he admits and others note, all of his life. While such theocratic priests are extreme cases (cf. Ott 1981), Don Efigenio embodied a religious ideology and style whose script was ever ready for performance during the Franco period. Don Efigenio played the part of Francoist parish priest to the hilt, and he played it as tragedy and as farce—as tragedy because he longed for a religious orthodoxy that was no longer enforceable, and as farce because, in trying to enforce religious orthodoxy by nagging and insulting villagers, he made himself ridiculous.

The Francoist style of religiosity, later disparaged by the liberal, Vatican II priests as "National Catholicism," was based on the public display of faith in processions, solemn masses, and elaborate ceremonialism reminiscent of the Counter-Reformation church. Reacting against the overt anticlericalism of the previous Republican state (1931–1936), in which burnings of churches and persecutions and murders of priests, monks, and nuns had been tolerated, Francoist religiosity encouraged the sort of adherence to external religious forms that the reforming priests, like Don Laurentino, later criticized and sought to replace with a more internal faith. Similarly, all the changes legislated by the Republic, from the separation of church and state and the creation of secular education—symbolized by the removal of crucifixes from schools—to divorce, were undone by Franco (to be brought back again only after his death, under the Constitution of 1978).

In parts of the rural north and center, where peasants felt their moral universe threatened by the Republican government's political anticlericalism, there had been much uneasiness and even fear about what the new secularism meant. A native Santa María woman who emigrated to Madrid after the Civil War, Polonia Robles, remembered how shocked people were in Santa María during the Republic when the schoolteacher, acting under state orders, gathered up all the religion books and burned them in a bonfire at the doorstep of the village council meeting house. She also recalled how the women gossiped around the fountain about "the new law" that decreed that one could not say "Adios" but had to say "*Salud camarada*," because "if they heard, they would take one prisoner."[7] In the Basque country apparitions in 1931 of the Virgin, who admonished "Pray the rosary daily," and later, "Save Spain," testified to rural people's fears about the loss of religion (Christian 1987a; cf. Harding 1988).

After the Nationalist victory in 1939 Franco consciously modeled his regime on that of Isabella and Ferdinand, the great defenders of Catholic orthodoxy, who brought the reconquest against Islam to a close with the defeat of Granada, ordered the first expulsion of the Jews, oversaw the inception of the Inquisition, and consecrated their empire, as far as the New World, to the salvation of souls (Payne 1984:177; cf. Elliott 1963;

Herr 1974). For the Nationalists their *movimiento* had been "nothing less than a holy war or righteous crusade—*cruzada* being the term they favored—on behalf of Christian civilization, with the Spanish Reconquista and Inquisition as its guiding precedents" (Lincoln 1985:245). While there were no longer Jews and Moors to crusade against in the twentieth century, in the Francoist view the Spanish body politic had been smothered by the accumulated weight of modern European thought that "had been borne, by trickery, to our soil," as one Leonese journalist put it in 1939. "The Renaissance, the Reformation, the Enlightenment, Progress, Democracy, Marxism—had poisoned Spain," he went on to say, and through the Civil War "Spain saved itself. And it saved Christian Europe, the Christian World, Christianity. Saving itself, Spain has saved the universe. Understand it once and for all; Spain is the flower of the universe, because it is culture, because it is Spirit, because it is Catholicity" (cited in Sen Rodríguez 1987:345–346).

This fusion of Catholicism with *patria* meant, in practice, that religious rites became the rites of statehood on both national and local levels. Always, in the churches of the cities he visited, Franco made a point of entering under the pallium like the Eucharist itself. Orthodoxy was imposed on people through numerous injunctions, reminiscent of Inquisi-

General Franco entering the Sanctuary of the Virgen del Camino in León under the pallium, like the Eucharist itself. Church and state power were closely allied in the early Franco period, and religious symbols were used to legitimate the regime. Reproduced from *Diario de León*, series on "La Guerra Civil Española en León," part 2, fasciculo 8 (1987), p. 275. (Courtesy of *Diario de León*)

torial concerns, that included prohibitions against working on Sundays and against uttering blasphemies in public.[8]

In Santa María during the postwar period the village was served by the priest of neighboring Barrillos, Don Germiniano. The priest's uncle, Maximino, a well-off peasant and fervent Francoist who had married into Santa María, acted as informer for Don Germiniano, keeping a record of all those who uttered blasphemies or didn't go to church on Sundays. Until the late 1950s one had to ask the priest for permission to bring home a cart of hay after Sunday mass; and those who were heard saying "I shit on God" or "I shit on the Virgin" had to listen to mass on their knees for several weeks in the front row of the village church or pay a costly fine. This image of the priest brandishing a moral whip contrasted sharply with the previous priestly style, exemplified by Don Simón, village priest during the Republic and Civil War. When the Nationalists took power during the war and came asking for "Reds," Don Simón is always quoted as having replied, "I am more of a Red than anyone here, and I say mass." While enforcing religiosity with zeal, the Francoist approach, as village people pointed out to me, was not necessarily in accordance with Christian ideals. Don Simón had always let passing families of Gypsies sleep in the portal of the church, but Maximino always threw them out. On one occasion Justa Llamazares, a devout Catholic in her eighties, remembered how Maximino coldly locked out a Gypsy woman who had just given birth and was hemorrhaging; taking pity on the woman and her family, she herself had brought them to her house.

The Francoist glorification of Catholicism, with its explicit forging of a link between religion and power, was tied to the glorification of rural life and the image of rural traditionalism. An article entitled "The Countryside in the New Spain," which appeared in 1937 in a Leonese daily, spoke of how "the new Spain has to reorganize itself by returning to the countryside. The city no longer has anything to give. It has given what it had: vice, desperation, frivolity, and revolutionary dreams. . . . Spanish life has to be disinfected with the healthy airs that blow in the fertile valleys of our mountains and in the ample horizons of our plains. . . . Tomorrow's peasant Spain will be the source of our greatness and of our virtues" (cited in Sen Rodríguez 1987:349).[9]

One of the greatest ironies of the Franco regime is that this ideological praise for rural life culminated, after the postwar hunger and scarcity, in a program of rapid industrialization, which led to a massive exodus from the villages to industrial centers at home and abroad. Under Franco's authoritarian regime, with the aid of foreign investment (mainly from the United States in exchange for four naval bases), tourism, and the remittances of emigrants gone to work in northern Europe, Spain took a dive into the seas of world capitalism (cf. Carr and Fusi Aizpurua 1979). By

Justa, a religious virtuoso from
Santa María, with her rosary.

the 1960s and 1970s the *pueblo* had become marginalized and dependent
on the world beyond its borders for money, entertainment, and models
of how to live a good, middle-class life, while the society as a whole, in
an act of resistance against the previous social asceticism, took refuge in
rampant consumerism (cf. Pérez Díaz 1987:404, 442).

At the same time that village life was being undermined, the base of
village culture—religion—was being changed and ultimately undermined as well by the reforming Vatican II priests anxious to undo the
damages of National Catholicism. As Stanley Payne observes, "In no
Catholic society did the dramatic new doctrines of Vatican II have such a
marked effect as in Spain" (1984:195). By the end of the 1960s, under the
influence of Vatican II and desiring to clear its own guilty conscience, the
Catholic church in Spain underwent a "political reconversion" (Pérez
Díaz 1987:454), distancing itself from the Franco regime, to which it, like
the Vatican, had initially granted legitimacy, and supporting the transition to democracy. Many priests, especially from the Catalan and Basque
clergy, were at the forefront of domestic political protest by the early
1970s, and a special jail was even created for such priests in Zamora
(Payne 1984:196–204). Following in the spirit of Vatican II, the church in
Spain relinquished its adherence to the notion of religion as a monopoly

and accepted the existence of an open market for religious beliefs (Pérez Díaz 1987:415).

Thus, in a matter of fifty years the Spanish church went through an extraordinary process of change. Observing this process, one has the sensation, as Victor Pérez Díaz remarks, of seeing a drama unfold in various acts, "with changes in scene, argument, characters, and even emotional tone": from the persecuted church of the 1930s, to the exultant church of the 1940s and 1950s, to the politically reconverted church of the last three decades (1987:42). What conclusions about the church, priests, and religion have rural people drawn from this drama? I turn to this question now.

THE DISCOURSE OF POPULAR ANTICLERICALISM

Priests versus Religion

People in and around Santa María draw a sharp dividing line between religion and God, on the one hand, and the clergy, on the other. When I asked Isolina de la Puente, a sixty-year-old Santa María woman still actively farming, whether priests had any special powers, she said that a priest is a person who has studied for a particular career, like a farmer or a schoolteacher, and that they have no special powers, and certainly not supernatural powers.[10] "Now who has the power? The one who is up there has it always, and will always have it. The one you have to pray to, when something happens, I bet you don't pray to the priest? 'Oh, priest, I'm suffering, save me from this! [laughing] Help me in this task, in this affliction!' You ask the Lord." In mass, as Monserrat Verduras, a farming woman from nearby Vegas del Condado, said, one thinks about God, the Virgin, the Gospels, not about the priest. Camino Aller, a schoolteacher in her late twenties from Villamayor, went so far as to say that anyone could say the mass as well as the priests; there is nothing holy about them.

Priests are men like any other men. They are viewed as functionaries of the church and of the state, a product of the long historical connection of the two in Spain. They are men with a career, whose business is religion. As an anticlerical chant from the Republic puts it:

La iglesia es un comercio	The church is a business,
el cura un comerciante.	the priest a businessman.
Al toque de la campana	The ringing of the bells
acuden los ignorantes.	calls out the ignorants.

People are not even willing to grant priests a higher status, viewing them as their equals. Venerable Prieto, a farmer of sixty-five who has long been retired because of his rheumatism, says, referring to priests: "It's a career like any other, and nothing more. They depend on that to earn their food and we depend on this [agriculture] to earn ours."

This feeling of equality with priests stems, in large part, from two factors: first, that in small, egalitarian communities like Santa María there is a disinclination to accept the hierarchical model of society offered by the church; and second, that parish priests in rural León are native sons from the villages, who often share the mentality of their parishioners, rather than outsiders from a different milieu or social class. In the past, young men from the villages went to the seminary in León because it was the only way to get an education, to become a professional, to better oneself. As Monserrat Verduras said, "It was like going abroad," the only way to escape the village and cease to be a peasant. Priests paid for their nephews to study, as was the case with Nicéforo Carral who went off to the seminary during the 1930s. When he returned to the village for a visit, everyone admired his nice suit; but then his uncle died suddenly, and the following day he was back, working the land. The seminaries in León were full of such young men of peasant stock. As a result, priests are not put up on pedestals, even if they are among those few in the professional class who are given the title "don." Their task is to attend to their "business": to provide the sacraments, lead the flock, and say mass, with a minimum of interference in the other domains of social life. Today, more than ever, people resent any intrusion of the priest in their private lives or in the activities of the community.

It is said that in church all priests are good and that when judging priests you have to consider what they do in church, not what they do in the street. In the street a priest is a person like any other: a man. Several people remembered how priests used to say in church: "Do as I say and not as I do." Leonardo Mirantes, a retired farmer of eighty-one who lived in Madrid for twenty years, noted: "A priest perhaps preaches one thing and then does another. Well, that's up to his own conscience. If there is anything, if there is a God, or there is something, well, then he will be held to account for whatever he has done." Or, in the words of seventy-year-old Sixto Mirantes, a farmer who still works in agriculture: "The priest's prayers are always valid. No matter what sort of person he is."

Sexuality of Priests

Aware of the humanity, mortality, and frailty of priests, people don't deny their sexuality either. María Ribero, a retired widow of sixty-five who manages the recently installed village telephone, put it bluntly: "If they have balls, if they haven't been castrated, then they can't be very different from other men." And, she went on to note, it is only when dogs are castrated that they have no sexual appetite. For this reason she felt

Francisco Goya, "Nadie nos ha visto" (No one has seen us), 1799, in the *Caprichos* series of etchings. Anticlerical satire: priests drinking and partying. (Courtesy of the Hispanic Society of America, New York)

that it would be better if priests could marry. To this effect there is a popular saying: "The priest doesn't have a wife, so someone has to give him one" (*El cura no tiene mujer y alguien la tiene que poner*).

In the nearby village of Villamayor the priest who was there around 1915 had an ongoing affair with a young woman; the local children used to watch the pair kissing and hugging from a tree that looked into the courtyard of the priest's house. After the woman had a miscarriage people found the priest by her side, gathering up the blood in a bucket. In response to my question about whether anyone complained to the bishop, a Villamayor woman in her eighties, Delfina Aller, said that no one did because people felt that if he was going to have affairs that was his own responsibility. The next priest assigned to the parish also had an affair with a woman from the village, and after that, Delfina said, the bishop punished the village by not allowing it to have its own parish priest. For decades now, before the current decline in numbers of priests, Villamayor has been attended by visiting priests from other parishes. Thus, while the priest's doings may be his own responsibility, people feel that a village can be "punished" because of a bad priest.

Resistance to the Priest's Powers over the Sacraments

Since priests are men like any other, there is a great deal of resistance against their power to hear confession, provide Communion, and give the sacraments. At present much popular, pious, anticlericalism focusses on the confession. As Venerable Prieto, among many others, put it: "Confession is a tall tale. Why do I have to go to that man who is just like me and tell him what I've done? If I tell it to him, will he forgive me?" Still, Venerable says he likes mass, and for him a Sunday is not a Sunday unless he goes to mass. But confession remains a major point of contention with priests and can even lead to a complete rejection of the role of the priest.

José Antonio Llamazares, a forty-year-old contractor born in Santa María, who has a weekend house in the village, thinks that the way to approach religion is "to take the good and discard the absurd," confession being one of the absurd things. Even Communion in church verges on the absurd—Why not drink wine and eat bread in your own house? Can things be made sacred only by the priest? In his words: "The body and all that, and when there is no body, you eat a piece of bread in your house as though you had taken Communion. . . . The water that I drink everyday, I have faith that the God in which I believe will continue to provide me with this water that is the blood, if you want to interpret it this way. Without having to go there [to church]."

Ana Mari Gigante, a native of the wheat and wine lands of southern León and José Antonio's wife, said that she doesn't believe in the act of confession because the wrongs you have committed must be revealed to another person who, being human like you, also commits wrongs. In particular she casts doubt on the ability of priests to maintain the secrecy of confession, which amounts to a superhuman injunction to rise above gossip. She recalled how her mother was raised in the house of an uncle who was a priest, and when the time came for the yearly Easter duty confession he would get together with other priests and laugh and joke about the things people had told them: "People before were so ignorant that I think if they had to make love to their husbands they would go and tell the priest how many times they had done it. And then the priests would get together, as my mother told me, and have a great time. 'Well, what do you think, that dummy told me this, and the other one told me that.' They made fun of what people told them."

Confession, like other aspects of official religiosity, is viewed now as an institution that has been maintained in part by force and in part by the ignorance of the people, who did as they were told because they did not know any better. Much anticlerical critique today stems from the desire of people to disassociate themselves from what they perceive to be the unquestioning religious traditionalism of the past. People want to assert their modernity, a modernity that is equated with an awakening of critical consciousness. Leonardo Mirantes, the elderly retired farmer we heard from earlier, spoke of how he had little faith in the idea that if you missed mass and confessed you could be "forgiven" by whatever "penance" the priest told you to fulfill. "Do you think that because they tell me to fulfill a penance, say, to go to twenty rosaries, that with rosaries I'm going to get anywhere? If I kill someone . . . I will carry that responsibility with me always." Rather than seeking the priest's pardon, he prefers to think about the notions of conscience and forgiving expressed in the Lord's Prayer, which emphasizes the relationship between God's pardoning of us and our pardoning of one another: "Listen, if we don't forgive our debtors, how are they going to forgive us? Just reciting that is enough. I have a bit of faith in these things. I'm not one of those who goes everyday to confess."[11]

Sin, says José Antonio, is to do a wrong and to take cognizance of it and feel repentant: "A moment comes in which you say, I did this, but I won't do it again, because it was wrong. Fine. That is your repentance and your confession. . . . It doesn't seem logical or just to me to go tell you about it. Or someone else. If I tell you about it because I want to tell you about it, but not for you to forgive me—you are like me." Only the person you hurt can forgive you, or you yourself must repent within yourself. The mere act "of humbling yourself and kneeling before something," says Balbino Llamazares, a Santa María farmer just turned sixty-five, "that's enough already. Even if you haven't confessed properly. If you go with a true faith, wanting to repent and be as good as you can, simply by that act you have done enough."[12]

If traditional confession is rejected, the whole chain—sin, confession, Communion—starts to fall apart, as José Antonio nonchalantly notes in his remarks. It seems to be the case here, as in northern Portugal, that people resist, and even deny, the priest's authority "as the sole disseminator of the sacraments," which, as Riegelhaupt had noted, "is built into the structure of the religion" (1984:106). People seem unwilling to grant the priest any sort of power over them, and especially "the power to condemn or forgive" (Riegelhaupt 1984:109), which is God's alone, *if* there is a God.

Priests versus Christ

The rejection of the role of the priest is taken to its furthest extreme in comments often made about the way priests—in this case, Jewish religious leaders—persecuted and ultimately rejected Christ. There is a fundamental mistrust of the priesthood as an institution. Leonardo Mirantes explains: "Jesus Christ didn't preach evil. He always preached good. Love of one's neighbor. Why was such a man punished? Because, my friend, the priests themselves who existed then, Sanhedrin and all of them, well, they were the ones who punished him, because, of course, he threatened them. It's the same thing now with priests. Why do they preach religion? Because if you take away all of that [if you take away] religion, well, they're left without anything."

Similarly, in a conversation about the apocalypse Balbino Llamazares said that this time "the world would end in fire," just as in the time of the Flood it ended in water, because there are so many sophisticated weapons now that we will end up destroying the world. Manuel Llamazares, a fifty-year-old bachelor farmer and distant kin of Balbino, responded that the world would end only if God wills it; though the Holy Scriptures say that there will be an end, no one can know when it will be. Balbino was more skeptical and said, "But the Scriptures, who do you think wrote them? Well, the priests did, and then it turns out that they killed Christ and now they believe in him." Manuel, who tends more toward religious orthodoxy, immediately responded that the Scriptures were written under the inspiration of God and that they are the teaching of Christ. But Balbino was not convinced.

It is interesting that Balbino and Leonardo equate Old Testament (Jewish) and New Testament (Christian) priests, treating them essentially as playing the same structural roles in relation to religion. Insofar as priests—making no distinction between Jewish or Christian priests—found Christ a threat to their institutional religion and now act as his ministers, they are hypocritical in their faith. If we follow Balbino, the priests, who once abandoned Christ, are perhaps not even worthy of the religion they profess. The implication of both Balbino's and Leonardo's comments is that it was the people who recognized Christ as the Messiah, while the priests themselves, the religious authorities who had special interests and a hierarchy to protect, failed to do so.

Given this conceptual separation of the priests from the religion they represent—this mistrust of priests as bearers of the true faith—there is a sense (especially among those brought up before Vatican II) that the priests have no right to change anything within the religion. Saturnina Llamazares, a sixty-year-old devout Catholic who never married in order to care for her widowed mother, remembered a conversation at the fountain between two older women after the introduction of Vatican II changes. Commenting on the switch to the mass in Spanish and the new norm allowing women to go to mass without wearing a veil, Saturnina recalled how one of them exclaimed, "But who was the Pope to do all of this?" Saturnina pointed out that those were things people could change but that the religion remained the same. Yet she could not convince these women, true religious virtuosi, who continued to fast on Christmas Eve and Holy Thursday and continued to ask scornfully, "Who were they to change things?"[13]

More than mere resistance to change, these views are based on the idea that religious practices are divine and eternal (cf. Brandes 1976:24), not a creation of human beings with an authority structure of their own. Bene Verduras, from Vegas del Condado, whose father was the Republican mayor of the municipality during the 1930s, noted, as many others have, that religious faith has been lost because too much has been changed: "Since everything has changed, people believe less in ecclesiastical things. They say, these people [the priests], when they want to, change everything. So what remains?"

This resistance to change is not a question of mystification or false consciousness but of power: Who has the power to know what God really intends for his church? While the Pope, and consequently the priests, often act as if they "own" the church, people resist this intervention by treating it as "their church" (cf. Riegelhaupt 1984:101), finding ways to circumvent clerical control over religious belief and practice. People even doubt whether priests know everything about the religion they profess to be authorities of. They note that priests don't understand all the mysteries of Catholicism, either, like the virginity of Mary or the unity and separateness of the Trinity, which are mysteries that are beyond human understanding. Priests, therefore, are not even conceded a superior wisdom; the religion, which is greater than the priests, rises above, enshadowing and engulfing them.

RECIPROCITY AND POPULAR RELIGIOSITY

A Doubting Faith

According to the philosopher-novelist Miguel de Unamuno, only a doubting faith is a living faith. Unamuno, who was fond of quoting the Gospel passage "I believe, help my unbelief!" (cf. Unamuno 1930:34) felt that this tragic, "agonic," sense of life was characteristic of popular Spanish Catholicism. Yet in his novel *San Manuel Bueno, Mártir* (1979) he created the character of a parish priest, "the saint," who tragically kept secret the fact that he could not believe, so as not to sow discontent in the hearts of his parishioners, for whom the opium of religious certainty gave them the will to go on living and the peace to die well. Unamuno, like many of the reforming clergy today, underestimated the doubting, contradictory quality of peasant faith. The truth is that even students of folk Catholicism have not focussed sufficient attention on the question of peasant faith (Freeman 1978). Here I will try to shed some light on this question by briefly looking at peasant ideas of death and salvation and the practices surrounding the cult of Saint Anthony.

While the discourse of pious anticlericalism would seem to make priests completely irrelevant to the practice of religion, there is one point in the life cycle of the individual when a priest is thought to be absolutely essential: at the moment of one's last agony, when one is on the threshold between life and death.[14] People both fear and doubt that there is a God and they are skeptical of Catholicism's promise of an afterlife, the doctrine at the heart of the official religion (cf. Schneider and Lindenbaum 1987:2). They want to believe and yet they cannot believe. Asked in catechism class, "What is death?" Amabilia Mirantes responded, "To stretch out your legs and grit your teeth." Rather than a blind faith, people have an earthy conception of life and death, and they take a very practical "just in case" attitude toward the measures provided by the official religion for gaining personal salvation.

This attitude is given expression in the numerous stories told about nonbelievers asking for a priest in their last agony. In one story told to me by Sixto Mirantes three friends agreed over coffee that it was foolish to believe in priests and religion. Among themselves they affirmed that when one dies that is the end; there is nothing more. Then one of the friends became ill. When the other two went to visit him, they found him on his deathbed, asking for a priest to make his last confession. Hearing this, the two friends turned to him and said, "Don't you remember the agreement we came to, while we drank coffee? And he said to them, "Yes. Yes, I remember. And there may not be anything, but just in case—. Just in case. There may not be anything. But just in case, I'm going to prepare myself."

It is with this cautionary attitude toward the fate awaiting the Christian after death that many village people who grew up before Vatican II go to mass. For them the core of Catholicism is the Sunday mass and the uncertain expectation of personal salvation that being present at the weekly sacrifice of Christ may bring should there, indeed, be an afterlife and a God who judges and condemns. In the words of Balbino Llamazares: "If it turns out there is nothing, then you have lost nothing. . . . Who knows if there is or isn't something? No one. So what I'm saying is, by doing it, if there's nothing, nothing is lost. And if there is something, then one can be recompensated for it, right? In the other world." Thus, while people

Francisco Goya, "La última Comunión de San José de
Calasanz," 1819. Reproduced from *Goya en las Colec-
ciones Madrileñas* (Madrid: Amigos del Museo del
Prado, 1983). While fiercely anticlerical, Goya here
captures a key element of popular religiosity. There is
one point in the life cycle of the individual when a
priest is thought to be absolutely essential: at the moment of one's last agony, when one is on the threshold
between life and death. (Courtesy of Amigos del Museo
del Prado)

have accepted some of the features of official religion as taught to them
during the Franco period and before, such as the importance of going to
mass and of dying within the church, they have reinterpreted these doctrines in such a way that the meaning given to them by the institutional
church is subverted. Here, for example, salvation is not the key idea but
"recompensation," a notion of exchange or reciprocity—of attendance at
mass traded for a good afterlife.

This notion of reciprocity has two sides to it. On the one hand, faith in God and the saints and proper participation in the rites and cults that honor them are repaid with the promise of a good afterlife or a request fulfilled; on the other hand, acts of profanation against the holy put the individual at the mercy of the divine hand, which is powerful when it punishes. Again, much wisdom about these matters is contained in stories "about things that really happened" and in the commentaries people make after telling the stories. Hilaria Carral, a sixty-year-old Santa María woman, told me a story about three friends who, one night after a fiesta, stopped in front of a Christ shrine and profaned it by uttering blasphemies against Christ and throwing stones and bullets at the door. Soon afterwards one of the men died, the second went blind, and the third was paralyzed. People began to wonder what had happened to make these three friends suffer such a fate so suddenly and all at once. Finally, one of the men confessed what they had done, and everyone understood that they had been punished by God. Hilaria commented:

> That was a punishment. It is one thing not to have faith. You don't have faith, well, you don't have faith. But to go there and say there is neither Christ nor anyone. And boom, bullets. And stones. That is to say, I am more than you. I always heard my father say that God forgives, that God is very good. But when he gets angry and tired, he punishes. Without a stone or a stick. He would say, you got this far, but you won't go any further. Look, we are not more powerful than them. We don't understand that. That, we don't understand.

As we saw earlier, people feel that it is God that has power and not human beings; to ridicule or profane the faith is to invite God to use his power to reassert the proper order of things. Don Laurentino's burning of the Saint Tirso image, while not a profanation in his view, was from the village perspective just such an audacious taking on of power. It is for this reason that the villager claimed he could never have gotten up the nerve to perform such an act.

The Cult of Saint Anthony

In viewing their relationship with God as a reciprocal relationship people are expanding upon the kind of reciprocity that has existed for centuries between local communities and their local saints and that is vibrantly dramatized in yearly village fiestas honoring the patron saints (cf. Christian 1972, 1981a). Here I would like to discuss one particular cult, that surrounding Saint Anthony, to whom people are very devoted in the Santa María area. The cult of Saint Anthony has been given a thoroughly agricultural basis, and it fuses, in a creative synthesis that local priests scorn, belief in the two Saint Anthonys recognized by the church: Saint

Anthony, the Abbot, whose feast day is celebrated on 17 January, and Saint Anthony, the Preacher of Padua, whose feast day is celebrated on 13 June. The first Anthony left his material possessions and went to live in the desert in A.D. 285, founding the first community of monks; in Christian art he is often depicted undergoing the test of temptation with a pig by his side, and he is known as a protector of animals. The second Saint Anthony was a Franciscan renowned for his sanctity and his teaching who died in 1231; he is always depicted with the Christ child in his hands and is popularly viewed as an intercessor for lost people (especially children), lost animals, and lost things, as well as for helping women find mates.

There are three different aspects to the local cult of Saint Anthony. First, people will recite the prayer to Saint Anthony when an animal is lost or otherwise in trouble. Several people told me the story of Victoriano's burro, which got lost in the woods and returned the following day with a chunk of its hind parts bitten off by a wolf; Saint Anthony had come to its rescue but a little late, they said, because Victoriano had not recited the prayer right away. As a protector of the health and welfare of farm animals, a picture of Saint Anthony (but Saint Anthony of Padua rather than the abbot), torn from an old calendar of the Capuchin magazine *El Santo*, which almost everyone subscribes to, hangs in most of the stables. Sixto Mirantes told me about his prayer to Saint Anthony when a cow of his was having difficulty giving birth on the day that an anniversary mass was going to be said for a former neighbor:

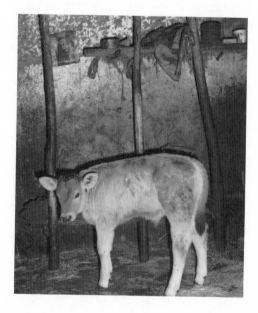

Calf in a Santa María stable, watched over by a Saint Anthony image posted on the wall above.

The cow, nothing, there was no way. And then I recited the prayer to Saint Anthony and had faith as I've told you, the faith I have in him. I went from here to there. I took off my clothes, put on slacks to go. To the funeral mass, the anniversary mass for Emilio. I hardly took any time. When I returned to the stable, the cow was already giving birth. I just had to clean up, the cow had already given birth. All I know is that the cow was at it all day and there was no way. And nothing, nothing, nothing. And nothing was wrong with her. The cow was giving birth and it was going badly. It's going badly and we have to call the veterinarian. And that was when I tried that.

With Saint Anthony, too, the same notion of reciprocity holds that does with God. To challenge the saint's ability to care for animals is to challenge his power and provoke him to manifest it. Hilaria Carral and Balbino Llamazares told me about a man who, after losing his burro, went out into the street and rather than saying the prayer to Saint Anthony properly, did so in jest, saying, "You animals who roam the woods, with your mouths open and your tails stretched out, eat the burro which this evening has gotten lost!" The next morning, sure enough, the burro was found dead, eaten by the wolves. As Balbino explained: "He wanted to prove that the saint doesn't perform miracles. To make it reappear or to save it. Let's see if my little animal, my *burra*, my cow, will reappear. And you say the prayer the correct way and it reappears the next morning. But he said it making fun of the saint." Here, too, what is punished is not only the profanation of the holy but dissension against the religious customs of the *pueblo*.

In the recent past another facet of praying to Saint Anthony was to promise him a pig's ear or foot on his feast day and go around the village collecting more pig parts for him on the eve of his day if he interceded in one's request for help—and especially if he cured a sick pig. This custom, known as *pedir para San Antonio*, was part of a group of food-sharing or commensal customs that involved gathering offerings of food from the whole village.[15] Here the social organizing principle of circular rotation so common in northern Iberian communities was followed, as occurs today with a Virgin image that is circulated around the houses. The pig parts that were gathered from all the houses were auctioned by the *concejo* (the village council) following the mass for Saint Anthony on 13 June, and the money was used to pay the priest for the mass. Thus an individual food offering to Saint Anthony was turned into a collective one, with the village as a whole entering into a kind of contract with the saint. While it is Saint Anthony the Abbot who is represented accompanied by a pig in the desert, the offerings of pork were made on the feast day of Saint Anthony of Padua—in popular religious practice the two Anthonys

Jerónima posing with a Virgin and Child that circulates around the houses of the village. The image was brought to Santa María in the 1950s by a priest born in Santa María.

have been fused into one who both protects and cures animals and brings them back home when they are lost.

On the feast day of Saint Anthony of Padua people don't yoke their cows or work with any of their animals. It is a day of rest for the animals, of thanks and veneration for the services they provide their keepers; it is their "Sunday." To work with one's animals that day is to risk having something happen to them or to oneself. Saturnina Llamazares said that once when her uncle Láutico yoked his cows and took them to gather hay on Saint Anthony's Day, a gust of wind blew down on the field and carried all the hay away, not leaving anything. Devotion to Saint Anthony is such that no villager misses the mass on his feast day, and in addition masses are requested for him throughout the year by individual families. Both Don Efigenio and Don Laurentino have sought to teach people that a Sunday, as the Lord's Day, is more important than Saint Anthony's Day; that Saint Anthony is only an intermediary with God and not the source of supernatural power, and therefore should be seen as the "cup and not the spring"; that the saints are not vengeful nor should they be treated as dispensers of miracles; that people are confusing the two Saint Anthonys; and that, finally, that sort of veneration for one's beasts of burden verges on superstition. Among those older farmers who still work the land, or have worked it until recently, these scoldings are heard and even repeated. Nevertheless, the beliefs continue that give magical powers to saintly priest figures while disparaging the political and religious powers that contemporary priests dare to take on.[16]

CONCLUSION

Until Vatican II the Catholic church, as a hierarchical institution based on priestly domination, taught the faithful that it was the eternal receptacle of Christ's teachings. What was radical about Vatican II was that it offered, as a new orthodoxy, a historicist outlook on the practice of religion. This meant that practices or traditions that had become anachronistic in the eyes of the church could be "modified or even eliminated" (O'Malley 1974:689). There was a new recognition that religious doctrines and practices grow out of a given culture and a given historical moment, that, for example, the Immaculate Conception of Mary was not an eternal truth but a dogma that was unknown to early Christians.

To the peasant populations of Santa María and other small farming communities in northern Iberia, this new outlook was a strange kind of heresy, uttered by the church itself. Their initial shock, followed by resistance and resentment, stemmed from the fact that so many aspects of religious practice had become for them an integral part of an undisputed life-world, a taken-for-granted part of daily life, the doxa of Bourdieu (1977:159–171). While they questioned the very existence of the institutional church, the rites of Catholicism, on the other hand, as they had always seen them practiced, were eternal and divine and not something to be changed by mere humans.

With Vatican II rite and belief were moved from the domain of doxa to the domain of the contestable. For older people in the Santa María area it seemed that the church was changing everything, that nothing was being left of religion as they had always known it. This led, initially, to resistance in the form of angry statements and efforts to continue practicing religion as they had always practiced it. More recently it has led to a certain self-consciousness about religious practice that has brought about disenchantment and, on the positive side, a critical political awakening.

Leonardo Mirantes recounted how, when he took his First Communion in 1916, he went home in tears because the Host had stuck to the roof of his mouth and he didn't dare move it with his tongue for fear of biting down on it. "We used to view the Host as something sacred. Body and blood of Jesus Christ. They used to fill us with such fear, that you couldn't touch it with your teeth, that you couldn't bite it. . . . Oh, what worries. And what fear. There I was, during the entire mass, with the

Host stuck up there. Today one laughs, but at that time one didn't laugh." His aunt gave him a glass of water and he gulped down the Host, glad that he had finally swallowed the body of Christ. "We had faith, such faith in all those things."

The recognition of this loss of faith stems from a new consciousness that the church adapts itself to changing political situations and that religion and power, therefore, are inextricably linked. Juan Robles, a bachelor farmer in his forties who returned to work the land after an extended stay in Paris, remarked: "The Gospels used to be preached to create fear, so that people would be afraid, and in the past there was more fear because the political system was also based on fear." Can we say that a long history of spiritual conquests, inquisitions, and national Catholicisms has left a legacy of faith based on fear? At least in this corner of Spain many people still go to mass *just in case* there is a God who judges and condemns. As William Christian notes, the "notion of a stern God subsisted in that part of rural Spain which remained Catholic, nursed by missions, well into the twentieth century. Indeed, in the depths of the post-Civil War period it was once again dominant" (1981a:264). This conception of the "terrible God" meting out punishments, which Jean Delumeau suggests was behind "the revolt against Christianity" that began in the seventeenth century (1977:230), is today being contested in Spain by a younger generation of priests and lay people who are calling for a transformation of the "theology of fear" into a "theology of love." Juan's mother, Julita Llamazares, who has lived and farmed in Santa María all of her life, gives voice to this change in rhetoric: "Now the priests have to open up, too. They have to explain the Gospel with more love. With more freedom. So that whoever wants it will truly want it."

The current discourse in Spain about the "theology of love" stems from the church's relinquishing of a monopoly over the faith and its acceptance of a market for religious ideas. Younger priests now say that they make an "offering" of the faith to people, and everyone is free to take it or leave it. Since religion has become contestable, since one can say yes or no, many in Spain today, especially the young, are saying no to religion and declaring it irrelevant to their lives—even as the new "young church" struggles to make it relevant. To the shock of village elders unprecedented numbers of young people from the area are no longer marrying by the church, and consequently they are not raising their children in the body of the church, a state of affairs that earlier in the century was mainly typical of those who held radical anarchist ideas (cf. Mintz 1982). These elders blame the church for having lost the young by changing too much too quickly, thereby tearing down the scaffolding that kept religious faith in place.

For, despite the pious anticlericalism of peasant people in Santa María and elsewhere, they view themselves, profoundly, as Catholics. Their discourse of anticlericalism is not an indication of a loss of religion but of a deep questioning of the institutional church as an arena for the practice of the true faith (cf. Freeman 1978:120). Theirs is, as Joyce Riegelhaupt noted, "a balanced stand-off in the acceptance and rejection of Catholicism" (1984:111). In this account I have tried to show how both the Francoist church and the new "young church" asserted two different visions of the relationship between religion and power and how people have resisted both of these visions of official religion by subverting their meaning, refusing to participate, and by developing alternative religious practices that help them contend with the problems of their own social reality.

In focussing on the relationship between religion and power, I may appear to be placing "the church" too much in the position of being "that which asserts" and "the people" in the position of being "those who resist." Obviously the interaction of clergy and laity has always been more complex and circular than this division between active and passive agency might suggest. Nor should the clergy and the laity be viewed as solid blocks of social structure but as loosely linked groups of actors who represent a broad spectrum of attitudes, styles, and ideologies. This is clearly seen in the contrast I made between the religious ideologies and priestly styles of Don Laurentino and Don Efigenio as expressed in their interaction with village people.

By downplaying the importance of attendance at mass and the cult of the saints, Don Laurentino shares and gives voice to the religious ideology of a younger, urbanized generation of village people, for whom external forms of religiosity are secondary to a deep inner faith. Older villagers, schooled in a pre-Vatican II religiosity, on the other hand, criticize Don Laurentino for being away on excursions a bit too often, rather than paying serious attention to his religious obligations. They appreciate the fact that Don Laurentino meddles less in village affairs (largely because he does not reside in the village), keeps his masses short, and does not attempt to enforce religious unity. But, at the same time, they admit to feeling spiritually and ritually shortchanged. While Don Efigenio said daily mass and rosary and celebrated all the fiestas, novenas, processions, and litanies, these villagers point out that Don Laurentino has not led a rosary since his arrival in the village. Yet even as they express their regret that religious practice is being watered down, they recognize that Don Laurentino represents a modern style of religiosity more in accord with modern life and that Don Efigenio represents a style that is as backward as harvesting wheat with the sickle, and should, likewise, be superseded. In this case, as in others, we find not a simple dichotomy of people versus priests but a slowly changing relationship. It is a relationship set in a historical moment, rather than a dichotomy, that I have tried to highlight here.

This relationship between village people and the priests who minister to them seems to me to be based on mutual misunderstanding and a mutual devaluation of each other's religious practice.[17] On the part of the people there is a continuing mistrust of priests as the "owners" of the church, and of the church itself as a power structure. On the part of priests, even those trained in Vatican II ideas, there is still an attempt to maintain an intellectual distance, a separation between the "simple" faith of the people and their "post-Christian paganism," and the "adult" faith of the priest.

We have seen how Don Laurentino continues to construe a model of "peasant religion" that represents "an 'other' against which both ortho-doxy and civilization can be measured" (Christian 1987b:273). As we have also seen, village people are much more radical in their religious beliefs (I almost want to say, theology) than such priests imagine. Theirs is not at all a hollow faith tied only to external images. Aware more acutely than ever before of the larger world beyond the village, the elderly peasants of Santa María, as elsewhere in northern Spain, have internalized the modern chastisement of traditional religious practices; they experience a form of "bicultural insecurity," such that these practices become "other" to them, too (Christian 1987b:273). Interestingly, however, those aspects of traditional religious practice they find most anachronistic are not the same ones that the priests do. Energized by the religious freedom granted the laity by Vatican II and the political freedom of a democratic government, they openly question the notions of sin, confession, and Communion so fundamental to the official religion because of the exces-sive power over the holy that they give a particular group of human be-ings who are just like them. With their anticlericalism they take the pre-cepts of the church and the desire for reform a step further than the priests themselves and make the case that, indeed, they, and not the priests, are truly the bearers of the faith.

Notes to Chapter 4

This paper is mainly based on interviews about religious belief and practice carried out among residents and priests in and around the Leonese village of Santa María del Monte during the summer of 1987. I am grateful to all the participants for speaking so frankly with me; I hope I do not betray their confidence here. My long-term research in Santa María, which began in 1978, has been funded over the years by grants from the United States-Spanish Joint Committee for Cultural and Educational Cooperation, Fulbright Hays, the American Association of University Women, the Society of Fellows at the University of Michigan, and the Harry Frank Guggenheim Foundation. I thank all these organizations for their support of my work. Finally, for extremely helpful comments and criticism on earlier drafts of this paper I would like to thank Ellen Badone, William Christian, Juan Diez, James Fernandez, David Frye, Carmelo Lisón-Tolosana, Bruce Mannheim, Mary Elizabeth Perry, Teofilo Ruiz, William Taylor, and the Anthropology Colloquium of the University of Michigan.

1. The high rate of church attendance in Castile-León has been attested to by several surveys on religious attitudes and practices that have been carried out in Spain in the 1980s. Table 1 details the results of one survey, which was conducted among farmers in six major agricultural regions. Similar results can be seen in surveys conducted among people of all walks of life, such as that on "The Church, Religion, and Politics" carried out by the Centro de Investigaciones Sociológicas in 1984. The latter survey also elicited responses to questions about Catholic belief which seem to indicate that the difference between Castile-León and the other regions lies more in the realm of practice than in that of belief (see Table 2). For most of the questions the number of "believers" is only slightly higher in

TABLE 1
Farmers' Religious Attitudes and Relations to the Church by Region, 1983

	Practicing Believers	Nonpracticing Believers	With Relatives in the Clergy
Duero Basin (Castile-León)	85%	12%	48%
Rioja and Navarre	73	12	36
Lerida	42	42	27
Levante	44	38	11
Almeria	34	55	10
Lower Andalusia	28	46	10
Total	51	34	25

Source: Pérez Díaz 1987: 497.

TABLE 2
Do You Believe in the Following Dogmas of the Catholic Church?

	Yes, Completely	With Doubts	Not at All	Don't Know/ No Answer
God Created the World	59 (63)	19 (17)	13 (6)	9 (14)
Jesus Christ is God	56 (57)	19 (20)	14 (9)	11 (13)
Existence of Heaven	50 (52)	21 (21)	18 (14)	11 (13)
Existence of Immortal Soul	46 (48)	20 (19)	19 (15)	14 (17)
Virginity of Mary	46 (52)	18 (14)	22 (13)	14 (18)
Existence of Hell	40 (41)	20 (23)	28 (19)	12 (17)
Ressurection of the Dead	41 (42)	20 (21)	25 (19)	14 (16)
Infallibility of the Pope	37 (47)	18 (18)	31 (19)	14 (15)

Source: Centro de Investigaciones Sociológicas 1984:309–313.

Note: The first number in each column is the percentage for all Spain, and the number in parentheses is the percentage for Castile-León only.

Castile-León. On the other hand, the number of "nonbelievers" is significantly lower, while the number not answering is significantly higher—which leads one to suspect that those who do not believe are more likely to keep their views to themselves in Castile-León, at least in a survey setting.

2. In 1985 the Spanish farming population consisted of .3 percent farm owners who employed salaried workers, 12 percent farm owners without salaried workers, and 4.9 percent salaried farm workers. The decline in the farming population has been taking place steadily: in 1950, 48.5 percent of the population was involved in farm work; in 1960, 39.8 percent; in 1970, 24.5 percent (Tezanos 1986:52–53). Also relevant is the decline in population in small communities; by 1981 only 8.6 percent of the population was living in municipalities of less than two thousand inhabitants (ibid.).

3. Even within the rural scene, diminished as it is, there are tremendous variations in religious beliefs, practices, and histories, and in the relationship between priests and their parishes. Similarly, within northern Spain itself there is a great deal of variation. In Galicia any description of religious life would have to take into account the elaboration of witchcraft beliefs and concepts of death linked to the house, lineage, and ancestors found there (Lisón-Tolosana 1979). In the Basque country, priests have been politically involved in the struggle for autonomy since the Franco period, so that the clergy have enjoyed much popular support (Payne 1984:196–197). In Asturias, where cattle herding and mining have coexisted for decades, there is both political anticlericalism and a keen sense of being situated in "the cradle" of Christian Spain (Fernandez 1986 and personal communication). In Santander traditional forms of religiosity embedded in the local landscape have remained strong (Christian 1972). Towards the east and south of Spain, in the more stratified towns of Aragon and Andalusia, traditions

of religious practice, anticlericalism, and antireligion have been linked to class tensions and class consciousness (Lisón-Tolosana 1983; Driessen 1984; Gilmore 1984; Maddox 1986), to involvement in political movements such as anarchism (Mintz 1982), and to the elaboration of folk saint traditions (Slater, in press).

4. Pulling the saint images out of the local context, they become things to behold for the price of an admission ticket to the museum, at once tied into the consumer market and lifted above it. The images cease to be vessels for dialogues with supernatural intercessors, reciprocal exchanges, and urgent requests for help and become fossilized as "art." In this sense their quality as external forms is, ironically, emphasized even more; demystified, they can be seen for what they are: just wood.

5. In former missionary outposts in Latin America the cults surrounding locally canonized "saints" not recognized by the official church have blossomed into popular religious movements. The cults surrounding Niño Fidencio in northern Mexico (cf. Macklin 1974) and Padre Cícero in northeastern Brazil (cf. Slater 1986) are two interesting examples.

6. One is reminded here of how the priest of the Portuguese village where Riegelhaupt did her fieldwork, to the shock and disdain of villagers, reburied the bones of the village dead in a football field to make room for a meeting hall that he built and controlled (Riegelhaupt 1984:108).

I wonder whether the shock of the village president might also have stemmed from the strange inversion posed by a priest destroying a religious image. At the start of the Civil War anticlericalists seeking to create a new social order not only exhumed the bodies of priests, nuns, and saints long-buried in churches but destroyed devotional objects, including works of art. Nationalist writers focussed on this "martyrdom of things," and among their most effective forms of propaganda were photographs of severely damaged religious art (Lincoln 1985:256).

7. León, during the Republic and the Civil War, was divided into two regions: the area south of the mountains from La Vecilla, taken early by the Nationalists, was basically conservative, rural, and orthodox, except for the city of León, where anticlerical magazines flourished from the turn of the century and throughout the Republic; north of La Vecilla, in the mountains near Asturias, where herding and mining coexisted, anticlericalism was stronger, and at the start of the war this area was still under Republican control. In the mountain region priests were persecuted and churches burned during the war; in the foothill region around Santa María, many who had displayed Republican loyalties were killed or persecuted, but in Santa María no one died as a result of the war.

8. Gregorio Boixo, the veterinarian for Santa María and surrounding villages, remembered how signs saying "Blasphemy is Forbidden" were posted up in bars and bus and train stations; of course, as he noted, this didn't keep people, men especially, from uttering blasphemies, at least in private, far from earshot of the priest or other watchful authorities. He found especially striking the various injunctions concerning female modesty, which enforced a strict dress code for women in the street, on the beach, and in church; in this sense, he says, Spain during the Franco period was rather like Khomeini's Iran.

9. This and the previous quote from the Leonese newspaper *Diario de León*

have appeared in the same newspaper in a series of Sunday magazine articles reevaluating the impact of the Civil War on the province of León. They form part of the critical reappraisal of the Civil War and the Franco period now taking place in Spain.

10. The Leonese image of the priest as lacking supernatural powers contrasts sharply with the Irish and Breton view of the priest as having special supernatural powers to cure as well as to harm. For these contrasts see the chapters by Taylor and Badone in this volume. Similarly, in the Alto Minho region of northern Portugal *"bruxo* priests"* in remote hamlets use white witchcraft to cure diseases caused by envy, just as "old-fashioned priests" until recently used the spiritual power they gained through esoteric knowledge to exorcize "souls in pain" with Latin prayers (Pina-Cabral 1986:206–207). Throughout Spanish history priests probably always appeared similar to functionaries because of the way in which the church has long served virtually as a branch of the state bureaucracy. It may be for this reason, at least in part, that the Spanish sensibility about priests emphasizes their "business" as opposed to "magical" functions.

11. In the village setting people who are too orthodox, too *beata* (a holy person), who insist on confessing constantly and hanging around the church, are viewed with suspicion. There is a fine line between being too religious, so that people begin to say, "That one is a friend of the priest," and not being religious enough, for even while voicing anticlerical ideas people will still go to church regularly. To hang around the church too much is to set oneself up above the community, as being better than others, and the community responds by pointing to the hypocrisy of the ultrareligious person—just as it points to the hypocrisy of priests. In illustration of this point Leonardo Mirantes told me about a woman named Gregoria, who used to confess and take Communion every day, but "when she came home she would open the door so that all her chickens could go eat the cabbage belonging to others. . . . We, as children noticed this. You know, children are children, but they are always aware of what goes on. And, damn, going to Communion so much, and then she would let her chickens out to eat other people's cabbage." When two villagers argue, the first insult to be cast at the devout Catholic is always, "You who take Communion are the worst!" In line with these ideas people generally find the Jehovah's Witnesses who come to the village seeking new converts both ridiculous, because they take their beliefs so seriously, and suspect, because they are so self-certain about where lies the path to the true faith.

12. Not everyone is critical of confession. A few people suggested that it allows you to take Communion with a cleaner spirit. María Ribero says that confessing to a crucifix or image is not the same as confessing to a priest because you need to be shamed in front of another person in order to feel the sinfulness of what you did. Maribel Llamazares, a single nurse from Santa María who is thoroughly immersed in base community work in the city of León, says that she has her particular confessor, to whom she talks about whatever is on her mind every day. Clearly, however, those in favor of confession are in the minority, and, as Camino Aller points out, the church may in the future have to do away with it completely.

13. A number of people in Santa María, now in their sixties and seventies,

remembered how their grandmothers, the religious virtuosi of the past, were often more fervent about religious practice than the priests themselves. In particular, these virtuosi emphasized abstinence and penance. Hilaria Carral recalled how her maternal grandmother was constantly dizzy and faint throughout Lent because she fasted mornings and barely ate. Instead of gaining indulgences she was actually sinning, the priest would say to her, because she was damaging her health. But her grandmother, who had her own ideas, paid no heed to the priest's scoldings.

14. Lisón-Tolosana found a similar view of death and religion in his native Aragonese town: "Nobody, not even the most miscreant, dies without receiving the Sacraments unless death is sudden. To receive the last Sacraments at the hour of death is the best technique of all for securing salvation and everlasting life. The desire to survive after death, to continue existing, makes them at the moment of dying cry out passionately: 'The priest, the priest!' because he alone can satisfy that yearning for personal endurance, for transcendence. This tragic sentiment of life—thus Unamuno names one of his books—when faced by its inherent poverty and the *mysterium tremendum* of death, makes the religion of salvation the fundamental and intimate expression of religious belief in the *pueblo*" (Lisón-Tolosana 1983:310). Or, as an informant of William Christian's put it, "Those who do not die in the grace of God die like animals" (Christian 1972:139).

15. A related custom is that of *pedir para las ánimas*, to collect for the souls, which used to be a weekly collection of pieces of bread that were auctioned off after Sunday mass; the money went for masses for the village dead. *Pedir para los lobos*, while not a religious custom, is also similar: when a wolf was caught in the woods by a group of hunters or by the shepherd, it would be taken around from house to house hung to a stick and people would give eggs, bread, and sausage as a token of thanks for having spared their animals. These commensal customs, involving food sharing and an identification of community with food, recall the close association between feasting and religious practice that was common before the Counter-Reformation (Bossy 1970:61–62). For a recent account of commensal customs viewed within the context of Iberian rotation systems see Freeman (1987).

16. For the most part the younger people from the villages (age thirty-five and under), all of whom have either been raised or schooled in urban centers, place little faith in the saints, or even in Mary. If asked about the saints or the Virgin, they will say that in moments of distress they appeal directly to God. While the God-centered view of religion is gaining strength among the older generation as well, men and women who grew up in the pre-Vatican II era have an easy familiarity with the lore and calendrical cycle surrounding the saints and their cults that is simply lacking in their offspring. I have found that in this part of Spain age rather than gender is the key differential of religious belief and practice. While religious virtuosi tend to be female, both men and women of the older generation attend mass and take Communion about as frequently and share equally in the elaboration of discourses about the miraculous powers of saints.

17. In contemporary urban settings the relationship between the clergy and the laity appears not to be based on this kind of antagonism. Even in the village

setting the relationship between urban-educated village youth and Vatican II parish priests tends to be much more harmonious. Parish priests, even though they come out of the same rural milieu as their parishioners, acquire in their seminary training certain prejudices about the "pagan superstition" of peasant religion in contrast to the learned concept of "theology." With education, by means of which they gain a wage, priests rise to a higher status and essentially become part of a middle class, even though they may maintain some aspects of a peasant mentality. Part of the conflict between priests and village people has to be seen as a product of class conflict and class consciousness. Educated village youth become part of the same social class as the parish priest because by virtue of their education they likewise move into the middle class, leaving behind, or becoming ambivalent about, their peasant identity. But the conflict between village people and their priests needs to be seen from another perspective as well. In a peasant village, where the control of the community comes under two overlapping structures—the parish, on the one hand, and the village community, on the other— more is at stake than in the city, where the question of control is superseded by the fact that local authority is subsumed under larger structures of power beyond the province of the priest or the people. In the village setting the real stakes are political; thus the struggle for the church is played out with greater intensity.

CHAPTER 5

Pilgrimage and Popular Religion at a Greek Holy Shrine

Jill Dubisch

THE Roman Catholic church and the Eastern Orthodox church, officially separate for over nine hundred years, differ in ecclesiastical organization and points of doctrine, as well as in the geographical distribution of their adherents. The Orthodox church has no single prelate with authority over the entirety of the church but is organized into a number of self-governing local churches, some of which coincide with states and some of which do not (Ware 1963:15). Followers of the Orthodox faith are found worldwide, but the greatest concentration of adherents, and of churches, is in Eastern Europe, and within the variety of nationalities and cultural traditions represented in Eastern Orthodoxy "the primary cultural influence has been that of Greece" (Ware 1963:12). Hence the Orthodox church is sometimes termed "Greek Orthodox." Orthodoxy, in turn, played an important role in the formation of the contemporary Greek state in the early nineteenth century. Although within Greece to-day there is a small percentage of Greeks of other faiths, to be Greek and to be Orthodox are very nearly synonymous. Moreover, "Greece is now the only country in the world that is officially an Orthodox Christian country" (Campbell and Sherrard 1968:189). This does not mean, how-ever, that the church and the laity are always in harmony. As in the Cath-olic countries of Europe, conflicts and discrepancies occur between offi-cial and popular practices and beliefs.[1]

This paper explores some of the aspects of this complex relationship between nationalism, official religion, and popular religion in Greece by focussing on a particular ritual setting—the church of the Annunciation (*Evangelismós*) on the Cycladic island of Tinos, home of a miracle-work-ing icon of the Madonna (*Panayía*)[2]—and upon a particular incident that occurred during fieldwork at the church—the folk exorcism of a woman possessed by the devil. The paper is not concerned so much with con-trasting "official" beliefs and practices with those of the "folk," or with a discussion of anticlericalism and attitudes toward the church. Rather, it draws on fieldwork observations in order to suggest some of the ways in which "folk" or popular practice is carried out in the context of an "official" shrine and serves to give that shrine its popular form, or what I have termed its "folk shape"—that is, the pattern of ritual activities which are the most striking feature of pilgrimage to the shrine.[3] I begin with a discussion of the history of the shrine and its place within contemporary Greece and contemporary Greek Orthodox religious practice. This is followed by a description of an observed incident of possession at the shrine. This description is then used as a basis for a discussion of certain aspects of popular or folk religion in Greece.

BACKGROUND

Pilgrimage is a common religious activity in Greece, as it is in many of the Catholic countries of Europe.[4] Regional shrines throughout Greece draw large numbers of pilgrims on their particular saint's day or festival, and such shrines and the saints they commemorate may serve as foci of local identity (see Kenna 1977). Shrines are often associated with some account of miraculous origins or other marvels performed by the saint.

The Church of the Annunciation on the Aegean island of Tinos, though a source of local pride (see Dubisch 1988), is also an important national symbol and the most visited of contemporary Greek pilgrimage sites. The stories of the church's origin state that it was founded in 1823 when a miraculous icon of the Annunciation was discovered in a field where the church now stands. Since then the church has been the object of pilgrimage for thousands of Orthodox Christians (both Greeks and non-Greeks) each year. These pilgrims come to request healing and other divine favors, to render thanks for prayers fulfilled, or simply to seek the grace (*hári*) of the Panayía. Pilgrimage reaches its peak twice a year at the two major festivals of the Panayía: the feast of the Annunciation (*Evangelismós*) on 25 March and the feast of the Assumption or Dormition (*i Kímisis tis Theotókou*) on 15 August.

The discovery of the miraculous icon which gives the church its fame occurred during a crucial point in the history of the modern Greek state. It was found in the beginning of the third year of the Greek struggle for independence from Turkey (*Epanástasis*). The bond of Orthodox Christianity served as an important unifying force for the Greeks in this struggle for nationhood, and the heroic contributions of local church officials as well as the role of local priests in keeping alive Greek religion and culture during the years of Ottoman rule (see Campbell and Sherrard 1968:193–194) are well-remembered.[5] The Greek church became independent of the Patriarchate of Constantinople in 1837 (Herzfeld 1982). Under the new Constitution of 1833 the church of Greece became a department of state.

Many of the Westernized elite who formed the first government of

Greece approved efforts to limit clerical autonomy, seeing Hellenism, not Orthodoxy, as the foundation of a modern state. "They expected the attachment of the population to religion to be replaced rather quickly with nationalism as had happened in the west. What they misjudged was the ability of their Greek countrymen to absorb both Hellenism and Orthodoxy, in fact, to identify them" (Frazee 1977:134).[6]

This ability to combine Orthodoxy with the heritage of ancient Greece is clearly demonstrated at the Church of the Annunciation, which is not only presented as the spiritual heir of the nearby ancient island of Delos (marble from which was used in building the church) but was also purportedly constructed on the site of an ancient temple. Such accounts thus present Hellenism and Orthodoxy not as opposing world views but as stages in the evolution of modern Greece.

While some other popular Christian pilgrimage sites (such as Lourdes) have resulted from miraculous manifestations only reluctantly recognized by the church, the shrine at Tinos seems to have been both officially promoted and controlled from its beginnings. In fact the timing and location of the discovery of the icon were remarkably fortuitous, a point not overlooked by the skeptical (see, for example, Bent 1965). Not only was the icon found at a time of national crisis, it was found in a region with a fairly substantial Catholic population, the consequence of a long period of Italian rule. The Catholics, fearful of what their standing might be under a new—and Orthodox—Greek state, were not enthusiastic supporters of the war (Frazee 1979). Even though the first constitution (adopted in 1822) stated tolerance for all religions, it made the established religion of the new Greek state the Eastern Orthodox Church (Frazee 1979:321). The announcement of a miraculous icon in a region of resistance to the idea of an independent Greek state thus had important political overtones.

The icon of Tinos was found as the result of a series of visions, culminating in the appearance of the Panayía to a humble nun living in a local monastery. The nun relayed her vision to her superior who in turn sent her to the local bishop. It was the bishop who subsequently directed the proceedings that eventually, after a series of delays and the occurrence of several other miracles (including the uncovering of a holy spring), led to the finding of the icon itself. A lay committee (sílogos) was organized to coordinate efforts to build a church on the site.

Retrospectively, at least, and possibly contemporaneously as well, nationalistic significance was drawn from the fact that the icon was found during the turbulent years of the Greek struggle for independence, and the miracles that the icon was claimed to have performed were taken as a sign of divine favor toward the Greek cause. The fact that the icon depicts the Annunciation, and that the day of the Annunciation (25 March)

Inside the church on Tinos the icon itself is obscured by offerings of jewelry and adorned with flowers and *támata*.

is conventionally (though perhaps inaccurately) claimed to be the day the flag of rebellion was first raised, has added a further layer to the symbolism of the icon:[7] the announcement of the savior's birth represents the announcement of a new nation as well. The shrine acquired additional patriotic associations in 1940 when the battleship Elli, stationed in the harbor of Tinos for the 15 August Feast of the Dormition, was torpedoed and sunk on the day of the festival, presumably by an Italian submarine. (This was before Italy had officially declared war on Greece.) A mausoleum for those killed in the attack is located beneath the main part of the church.

Nationalism is also expressed through the presence of state officials and the armed forces at the shrine during the major festivals. The speeches delivered on such occasions emphasize the church's connection to the nation of Greece and the dual nature of the celebrations as both a patriotic and religious holiday. At another level the national and Panhellenic character of the church is demonstrated by the presence not only of pilgrims from distant parts of the country but of Greeks from abroad as well. In fact, since its establishment the church has served as a gathering point for Greeks, regardless of the particular government under which they lived (Bent 1965).

In addition to regular church services, prayer services for pilgrims, and all-night vigils on the eves of certain holy days, there are also processions that take place on the holidays specifically connected with the church (including the day of the Annunciation, the day of the Dormition, and the saint's day of Pelayía, the nun whose vision led to the icon's discovery). On such occasions the icon is carried through the streets (and on St. Pelayía's day, up the mountain to the monastery where she lived). During these processions pilgrims may kneel to have the icon carried over them.

Pilgrims are especially numerous on occasions such as the day of the Dormition, but they may come at any time. Pilgrimage is thus a constant at the church, and despite the overwhelming physical presence of the church itself, and despite its extensive formal organization and ceremonial, much of the ritual activity is carried out at the initiative and pace of the pilgrims themselves, often without any intervention from, or even contact with, a priest. It is thus the pilgrims and their activities that give an on-going ritual and social "shape" to the shrine. This shape reflects both the specific characteristics of the shrine (that is, the presence of the miracle-working icon) and the larger set of beliefs and practices (both official and popular) that constitute Greek Orthodoxy. As will be shown,

On a busy day pilgrims on Tinos must wait in line before they can file into the church.

this particular "folk shape," if I may so label it, contrasts in certain ways with the "official" presentation of the church.

Since Tinos is an island, the rhythm of pilgrimage is very much set by the arrival of the daily boats (four a day at the height of the summer season; fewer in the winter time). The boats generally dock at the main harbor of the town, from which a broad steep street about a kilometer in length runs up to the church. Many pilgrims proceed directly to the church, perhaps stopping along the way to buy large candles (*lambádhes*) or the small bottles for holy water (*boukalákia*) hawked by the merchants whose shops line the street. Those who have vowed to ascend to the church on their knees may begin this arduous journey at the foot of the street, by the harbor. Others proceed on foot, often crossing themselves or praying along the way. At the top of the hill worshippers cross a paved outer courtyard and enter the inner precincts of the church. Here, after ascending a double set of marble steps, they arrive at the church itself. Filing in, they carry out the standard ritual acts one performs upon entering a church: dropping money in the offering box, lighting a candle, and passing in front of the icon to bend and kiss it and make the sign of the cross.

Though prayer services are offered to coincide with the main boat ar-

A stand near the church on Tinos sells a variety of *támata* as well as little bottles (*boukalákia*) for holy water and candles (*lambádhes*) for offerings.

rivals, these do not usually "center" the ritual activity taking place inside the church, and may even appear almost incidental to the "main act," which is the pilgrim's devotion in front of the icon. No priest officiates over this devotion—only a church employee whose task it is to periodically wipe off the icon with a cloth. Some pilgrims arrive at the icon on their knees, others may go down on their knees at the site; some kiss other parts of the icon stand in addition to the icon itself or pass a *táma* three times over the icon in the sign of the cross; some leave flowers or other offerings; and others simply kiss the icon and cross themselves (the minimal act that one may perform). On busy summer days the candles lighted by the pilgrims create an impressive bank of flames, and employees are kept almost constantly busy removing the old candles and cleaning the dripping wax from the floor.

Many pilgrims leave immediately after their devotion at the icon of the Panayía. Others make the rounds of the church, performing devotions in front of the other icons as well. Some pilgrims stay for the services, if they are being performed, and may make special prayer requests to the priest, perhaps writing their requests on small slips of paper and putting them in the wooden box available for this purpose. Many also visit the small chapel (the Church of the Life-Giving Well) that lies below the main church and is the site of a miraculous spring, where they collect a bottle of holy water. It is also not uncommon to see people on their knees in various parts of the church, touching their heads to the marble floor and performing their own private acts of devotion. Some pilgrims come only for the day, or overnight, while others may remain for days, or even weeks, perhaps sleeping outside or in rooms provided by the church, repeating their devotions every day.

The church is thus not a peaceful place, at least not during the main periods of pilgrimage. It is rather a place of movement, action, entreaty, emotion, a place of continuous and constantly varied activity, which on busy days especially is almost impossible to absorb.

Although I have used the term "pilgrimage" to describe a visit to the church, the Greek word—*proskínima*—is not entirely glossed by the English term. A more satisfactory translation might be "paying one's respects" or "performing devotions." When a Greek says she or he has gone to the church "*na proskiníso*" (the verb form of *proskínima*), the activities involved are those which accompany any visit to a church: lighting a candle, making the sign of the cross, kissing the icon(s). These activities are carried out regardless of whether or not there is another purpose to the visit, such as a special request or the fulfillment of a vow.

While pilgrims who visit the church may come simply for *proskínima*, often they have a specific purpose in mind. This purpose is most often related to the health or well-being of the pilgrim or a family member.

The visit may be undertaken in order to ask for the cure of an illness or some other physical problem, or in order to fulfill a vow (*táma*) that has included the promise of such a visit should the supplicant's request be granted.[8] The request or vow may be accompanied by an offering—perhaps an object of a personal nature, such as a piece of embroidery, or something purchased, such as a large taper (*lambádha*) or a small metal plaque (also called a *táma*) with a picture of a person or a body part or other representation of the individual's request or vow. Or the offering may be any one of a number of other items, ranging from icons to flowers to sheep, or one of the three basic symbolic foods: oil, wine, or bread.

The *táma* may also involve the more direct presentation of one's self. In a sense the very act of pilgrimage is an "embodiment" of one's request or vow. But this presentation may be elaborated in various acts, the most common of which is crawling up to the church on one's hands and knees. Less arduous activities such as walking barefoot to the church or wearing black clothes (which are left at the church upon departure) can also be part of a vow. At the other extreme, a pilgrim may choose to go on her or his stomach instead of knees, possibly the most difficult and painful journey of all.

As Turner points out, "All sites of pilgrimage have this in common: they are believed to be places where miracles once happened, still happen, and may happen again" (Turner and Turner 1978:6). The central feature that pilgrims say draws them to the shrine is the fact that its icon is miracle working (*thavmatourgós*). The most commonly cited miracles performed by the icon are cures of paralysis, blindness, barrenness, deafness, muteness, and madness, as well as innumerable cases of the saving of ships at sea from sinking.[9] In addition, though not common in twentieth-century literature, many cases of individuals cured of demon possession can be found in nineteenth-century accounts. In the following section I will describe my own encounter with a contemporary case of a woman possessed by the devil and then analyze the significance of this incident in the ritual context of the shrine in order to demonstrate some of the ways that popular ritual performed at the site of the church contrasts with the official ceremonies of the church.[10]

A CASE OF POSSESSION

The celebration of the festival of the Dormition on 15 August draws thousands to the shrine every year, and for several days beforehand the daily boats are packed with pilgrims for this event. Two days before the festival, at about eight o'clock in the evening, I was on my way up the street to the church when I noticed a woman dressed in black lying face down in the street about halfway up the hill, surrounded by perhaps half a dozen onlookers. At first I thought that the woman was elderly and feeble and had collapsed trying to fulfill her vow to reach the church on her hands and knees. But as I approached, I realized that she was young (about twenty-five years old, I later learned). My next thought was that perhaps she was ill. She would rise to her knees, crawl a few steps, and then collapse, crying out to the woman accompanying her, "Maria, I can't, I can't" (*dhen boró, dhen boró*). Her companion was staring straight ahead of her and praying, pausing when the other woman collapsed in order to make the sign of the cross over her with the crucifix she was carrying. Passers-by and several people watching from the doorways of the shops lining the road came up to the woman to encourage her, telling her to have courage and perseverance (*káne kouráyio*), to go on and complete her *táma*. A Gypsy woman with scabbed knees stopped to say encouragingly that she herself had done it and surely the young woman could too. The lights of the church at the top of the hill had just been lit as I arrived on the scene, and a man was telling the woman on her knees that they had been lit for her. "The Panayía is waiting for you" (*i Panayía se periméni*), several people added.

At this point the comments of the onlookers suggested that they viewed the woman's behavior as somewhat extreme. She was, after all, engaging in an endeavor that is almost commonplace at the shrine, and one that is carried out successfully by many women older and more feeble than she. The woman accompanying her (who, it turned out, was her

A lone woman on her knees begins the long ascent to the church on Tinos attracting the glances of passers-by.

sister) kept encouraging her to go on, and at one point looked around almost in embarrassment at the crowd that had gathered to watch, telling her companion (who had again collapsed) to get up and go on. Look, she said, people (*o kósmos*) are watching you.

The woman on her knees, however, continued to have difficulty. She would get up and crawl rapidly for a few yards on her hands and knees and then collapse again, crying out. At one point she called out, "My head! My head!" and her sister bent to make the sign of the cross over her head. At another point she cried, "He'll kill me!" As she collapsed once more, face down on the ground, a middle-aged woman in black pushed through the crowd to the young woman's side and slipped a protective amulet of colored string around her wrist. She then took the crucifix from the sister and made the sign of the cross over the fallen woman and applied holy water to her face. People were now beginning to ask the sister what the young woman had, as it became evident that her difficulty was no ordinary one. "She has her cross" (*éhi to stavró tis*), the sister replied. And "she has a sin" (*amartía*).

By this point the number of people around the woman had grown quite large, and the spirit of the crowd had turned into one of active participation, with people shouting encouraging words: "You're getting close" (*kondévis*), or even "You've arrived" (*éftases*). About seventy-five people were in the crowd at this point, with perhaps thirty directly engaged in helping the young woman, verbally or otherwise. In a period of about an hour and a half the woman had covered perhaps a quarter of a kilometer, reaching a point about three-quarters of the way to the church. (A healthy woman is normally able to cover the entire distance on her knees in thirty to forty-five minutes.)

At this point the word had begun to spread through the crowd that the woman was possessed by the devil (*dhemonisméni*), that the devil (*o dhiávalos*) had got inside her head (*bíke mésa sto kefáli tis*). It was the devil who was holding her back to prevent her from getting to the Panayía and the miraculous icon. He had entered her, it was said (the story circulating around the crowd and being relayed to newcomers), when at the age of eighteen, finding herself not yet engaged, the young woman had resorted to magic to remedy her state. This had afforded the devil his opportunity. "The magic did it to her" (*i mayía tin ékane*).

While all of this was going on, there was no sign of activity from the church itself. Vespers had ended, the exterior church lights had been put on, and the priests had gone home. The only encounter the possessed woman had with anyone "official" came when the crowd accosted a young nun walking down the street, her briefcase in her hand. They urged her to speak to the possessed woman, and somewhat reluctantly the nun let herself be led to the young woman's side. I couldn't hear the exchange between them, but the nun knelt beside the possessed woman for only a few moments, and then she got up and left.

The crowd seemed to have much more definite ideas of what to do than the nun did, for they continued to try to help the possessed woman in her endeavor to reach the church. They made the sign of the cross over her, sent children running up to the church to fetch holy water, and chanted prayers. As the crowd continued to grow, augmented by the Gypsies who were camped at the top of the hill near the church, the woman was surrounded on all sides by onlookers, and there were constant cries of "Open up! Open up!" (*aníkste to!*) to try to part the crowd so that the woman could see the church and the lighted cross ahead of her.

By the time the young woman began to make her way up the first set of steps and across the outer courtyard of the church, the crowd had grown to perhaps one hundred fifty, or more, many of them Gypsies. Two men had begun to take charge. (Until this point the participants in the drama had been almost all women.) They yelled at the crowd to step back and make way so that the woman could go up the main stairs. There was some discussion about whether or not the church would be open when the woman got there, and several people agreed that even if the

On Tinos a group of women on their knees makes the final ascent to the church.

doors were closed, she could at least see the icon through the window, and then she could come back the next day for her *proskínima*. (There were also some expressions of indignation that the church would be closed at all, and several people wondered what those who arrived on the late evening boat were to do.)

From the time she had drawn near to the church, the possessed woman had begun to move more rapidly, and it did not take her long now to crawl up the two flights of steps to the balcony encircling the upper level. Several pilgrims sleeping on the balcony just outside the church doors were rather rudely awakened from their slumbers by the crowd and told to make way for the woman approaching on her knees.

The church was in fact closed. (The doors were normally locked at ten o'clock that summer, and it was by this time ten-thirty. It had taken the woman two and a half hours to make the journey from halfway up the hill to the church.) When she reached the church doors, the woman stood up and kissed the doors and prayed, the crowd pressing around behind her. Shortly after that I had a glimpse of her being led away down the hallway by one of the women in the crowd. They were chatting normally together as they walked. Obviously the devil no longer held her in his thrall.

INTERPRETATION

The inherent dramatic fascination of this incident is obvious. Yet it has a particular anthropological significance as well. It was a folk drama of the battle between good and evil, between the Panayía and the devil. The woman's body was the battleground,[11] with the onlookers helping her to do battle, utilizing their repertoire of spiritual techniques, from amulets and icons to holy water and prayers. It was a drama enacted entirely spontaneously, with no participation or direction provided by the church. In effect, the crowd, acting on its own, and with the unmediated help of the Panayía, had defeated Satan's power.

Defeating the devil in so direct a fashion is not an everyday occurrence in either popular or official ritual. Yet the incident just described does illustrate certain general features of popular Greek religious belief and practice. These include the belief in divine intervention in everyday life, the use of vows and pilgrimage as a means of individual connection with the divine, the public and external nature of religiosity, and the importance of women's participation in religious life. Each of these will be discussed in turn.

The Divine in Everyday Life

While the term miracle (*thávma*) is generally reserved for those acts which alter seemingly hopeless and generally medically untreatable conditions, in a sense any answered prayer that changes existing conditions (for example, effects a rescue or cure) could be termed a miracle.[12] In fact when we speak of "miracles," we must see them within a larger context of a perceived world in which divine beings can and do intervene in daily life and in which it is common to look for the significance of events in their temporal or spatial association with a saint or the Panayía (cf. Pina-Cabral 1986:167). For example, the raising of the Greek flag of independence is given divine significance by its association with the day of the Annunciation. This connecting of important events with the nearest holy day is also found in everyday life. For example, a woman whose son survived an accident told me that she planned to build a little church in thanks to St. Dimitrios, the saint whose day fell nearest the day of the accident and who was therefore the saint most likely responsible for the young man's having been saved.

In the incident of possession just described, the normally invisible was made dramatically visible and real. For the people participating, the devil was unquestionably *there* in the body of the woman. Among other things this provided an occasion for religious interpretation and commentary. Several people, for example, used this incident for the edification of children. One woman commented several times "and to think our children don't believe . . . ," while another explained to several young girls how when the devil got inside someone, that person could do whatever she or he wanted (óti théli) except go to church. That's why the harder the young woman on her knees tried to get to the church, the more the devil sought to hold her back. One little girl who shrank back in fear as the possessed woman crawled past her up the steps of the church was reassured by her mother that she had nothing to be afraid of, for the devil could not hurt her if she had a strong belief in God.

The emotional impact and cathartic effect of the incident upon the possessed woman were obvious. Her progressive loosening and eventual removal of her headscarf as she crawled her way up the street to the church, a gesture often preceding the expression and release of emotion among Greek women (see Caraveli 1986), was an indication of the evolution of her own emotional state. The event was also emotional for members of the audience. I saw several women crying as they watched the young woman's struggle, and others turned away, sighing and crossing themselves and calling on the Panayía. Ordinary events, then (in this case, a young woman's failure to become engaged and her resort to magic as a remedy), can lead to demonstrations of the power of the other world.

As the example of the possessed woman illustrates, what happens at the Church of the Annunciation is an intensification of forces already present in everyday life. Spiritual powers, both good and evil, can be called upon or revealed at any time or place. At the site of the church, however, the divine is more likely to be manifest and to be manifest in greater force (in this instance strongly enough to defeat Satan's power). The possibilities of such manifestations—though always present—are increased around major holy days such as the day of the Annunciation. During the all-night vigil, miracles of healing may occur and the Panayía herself may appear to those who truly believe. "There are many things here that we don't understand," a woman who worked at the church said to me wonderingly after recounting to me some of the icon's most renowned miracles.

The relationship between the popular conceptions of such happenings and official accounts is complex. Pamphlets distributed by the church describe some of the shrine's most famous miracles, and these may be recounted to the visitor by both pilgrims and inhabitants of the island. "Official" miracles are medically substantiated before they are inscribed in church records. At the same time there is also a large oral tradition, consisting of pilgrims' own experiences and those relayed to them by word of mouth, a large part of which is not found in literature on the church (compare Slater 1986). The recounting of such stories (as well as tales of unusual vows or other dramatic incidents) is a common type of exchange among pilgrims, especially at major festival times when the crowds are large and people are more likely to fall into conversation with each other. In the summer of 1988, for example, at the festival of the Dormition, I heard the following story while I was standing with a group of pilgrims just outside the church. A child who had been "vowed" (taméno) to the Panayía had fallen overboard from a ship on its way to Tinos. The ship had not turned around but had sailed on. However, the Panayía was watching over the child, and it was picked up by another ship which was passing by and brought to the church. When the grieving parents arrived, they found the child waiting for them beside the icon.

Such tales, individually and collectively, reinforce faith and give hope to those to whom they are told.

The Vow

One of the most important components of pilgrimage to the church of the Panayía of Tinos is the táma or vow. William Christian has suggested that the fact that vows, by their very nature, tend to be unmediated and personal often results in their not being given the attention they deserve as an important religious phenomenon (Christian 1981a:31–32).[13] At pilgrimage sites such as that at Tinos, where individual vows become part of a collective (though not necessarily communal) activity, the significance of the vow in Orthodox religious life becomes apparent.

The making of a táma is entirely between the person making it and the spiritual being in question (in this case the Panayía). It is made "inside oneself" and often not revealed to others until its fulfillment, if then.[14] Some of the conventional things one might do in fulfillment of a vow have already been mentioned, but a vow can, in theory at least, be whatever the person wishes it to be. The fulfillment of the vow may represent in some way the vow itself (for example, a replica of a ship presented for a rescue at sea, a cured child carried up the hill on its mother's back as she crawls on her hands and knees), or it may not. In any case, these vows are not overseen by a priest, either in their making or their execution, though they may be recorded by the church, especially if they involve the presentation of a gift to the church, or are especially dramatic in form. As examples of such gifts one may observe in the church a gold and silver orange tree (gift of a dying Greek abroad, miraculously restored to life), a silver ship with a fish stuck in a hole in its side (representing the rescue of a sinking ship at sea), and a marble fountain in the inner court-yard (presented by a Turkish official cured of syphilis).

The Sacred and the Profane

Turner has spoken of the increasing "sacralization" of the pilgrim's route (1974:182). At Tinos this sacralization is a combination of official direc-tives and the pilgrims' own activities. At one point in the past church officials forbade miniskirts on passengers who disembarked on the island. Today, while topless bathing and discos have invaded Tinos, there is still a zone around the church where the more raucous activities are forbid-den, and islanders continue to contrast the "quietness" of Tinos and the quality of their visitors with the nearby decadent and "dirty" island of Mykonos. Moreover, writings on Tinos suggest an ancient lineage of the sacred, for Tinos is presented as having replaced Delos as the holy center of Aegean Greece.

The church itself is, of course, a sacred precinct, and at the entrance-way to the courtyard that surrounds the church an employee stands guard to make certain no one enters inappropriately attired. (No shorts are allowed for either men or women, and no short skirts. Though some-times women in pants enter, some bring skirts to pull over their pants.) In other respects it is the pilgrims themselves who determine, through their own behavior, the degrees of sacredness of their route. Many cross themselves when the church first comes into sight, others as they dis-embark from the boat. For those going on their knees the waterfront or the beginning of the road up to the church may mark the start of their entrance into the sacred realm. For others this occurs at the steps up to the church itself.

In the case of the possessed woman the sacred was viscerally dis-played. At the beginning of her long struggle up the hill to the church, she could barely move, so strongly did the devil hold her back. Then as she drew closer, the power of the Panayía gradually began to prevail, the devil loosed his hold, and she started to move more freely up the hill. And even though the church doors were locked, it was sufficient for her merely to behold the icon stand through the glass for her exorcism to be complete.

We must not be misled by such observations, however, into seeing some sort of absolute demarcation between the sacred and the profane, between religious and everyday life. Brettell points out (this volume) that in Portuguese Catholicism the sacred and the profane are "complexly intertwined," and this observation holds true for Greece as well. Religious holidays are occasions for socializing and entertainment, and pilgrimages likewise are excursions as well as religious events. Among the pilgrims I met, for example, were two middle-aged sisters who had vowed to spend a month in Tinos every summer in gratitude to the Panayía for curing various family members who had been ill. While the two women did visit the church frequently during their stay and also made excursions to the monastery, they also spent a considerable amount of time relaxing and eating and enjoying themselves. The fact that their vow provided them with an opportunity for a vacation should not be viewed cynically, however. Religious and recreational activities are not regarded as antithetical. In traditional village life religious holidays are the main recreational events, and churches are often sightseeing destinations for vacationers. It is very common for pilgrims to Tinos to visit other sites on the island (including the monastery where the nun Pelayía lived), take excursions by boat to the nearby islands of Delos and Mykonos, and go swimming and shopping, in addition to carrying out their *proskínima*. The common route of pilgrimage, especially for those who come only for the day, is to ascend to the church by the main road and return by a parallel secondary road that is lined with shops. (I have heard merchants refer to this portion of the pilgrim's progress as "the return"—*epistrofí*.) These shops offer a wide variety of religious and secular souvenirs, and icons and incense may be displayed side by side with suntan lotion and snorkling gear.[15] It is a rare pilgrim who leaves Tinos without some material remembrance of the visit, and the buying of gifts and souvenirs is sometimes given as much attention as the devotions at the church.

Inner State and Public Act

The relationship between the inner state of the performer and the religious act itself, and the relative importance of each within Greek Orthodox Christianity is a complex issue. Discussions of Greek popular belief often emphasize the importance of ritual, and I found that Greeks comparing their religion with that of Americans were less interested in what Americans believed than in what they did. Their questions were often concerned with whether or not saints' days are celebrated, what is done at funerals, do Americans have icons, and so forth. Thus to a great extent the Greek Orthodox religion, in its popular form at least, is defined for its participants by its external, rather than its internal, manifestations. However, one should be careful not to take this too far, for faith is important too. As the onlookers commented while the possessed woman crawled up to the church, one must have faith to hold the devil at bay. It is because people no longer have faith, another woman told me, that so many bad things are happening in the world now, and I have heard local people commenting that today's pilgrims no longer really believe and just come to Tinos for a holiday. Other informants, in describing the miraculous visions of the Panayía that appear in the church, stated that such visions come only to those who believe. In addition, vows are made "inside oneself," and the exact nature of the vow may never be publicly revealed.[16]

Nonetheless, it is fair to say that, in general, popular religion in Greece, like popular religion in Portugal (Brettell, this volume) and in other Catholic countries as well, is more outward than inward looking, more concerned with external images, with the public and communal than with the interior or the mystic. We can tie this in turn to a more general emphasis in Greek society on outward appearance as opposed to inner state or, as Herzfeld has put it, to a "fundamental concern with display and concealment" (Herzfeld 1986). In small communities, for example, morality is defined not so much by what one does as by whether others know about it. Juliet du Boulay quotes a Greek village woman who had successfully concealed the indiscretions of her daughter-in-law as saying, "God wants things covered up" (du Boulay 1976:406). In other words, the daughter-in-law was not immoral simply as a consequence of what she had done but only if other villagers learned about it and the family's reputation was stained.

This does not mean that Greeks feel that inner states do not exist, only that one cannot know the inner state of another with any accuracy or confidence (see, for example, Herzfeld 1985). Hence the importance of the public act or performance through which an inner state is made visible. Thus while a vow may be made "inside oneself," it finds expression in some type of public ritual act, whether this be as simple as lighting a candle in a nearby church or as dramatic as crawling up to the church at Tinos on one's knees. For the young woman possessed by the devil her suffering was made visible and public, as were her sin and her redemption. Moreover, her audience was engaged with her and, as so often occurs in such public situations, ready to offer both advice and aid.[17] The votive offerings that can be found in most Greek churches and that line the walls and ceiling of the church at Tinos are another visible, public manifestation of the vow.

In general, one might say that Greek Orthodoxy is a highly "visible" religion in the sense that it is represented in a variety of material objects: churches, the votive offerings and icons that fill these churches, the icons that are an essential part of any village home, and the many prophylactic objects that are used to protect valued property and persons from harm.[18] This popular, public, and material manifestation of religiosity is also found in the Greek landscape itself. Many of the islands, and parts of the mainland also, are dotted with tiny churches that are individually owned and meticulously kept. Such churches may be erected as the fulfillment of a vow or as an offering of thanksgiving (as for example, by a sailor returned from the sea). Although a priest is required if a liturgy is to be performed at such a church, the initiation, building, and maintenance (including lighting of the oil lamps on the eves of holy days) are entirely in lay hands. Similarly, the roadsides of Greece are dotted with tiny shrines (proskinitária), often erected as memorials to people who have died in accidents at that spot (see Hurlbutt 1985). Again, these are public displays, constructed at individual initiative and privately maintained.

Material objects are one way of making divine power both visible and available. Sometimes people speak of the Panayía, for example, as if she were resident in the icon itself, and instead of saying they are going to the church, pilgrims commonly say simply that they are going "to the Panayía" (stin Panayía). Objects in contact with, or proximity to, the sacred can become embued with therapeutic or protective power. In addition to holy water and consecrated oil, for example, pilgrims may also take away with them a piece of cloth or cotton or some other item with which they have rubbed one of the icons. Incense from the services, dried remnants of flowers brought for offerings, or pieces of the cloth used to wipe the glass front of the icon are sewed into tiny filactá and sold in street stands and at the monastery. Throughout Greece, cars, buses, trucks, and shops display medallions, icons, filactá, and blue beads against the evil eye, and every house has its iconostasis with its own protective icons. This variety of material objects is one way the power of the sacred penetrates and is manifested in everyday life.

None of this should be taken to mean that the variety of popular religious acts and objects observed in Greece are simply part of "empty" rituals, devoid of accompanying faith. Obviously this is not true. What it does mean, however, is that religiosity, expressed by a common performance of ritual acts that are carried out within a common framework of acceptance and understanding of such acts, may nonetheless conceal a

Small memorial shrines (*pros-kinitária*) such as this one dot the roadsides in much of Greece, erected and maintained by families or individuals.

diversity of beliefs. The emphasis on ritual performance may thus serve to mask the discrepancies that exist between popular and official interpretations. Greek funeral rituals, for example, which are extensive and elaborate (see Danforth and Tsiaras 1982), do not necessarily tell us what the participants believe about the afterlife. Once after a funeral I listened to several middle-aged village women discussing what happens when one dies. "Maybe it's just like falling asleep," one woman suggested. "Who really knows," another responded, and the others present agreed. None mentioned the Orthodox church's teaching regarding the afterlife, and yet all of these women, who faithfully performed the rituals of their religion, including those associated with the dead, would have been offended at the suggestion that they were not good Christians (cf. Caraveli 1986).

Religion and Gender

Except for the Gypsy men who stepped in toward the end, the drama of
the possessed woman was both staged and acted by women. This is not
so remarkable if one considers that the majority of pilgrims who come to
Tinos are female (though men participate too) and that Greek women are
in general more regular churchgoers than men and more involved in all
aspects of ritual. This gender difference is in part related to anticlericalism, which in Greece, as in many Catholic countries, may exist side by
side with strong feelings of religiosity. Such anticlerical feelings are usually most strongly expressed by men. One explanation which has been
suggested for this is that while religion offers an appropriate role model
for women in the form of the Panayía, the pure mother (du Boulay 1986),
Christ does not offer a similar model for men since the virtues he represents are inappropriate for Greek male behavior (Campbell 1964). In
particular, the exercise of restraint on sexuality, the institution of confession, and submission to the authority of other men seem to be sticking
points for men both in Greece and elsewhere in the Mediterranean.[19]
Thus not only does responsibility for the spiritual and physical well-being
of the family rest chiefly on women (see Dubisch 1983; Hirschon 1983)
but the most significant popular religious figure is a female one, the Panayía.[20] She is the holy figure to whom probably more churches are dedicated than any other, and, moreover, it is her church that is the chief
pilgrimage site in Greece and the symbolic representation of Greece itself.[21] In certain ways, however, this "feminization" of religion is in tension with the male-dominated institution of the church, a tension that is
manifest at the shrine itself. This is discussed further below.

CONCLUSION: "RITUAL ORDER" VERSUS "RITUAL CHAOS"

The account of a woman possessed by the devil, a single incident among
many which occur yearly at the Church of the Annunciation, illustrates
some of the ways in which pilgrims at the shrine create and carry out
their own religious rituals, both individually and collectively, independent of official direction and control. While such activities are not necessarily performed in defiance of church directives, and while the church
itself certainly celebrates and supports some of them, nonetheless the
church usually does not play an active role. Moreover, the way in which
the church chooses to officially portray the shrine is in some significant
respects at odds with the sort of popular religious activity that takes place
there. For example, official discussions and displays obscure the fact that
pilgrimage to the shrine is overwhelmingly female. Furthermore, wom-
en's offerings at the shrine tend to be ephemeral in nature—acts of sup-

plication such as crawling on their knees or the presentation of nondurable items such as flowers or oil or candles—while the offerings actually displayed at the church tend to be more durable and expensive ones which are usually presented by men (see Dubisch 1987).

The difference between official and popular ritual displays can be seen most dramatically, however, in the procession that occurs as part of the festivities of the Dormition on 15 August, the most heavily attended of the festivals at the church. This festival has over the years drawn an increasingly large number of Gypsies, as well as the more usual crowds of sick, crippled, and mentally ill. These pilgrims stream off the boats to fill the hotels, rooming houses, churchyard, and streets. At the church a continuous stream files past the icon of the Panayía. The impression is one almost of anarchy, with thousands of individual *proskinímata* carried out simultaneously and hundreds of individual dramas being enacted as pilgrims struggle up to the church on their knees, praying and crying out, each engrossed in his or her suffering and pain, sometimes drawing—as the possessed woman did—a small crowd of fellow pilgrims who stop to watch or to offer encouragement.

The formal climax of the celebration comes when the icon is carried from the church and down the main street to the harbor. It is accompanied by a military guard, and pilgrims kneel between two permanently marked lines in the street to have the icon passed over them. The rest of the street is cordoned off, and police pass up and down, trying to keep the eager crowds behind the ropes. The precision and rigidity of the military procession contrast with the highly individualized and unorganized crowd which it seeks to control so that the icon can pass. When I attended the festival in 1986, the procession was forced to halt several times to allow all the waiting pilgrims to stream underneath. Many people reached up to touch the icon as it passed over them, undeterred by officials who kept striking down their hands. Once the icon had passed, all order in the crowd broke down and the pilgrims streamed behind the procession en masse to the harbor where official sermons and speeches were delivered from the podium at the waterfront while military jets streaked overhead.

Such contrasts between popular and official activity, between "disorder" and structure, occur at other levels as well and may in fact be a general characteristic of such pilgrimage shrines.[22] Turner has suggested that religious leaders may have ambivalent feelings about pilgrimages: "Though operational on a wide scale, pilgrimages have somehow brought features of . . . the 'Little Tradition' into what should have been theologically, liturgically, and indeed, economically controlled by leading representatives of the 'Great Tradition' " (1974:188). He also suggests that pilgrimage represents a kind of "institutionalized or symbolic anti-

Preceded by a woman on her knees, a group of Gypsies on Tinos carries offerings of sheep and candles (*lambádhes*) to the church.

Surrounded by densely packed crowds, the icon is carried in procession through the street.

structure" (Turner 1974:187). We might then see major official events such as the festival of the Dormition as ways of counteracting this anti-structure, as occasions in which official ritual seeks to contain and control the massive and individualized religious behavior of the thousands of pilgrims who have descended upon the island at this time.

We gain a further insight into such tensions if we consider some of the reasons why certain groups are particularly in evidence at this particular pilgrimage site. The fact that such major festivals are heavily attended by Gypsies and women suggests that they hold a special importance for the socially marginal and oppressed.[23] By their (sometimes dramatic) identification with a major religious and national symbol, such groups seek both power and legitimacy. At the same time it is the activity of these groups which on such occasions give the shrine its "ritual shape," a shape that is not determined unilaterally by official activities or by individual acts but by a combination of both.[24]

What all of this suggests, then, is that the study of shrines such as that at Tinos may be a fruitful avenue for illuminating the nature of both popular and official forms of belief. The shrine is neither a "folk" nor an official phenomenon but both. The activities occurring there demonstrate that while the Orthodox church may exercise a kind of "hegemony,"[25] it by no means entirely contains or controls religious behavior at this sacred site. Nor is popular religious expression merely a corrupt or incomplete reflection of official dogma. Rather it is a powerful and creative force in its own right. This can perhaps best be summed up by a quotation from my own field notes, written after attending prayer services one August afternoon:

> As I was standing in the church today, I looked up at the elaborate vaulted domes of the ceiling, the many lamps and other offerings suspended from its heights—these offerings themselves are elaborate, some of them, and the effect of all of them is to fill the space above our heads with visible testaments to the power of the Panayía. . . .
>
> And yet I realized, looking around, that if one looks only at the structure of the shrine . . . one sees only the shell which encompasses the heart of the shrine, which is all those living, breathing, kneeling, praying people within it. It's true that these people have helped to build the shell—the offerings of the faithful not only adorn the church, they even contribute to various parts of its structure and furnishing, inside and out—but many offerings are of a poorer and more transitory sort. . . . Even the *lambádhes* are not allowed to be displayed for the length of their burning but are quickly snuffed, pulled from the holder, and thrown away. And the people themselves are offerings, are prayers—whether coming on their knees, walking barefoot, kneeling at the

iconostasis, lighting a candle. They are as bright and transitory as the candles they light—with them the church comes alive (8/24/86).

Investigation of ritual behavior at a shrine such as that of the Panayía of Tinos thus offers an avenue for exploring the multiple dimensions of religious phenomena within a particular society, including not only some of the contrasts and conflicts that may exist between "folk" belief and official religion and between individual and institutional levels of religious organization but also the ways in which religious ritual may reflect important structural, political, and symbolic features of the society itself.

Notes to Chapter 5

The research upon which this paper is based was carried out from May through November 1986, with return visits in the spring of 1987 and summer of 1988, and was made possible by funds from the Foundation of The University of North Carolina at Charlotte and the state of North Carolina and by a Fulbright Grant for research in Greece. An earlier version of this paper was presented at the 1986 meeting of the American Anthropological Society under the title "Pilgrimage and Folk Ritual at a Greek Holy Shrine." I am grateful to Raymond Michalowski, Salvatore Cucchiari, and Michael Herzfeld for their very helpful comments at various stages of the revision process.

1. Nor are church and state in Greece always in accord. The struggle between the two has been continuous since Greece became a nation (Frazee 1969, 1977). It is most recently manifested in attempts by the present socialist government to confiscate church lands and reorganize certain aspects of church government.

2. The term "Panayía" (All Holy One) is preferable to the usual English translation "Holy Virgin" or "Virgin Mary" since the virginity of Mary is not stressed in Orthodox theology, nor in Greek folk belief, in the same way it is in Catholicism. The term "Virgin" (*Parthéna*) is occasionally used in the liturgy or in religious writing, but I have never heard Mary referred to in this fashion in everyday speech.

3. In some ways the use of the term "folk" to describe pilgrims to the shrine and their activities there may be a little misleading, especially if the term is seen as referring to traditional rural peoples. People of all classes come to the shrine, including large numbers of Athenians, as well as villagers and townspeople from almost all areas of Greece. For this reason I have preferred to use the term "popular" or to put "folk" in quotation marks. Whichever term is used, there is at least an implicit tension, or dialectic, between such practices and official ecclesiastical models and forms (cf. Brettell, this volume).

4. Pilgrimage, although an important phenomenon in many religious traditions, has only recently begun to attract serious attention by anthropologists, beginning with the work of Victor Turner (Turner 1974, Turner and Turner 1978). For a recent study of pilgrimage in a Brazilian context see Slater (1986).

5. This does not mean, however, that official church support for independence was entirely enthusiastic. The Patriarch of Constantinople disavowed the revolution and excommunicated its supporters (an act that did not save him from Turkish reprisal, as he was later hanged). See Frazee (1977:129); also Campbell and Sherrard (1968).

6. For a detailed discussion of the complex relationship between Hellenism and Orthodoxy, including attempts to see in Christian practices the evidence of ancient roots, see Herzfeld (1982); also Campbell and Sherrard (1968).

7. Michael Herzfeld suggests that the accuracy of the date depends on where and with what event one sees the revolution as having begun (Herzfeld 1982:22). See also Herzfeld (1987).

138 · Jill Dubisch

8. The Greek word *táma* (pl. *támata*) refers both to the act (the vow and its fulfillment) and to objects that have been vowed (which may also be called offerings—*afyerómata*). The simplest form of *táma*/object is a little metal plaque depicting the nature of the request that was fulfilled (usually by a representation of a part of the body). The word *táma* seems to be used only in a religious context and is not applied to obligations and reciprocity in social relationships. Compare Pina-Cabral (1986:163–173) on the vow in Portugal.

9. On this subject see Florakis (1982).

10. Demon possession has not been widely discussed in the literature on modern Greece, and this was my first direct encounter with such an incident (though I have since heard about other cases). For one of the few references to this subject see Blum and Blum (1970), who interpret such cases as epilepsy or insanity. Early nineteenth-century discussions of cures of demon possession by the icon are mentioned in Pirgos (1865).

11. The symbolism of woman's body within Orthodox religion is an extensive topic in itself. It was through a woman's body that Christ entered the world, and at the shrine at Tinos women use their bodies in fulfillment of their *támata* to make symbolic statements about their own roles and relationships (Dubisch 1987). On the general symbolism of women's bodies in Greek village life see Dubisch (1986); Hirschon (1978); also Machin (1983).

12. An 1865 definition of a *thávma* states that it is something which does not get better by a doctor's skill but only through God (Pirgos 1865:9n).

13. Although Christian is discussing religion in sixteenth-century Spain, much of what he has to say about the nature of the vow fits the situation in Greece today remarkably well: the unmediated nature of the vow, the occasions upon which vows are made, the occurrence of important signs on or around saints' days, the building of chapels and shrines to fulfill vows, and so on. See also Christian (1972) on vows, shrines, and pilgrimage in contemporary Spain.

14. Nonfulfillment apparently is also a matter to be dealt with between the Panayía and the supplicant. For an account of what happened to a woman who tried to back out on a vow see Blum and Blum (1970:45–46). Nonfulfillment does not always invite drastic reprisals, however. When I asked people about what happens if one does not fulfill a vow the response I got was a shrug and the observation that one *ought* to fulfill a vow, but that sometimes, because of problems of time or money or health, it might take a while before one was able to do so. In other words, the obligation remains, but since a long time can elapse before this obligation is met, it is difficult to say exactly when a vow is really "unfulfilled."

15. The association of markets and secular celebrations with religious pilgrimage is, of course, an old pattern (see, for example, Turner 1974).

16. It would be tempting to see official religion as emphasizing the role of belief and faith, and popular religion as more concerned with acts, but this would be misleading. A more significant point of difference may be the sorts of acts considered religiously important. At a sermon on the eve of St. Pelayía, for example, the priest spoke not only of the importance of faith but of the necessity for faith to be manifested in deeds (*érga*) and not just in words. And in his sermon

on the day of the Dormition in 1988 the bishop railed against young women who came improperly dressed to the church and who had strayed from the proper road (*dhrómos*) in their lives.

17. On women's public religious displays see Dubisch (1987).

18. In many of these objects we see the ambiguous shading between the official and the "folk." Certain religious objects (medallions, holy items connected with the icon, et cetera) are used as prophylactics against the "eye" (*máti*), even though belief in the "eye" straddles the line between "folk" belief and official religion.

19. This is true in Latin America as well. For a discussion of the models offered to men and to women by the Catholic church in a Latin American community, and the effect of these models on ritual involvement, see Gudeman (1976). The conflict between cultural codes and religious codes for Spanish men is discussed by Brandes (1980:182–192).

20. Compare Giovannini (1981) on Italy.

21. On this aspect of the shrine see Dubisch (1988).

22. Compare Murphy (1987). I have put such terms as "disorder" and "chaos" in quotation marks to indicate that while I am using them as a contrast to the formal and hierarchically structured aspects of ritual, I do not mean to suggest that they are to be taken literally to indicate a complete breakdown of social order. Nor do I mean to suggest here that women necessarily represent disorder (though this has been suggested by Hoffman 1976). In fact in many ways they can be seen as the maintainers of order, including orderly relations between the human and spiritual world (see Dubisch 1986).

23. It is interesting to note in this context that the proportion of men visiting the shrine is higher among the Gypsies than it is in the general pilgrim population. Gypsies are not highly regarded by the local population, who see them as dirty and given to thievery. At the same time their devotion may be remarked. "They believe more than we do (*pyó polí ápo mas*)," several people observed when I asked about the Gypsies' presence at the church. It might be noted that from an anthropological perspective one of the interesting things about Gypsies is that they spill over boundaries (cf. Douglas 1966). They do not rent rooms but camp out in the streets or church courtyard, or in their trucks or vans, and Gypsy children roam about in "gangs," going freely where they please.

24. Gudeman sees vows and the making of votive offerings as transition rites since "they are usually undertaken to change some aspects of an individual's life" (Gudeman 1976:710). He contrasts these with revivification rituals, which are cyclical and predictable. One of the interesting things about the shrine of the Panayía at Tinos (and other similar shrines in Greece) is the way in which these two types of ritual mesh, especially for those who choose to fulfill their vows on one of the major festival days associated with the shrine. This may, in fact, be one of the significant ritual aspects of pilgrimage sites generally.

25. This term was suggested to me by Salvatore Cucchiari (personal communication), who has utilized it in his own analysis of folk religion in Sicily (Cucchiari 1985:97–128).

CHAPTER 6

Breton Folklore of Anticlericalism

Ellen Badone

CHURCH AND STATE IN FRANCE

FREQUENTLY described as "the eldest daughter of the Church,"[1] France has been a profoundly Catholic nation since the conversion of the Frankish king Clovis at the end of the fifth century. Despite the development of Protestantism in France sparked by the influence of Calvin, the Catholic church retained its dominance, particularly after the revocation of the Edict of Nantes in 1685, when Protestant worship was outlawed. Under the *Ancien Régime* Catholicism was the state religion of France, and the ecclesiastical hierarchy enjoyed a high degree of political power and economic privilege. However, serious questioning of Catholic doctrines was initiated during the Enlightenment by Voltaire and other *philosophes*. The Revolution displaced the church from its earlier position with the nationalization of ecclesiastical property in 1789 and the Civil Constitution of the clergy, introduced in 1790. During the most radical phase of the Revolution in 1793 and 1794 efforts were made partly by forced dechristianization to substitute for Catholicism new civic religions: first the cult of Reason and Liberty, then under Robespierre, that of the Supreme Being. This extremism provoked a revival of traditional religion in some regions, but the upheaval of the Revolution reinforced trends toward secularization in other parts of the country. Catholicism was given official recognition by Napoleon under the Concordat with Pope Pius VII as the religion of the majority of the French people, and the church's position was somewhat strengthened after the Restoration. However, deeply entrenched anticlerical ideas remained as a lasting legacy of the Revolution, especially among the educated bourgeoisie (McLeod 1981:1–15; Isambert 1972:175–176).

Throughout the nineteenth century and well into the twentieth French society was divided into two opposing ideological schools, the Catholic and the republican. Whereas the latter represented the forces of secular liberalism and anticlericalism, the more politically conservative Catholic sector was generally identified with the aristocracy and the royalist cause. During the second half of the nineteenth century one of the major struggles between these parties revolved around the issue of whether education should be controlled by the church or the state. The debate over education culminated in the Jules Ferry laws of the 1880s which reorganized the state school system, enshrining its secular character and removing public education from the clerical domain. The political and social power of the church was further restricted with the separation of church and state in 1905 (Anderson 1970; Dansette 1961:40–57, 220–248; Isambert 1972:175–176; Magraw 1970:195–217; Zeldin 1970).

In many parts of rural France during the nineteenth century the ideological differences between Catholics and republican anticlericals translated into power struggles between mayors—the representatives of secular authority—and parish priests. Conflicts of personality between priests and their congregations also played a part in fuelling anticlerical sentiments (Magraw 1970). Such tensions have continued to be expressed in certain regions, including parts of Brittany, through to the post World War II period.

CATHOLICISM IN BRITTANY

To the superficial observer Brittany would seem an unlikely candidate for a study of anticlerical folklore. Popular stereotypes depict Brittany as a devoutly Catholic region, conservative in terms of both *mentalités* and life style. As with most stereotypes, this one contains an element of truth. The geographical isolation of Brittany, the language barrier between Breton and French, and the poor development of transportation and communications networks linking the region to metropolitan France limited the impact of republican influences on Brittany during the nineteenth century. Many parts of Brittany did not experience until after World War II the types of social, economic, and intellectual changes that, as Eugen Weber (1976:357–374) has documented, posed a challenge to Catholicism elsewhere in France at earlier periods. Moreover, Lower Brittany, the western, Breton-speaking section of the region, was one of the few areas of France where the evangelizing efforts of the Counter-Reformation achieved a lasting impact (Croix 1981:1240–1241). From the sixteenth to the twentieth century Brittany has been noted for its extremely high levels of religious practice relative to other regions of France. As recently as the 1950s it was not unusual for Breton parishes to count 80 to 90 percent or more of their adult population as regularly practicing Catholics (Lambert 1985:8).

The image of Brittany as a region securely under the control of the church is, however, misleading for two reasons. First, it ignores the extent to which the Breton version of Catholicism has assimilated unorthodox elements of folk belief, some of which have parallels in Celtic regions of the British Isles. Catholicism in Brittany is marked by devotion to local saints and regional pilgrimage sites, as well as by the central importance accorded to death and the dead (Croix 1981; Croix and Roudaut 1984; Badone 1989). Second, the Catholic, conservative stereotype of Brittany overlooks the fact that political and religious attitudes vary widely among localities within the region. The present discussion is concerned with one area, the Monts d'Arrée, that has been noted for its tradition of anticlericalism and radical politics since the nineteenth century.

RELIGION AND POLITICS IN THE MONTS D'ARRÉE

The Monts d'Arrée, a range of craggy hills, extend from east to west across the north-central section of the *département* of Finistère. In religious and political attitudes the Monts d'Arrée region differs dramatically from the Léon, a region of fertile coastal plain directly to the north, and the Morbihan in southern Brittany, where the church has historically enjoyed high levels of support. Throughout the nineteenth century and well into the twentieth the interests of the church in these two regions were closely linked to those of the aristocracy and prosperous peasant classes. Through the confessional, priests in the Léon and Morbihan wielded con-

Parish church in the Monts d'Arrée, Brittany, with tombs decorated for *Toussaint* (All Saints' Day). Breton Catholicism is marked by devotion to the dead.

siderable influence over secular affairs within their parishes. Those who voted for electoral candidates not approved by the church, those who read books or newspapers condemned by the Catholic hierarchy, and those who sent their children to secular, state-run rather than Catholic schools risked refusal of absolution and hence damnation in the afterlife. The priest had authority to reject the godparents chosen by a family for their children and often arranged marriages among his parishioners. Social ostracism and economic disaster faced those who opposed him. The curé's influence was such that he could lead a boycott of stores owned by the anticlerical or prevent proprietors in the parish from renting land to tenants who defied the church. Moreover, with its masses, *pardons*, or saints' day festivals, and Catholic youth organizations, the church monopolized opportunities for recreation and socialization (Croix and Roudaut 1984:196–204; Lambert 1985:28–29, 158–160, 220; Siegfried 1913:115–117, 182–186).

The clerical domination of Breton society was highly successful in the Léon and Morbihan until the late 1950s (Croix and Roudaut 1984:217–218; Lambert 1985:237–270). In the Monts d'Arrée, however, efforts to challenge the social power of the clergy began much earlier, as a result of several factors. First, unlike the Léon, the Monts d'Arrée has traditionally been a region of small holdings, with no wealthy peasantry and practically no nobility. The pattern of land ownership in many parts of the Monts d'Arrée was characterized by a proliferation of small, relatively poor, but independent proprietors. Under such economic conditions an antihierarchical ethos of egalitarianism developed in the region (Siegfried 1913:174–175).

The second factor contributing to the growth of anticlericalism in the Monts d'Arrée was the early exposure of this region to intellectual currents from metropolitan France. The Monts d'Arrée is poorly suited to agriculture because of its acidic, heavy soils and relatively cool and moist climate. For this reason emigration developed during the nineteenth century as a solution to rural poverty. The *exode rural* continued through the twentieth century into the post World War II period. Emigration was given impetus by the high value placed on education in the Monts d'Arrée. In La Feuillée, the community where the major part of this research on anticlericalism was carried out, a supplementary course was established following World War I in the communal state-run school, enabling students to complete their secondary education without the expense of boarding away from home. As a result emigrants from La Feuillée were prepared for careers in metropolitan France as teachers, army and naval officers, and civil servants. Their interests were tied to those of the secular Republic rather than to the church (Chaussy, Emeillat, and Messager 1976:19–21; Siegfried 1913:175–176).

Influenced by the liberal and republican ideologies of their new professional milieux, the emigrants, who maintained close ties with their families in the Monts d'Arrée, provided a conduit for the transfer to the region of anticlerical sentiments originating elsewhere. Such attitudes also penetrated to the region as a result of the "nomadic" life style of Monts d'Arrée residents. In order to supplement their income from agriculture many peasants from the region became active entrepreneurs, travelling throughout Finistère and the Côtes-du-Nord to buy and sell grain, livestock, *sabots*, and other goods, or to collect rags for sale to paper manufacturers through middlemen in the Breton urban centers of Quimper and Brest. This economic pattern necessitated knowledge of French, which facilitated access to political ideas other than those approved and propagated by the clergy (Chaussy, Emeillat, and Messager 1976:18–19; Siegfried 1913:175–176).

A third reason for the weakness of the church in the Monts d'Arrée was the inadequacy of the clergy in the region. From the clerical point of view the region was undesirable, owing to the poverty and large size of its parishes, its inclement weather and rough terrain, the independent character of its residents, and its distance from cultural and religious centers. Priests were frequently appointed to parishes in the Monts d'Arrée as punishment for failings of character, such as alcoholism. Other priests sent to the region had physical disabilities, such as speech impediments, which made them unsuitable for "better" parishes. Still others lacked knowledge of Breton, further complicating their difficulties in developing rapport with Monts d'Arrée peasants (Le Gallo 1980:121).

All of these factors meant that priests in the Monts d'Arrée during the nineteenth and early twentieth centuries were frequently unable to command the respect accorded to their counterparts elsewhere in Brittany. Nevertheless, they sought to exercise the same degree of social control. This led to conflicts with their parishioners, particularly the local mayors and elected municipal councils. By the late nineteenth century a tradition of overwhelming support for left-wing political parties opposed to the church was firmly rooted in the Monts d'Arrée (Siegfried 1913:177–179). This tradition has continued to the present, with elections favoring Communist and Socialist party candidates throughout the twentieth century.

Despite the fact that elected officials in the Monts d'Arrée curbed the power of the clergy to some extent, parish priests in this region retained considerable real influence over the lives of their parishioners until the 1950s. The priest could serve as a patron, providing local people (or refusing to provide them) with the requisite letters of recommendation for jobs in Paris and other forms of assistance toward social advancement in the outside world. In addition, the priest was generally better educated than the majority of those peasants who remained in the Monts d'Arrée instead of emigrating to the cities. His superior education, social status, and ability to act as a patron made the priest in the Monts d'Arrée an object of resentment. Furthermore, priests were disliked for economic reasons. In a region where subsistence depended upon manual labor the clergy were seen as parasites, who made their living by demanding money or agricultural produce from the poor through "*quêtes*," or door-to-door collections within the parish, and by exacting payments for religious offices such as baptisms, weddings, and funerals.

Resentment for the clergy in the Monts d'Arrée was additionally generated by the perception that priests were allied by birth and self-interest to "*les gros*," or the wealthy peasant and noble classes of the regions to the north and south, rather than to "*les petits*," smallholders in the Monts d'Arrée. As such, priests were held responsible for perpetuating an unjust social order. This view was reinforced by the predominantly right-wing political sympathies of the church.[2]

Although the anticlerical sentiments outlined above are derived from experience of social conditions in the past, they continue to be vigorously expressed in present-day communities in the Monts d'Arrée. Religious and political *mentalités* are passed down from generation to generation and have come to assume symbolic importance. To a large extent they define community, family, and individual identity.

While less marked than in the past, the dichotomy between *rouges* and *blancs* remains a central feature of social life in contemporary Monts d'Arrée communities. The *rouges* are anticlerical, while the *blancs* (who constitute the numerically smaller group in this region), support the church. This cleavage extends beyond religion to include politics, life style, and values. Whereas the *blancs* vote for right-wing parties such as the *Rassemblement pour la République* (RPR), the *rouges* vote for the left-wing *Parti Socialiste* (PS) and *Parti Communiste Français* (PCF). *Blanc* families tend to consider themselves more refined than the *rouges*, who see themselves as the working people of the earth. While the *blancs* take pride in their association with the church, the *rouges* consider themselves to be morally superior despite their lack of formal religious practice. It should be noted that economic discrepancies between the two groups are no longer a substantive issue. It is not necessarily the case that all *blanc* families are wealthier than *rouge* ones. However, the *blancs* are *perceived* by the *rouges*, and to some extent perceive themselves, to be the wealthier group.

Support for the PCF in the Monts d'Arrée began prior to World War II but gained momentum during the *Résistance*, which was locally dominated by Communist party members. In 1943 tension between *rouges* and *blancs* erupted with the assassination by *résistants* of the Abbé Perrot, a local priest suspected of collaboration with the Nazis. Perrot was active in the Breton nationalist movement, which the Germans supported (Fortier 1980). His murder polarized *rouge-blanc* animosity, and continues to do so. Forty years afterwards, *blancs* from the Monts d'Arrée, Breton separatist sympathizers, and members of Perrot's family gather annually at a ceremony commemorating his death. Following World War II former *Résistance* leaders in the PCF emerged as the Monts d'Arrée political elite. They have continued to hold power in the municipal councils of the region to the 1980s (Le Guirriec 1984, 1986).[3]

It is thus against a backdrop of class tensions, rivalry between representatives of the church and those of the Republic, as well as personal animosity between priests and parishioners that the folklore of anticlericalism from the Monts d'Arrée must be interpreted. The folklore materials discussed in the following sections of this paper were, for the most part, recorded in La Feuillée, a community of 627 inhabitants located on the southern slopes of the Mont d'Arrée.[4] For the purposes of the present discussion the folklore texts have been divided into five categories, including:

1. legends about the "Red Monks" of the abbey at Le Relecq;
2. narratives and jokes about priests and sexuality;
3. narratives about the "mock" *pardon* of 1907;
4. narratives concerning tricks played by priests on their parishioners; and
5. memorates dealing with the supernatural powers of priests.[5]

THE "RED MONKS" OF LE RELECQ

The Cistercian abbey of Le Relecq, located in the parish of Plounéour-Ménez on the north slopes of the Monts d'Arrée, has been in ruins since the French Revolution. Prior to 1789, however, the Cistercians owned large tracts of land in the present-day *départements* of Finistère and the Côtes-du-Nord. According to present-day folklore in the Monts d'Arrée, the Cistercians, nicknamed the "Red Monks," were dissolute, unprincipled, and cruel in their dealings with the peasants living within their domain. Among other seigneurial rights they exercised the *droit de cuissage*, or the right to sleep with every virgin from their estate on her wedding night.[6] The first night of married life was ostensibly to be passed in prayer at the abbey. In reality, however, the monks took pleasure in deflowering the young virgins. According to the legend, one red-haired monk who was particularly active in enforcing the *droit de cuissage* has left a legacy of red-haired descendants to this day in the Monts d'Arrée. The power of the monks as *seigneurs* was so great that the *droit de cuissage* was rarely challenged. Finally, however, one woman from the village of Trédudon, which overlooks the abbey from the upper slopes of the Monts d'Arrée, refused to comply with the *droit*, claiming that she would rather die than spend her wedding night with the monks.

Several details of this story are significant. First, on at least one occasion it was told in the context of a conversation about the power of the clergy in the Monts d'Arrée prior to World War I. At that period, according to the retired agriculturalists from Trédudon who narrated the story, priests kept the poor in ignorance and robbed them of their hard-won savings through *quêtes* and payments for religious offices. The legend of the Red Monks can be interpreted in one sense as a metaphor for the powerless situation of the peasantry vis-à-vis the clergy during the recent past in Brittany. In the legend the emasculation of the poor peasant through the *droit de cuissage* stands for the actual social and financial constraints imposed on the peasantry by the clerical elite.

The second aspect of the legend that needs amplification concerns the identity of the first woman to resist the *droit de cuissage*. It is highly significant that she is said to have been from Trédudon. This village, well-known in the Monts d'Arrée for its independence and allegiance to the *Parti Communiste Français*, is locally reputed to have been the first in France to take up the *Résistance* cause during World War II. Moreover, it is also claimed that the first woman *résistante* in the country was a native of Trédudon. The parallel with the legend of the Red Monks is striking. It suggests that the sense of egalitarian independence and distaste for hierarchical authority that typify world view in the Monts d'Arrée lie behind both local opposition to the church and resistance to the German occupation. In fact, with the suspected collaboration of the Abbé Perrot during World War II the two struggles were temporarily united.[7]

PRIESTS AND SEXUALITY

The legend of the Red Monks obviously overlaps with the category of folklore texts dealing with priests and sexuality. As in a number of southern European contexts,[8] anticlericalism in the Monts d'Arrée takes the form of jokes about priestly celibacy and speculation that priests do not, in fact, abstain from sexual activity. As one La Feuillée man claims, "They make love too, when they get the chance."

In the Monts d'Arrée the church's campaign against sexuality was focussed on the dance.[9] From the early nineteenth century through the 1950s the church in Brittany sought to discourage all forms of dancing (Lambert 1985:103–106; Le Gallo 1980:1008–1019). Initially directed toward traditional Breton line or circle dances such as the *gavotte des montagnes* popular in the Monts d'Arrée, the crusade against dancing was later focussed on the modern couple dances that appeared in the area during the 1920s. These were condemned because the position of the dancers—*"kof à kof"* or "stomach to stomach" in Breton—was thought to provoke sexual passion. As jazz, swing, and other nontraditional types of music and their associated dances penetrated to the Monts d'Arrée after World War II, preaching against *"les bals"* continued.

The church's former rigor with respect to sexuality is suspect in the Monts d'Arrée, for it is deemed unlikely that priests themselves remain celibate throughout their entire lives. In addition, priests do not fit into the local system of gender classification. Their apparent celibacy makes them sexually ambiguous, neither female nor truly male. This ambiguity is expressed in joking conversations about one curé in the Monts d'Arrée, whose name coincides with a word that means "ten penises" in local folk-speech. "He doesn't even need one and yet he has ten," quips the *rouge* bartender in a Monts d'Arrée café. As this comment suggests, priests are viewed as being potentially oversexed, despite their theoretical chastity. If heightened sexual power can be taken as a metaphor for social power, the bartender's comment is additionally revealing. It conveys the anomalous position of the priest who presumably lacks the sexual prowess of ordinary men but wields considerable social power over them.

The sexual ambiguity of the priest is reinforced by the fact that, unlike "true men," priests—at least ideally—drink only in moderation. Drinking with friends over the course of an afternoon and evening is an important male social activity, which often leaves the participants in a state surpassing mere tipsiness. It is significant that the only priest in recent years to be well accepted in La Feuillée was an inveterate drinker, who enjoyed sharing a bottle of wine with his male parishioners. The majority of priests in the region do not socialize easily in the male realm.[10] At mixed social gatherings where men tend to interact among themselves separately from women, the curé's indecision about which group to join is frequently very clear. Most often he avoids the "men's groups" and joins a party of understanding women who attend mass regularly. Indeed, as in the Mediterranean, religion in Breton society is primarily the domain of women. The fact that the priest, as a man, plays a leading role in this typically female field serves further to alienate him from men in his parish.

THE "MOCK" PARDON OF 1907

With the exception of *Toussaint-la Fête des Morts*, the most important annual religious celebration in La Feuillée is the *pardon*, or festival of the parish's patron St. John the Baptist. The *pardon*, which takes place on 24 June, is marked by an afternoon mass, which culminates with a procession around the main streets of the *bourg*. The procession is

The *pardon* of Saint John the Baptist in La Feuillée, Brittany (Photograph by
Stephen Jones)

headed by a small boy dressed in a sheepskin and sandals to impersonate
St. John. The child leads a lamb symbolizing Christ, whom St. John baptized and recognized as the Messiah, proclaiming " 'Behold, the Lamb of
God, who takes away the sin of the world!' " (John 1:29). The focal point
of the *pardon* procession, the lamb is decorated with pink cloth roses
attached to its fleece, which has previously been scrubbed and bleached
to a pristine whiteness.

Despite the parish's anticlerical tradition, the *pardon* continues to be
a popular event in La Feuillée. According to the elderly, the *pardon* procession has "always been done," and the festival probably dates at least
to the early nineteenth century, when the raising of sheep was central to
the local economy. La Feuillée is the only parish in the region with a
pardon procession featuring an animal, and part of the ongoing appeal of
the festival lies in the fact that the procession with its lamb differentiates
La Feuillée from surrounding parishes, highlighting its distinctive identity.[11]

Whereas the regular Sunday mass in La Feuillée attracts fifteen or
twenty faithful, most of them women, a congregation of two hundred or
more attends the *pardon* mass. Moreover, at least one-third of those who
come to the *pardon* ceremony are men, generally the more vocally anticlerical of the sexes. Their presence in the church is less an endorsement

of Catholic doctrines than a statement of allegiance to the community. Attachment to the *pardon* stems from the perception that it epitomizes parish identity. As one twenty-one-year-old man enthuses, "The little lamb, that's us, that's La Feuillée."

The fact that support for the *pardon* exists independently of support for the church and the clergy is well illustrated by an incident that occurred in La Feuillée at the *pardon* in 1907. As the oldest members of the community recall, the parish priest determined that year to cancel the *pardon*. The diocesan newsletter for 1907 records that the bishop approved this course of action because in previous years the *pardon* had been the focus for "inconvenient and hostile manifestations" which the municipal council had refused to suppress (*La Semaine Religieuse* 1907a:461). The decision outraged the people of La Feuillée, however, and in protest a group of the parish youths organized a mock procession on 24 June, in which a fox decorated with ribbons was led through the *bourg*, followed by a crowd that forced its way into the church. Here the beribboned fox was "baptized" in the font. Throughout the parody the mayor ordered the church bells to be rung at full volume.

In its reversal of the ritual order the mock *pardon* represented a clear victory of secular over clerical authority. It was not the priest but the mayor who ordered the church bells to be rung. With his backing, not

A baptism in La Feuillée. This is the ritual that was parodied during the "mock" *pardon* of 1907, when a fox was placed in the font.

an innocent child, but the community's boisterous youth led a procession featuring a wild animal rather than the domestic lamb that represents Christ and signifies meekness and innocence in traditional Christian imagery.[12]

As a result of this anticlerical demonstration, which took place under one of the first left-wing municipal councils elected in La Feuillée, the curé and vicar fled the community and took refuge with relatives elsewhere. A six-month interdiction was placed on the La Feuillée church, following which a new priest was assigned to the parish (*La Semaine Religieuse* 1907b:876).

The mock *pardon* of 1907 demonstrates the depth of attachment to local religious traditions in the Monts d'Arrée, even when those traditions do not meet with full approval from the church hierarchy. As studies of anticlericalism elsewhere in Europe have shown, conflicts with the church often focus on the issue of whether priest or parishioners will control ritual occasions (Brandes 1976; Pina-Cabral 1986:131, 205; Riegelhaupt 1973, 1984). By trying to cancel the *pardon* in 1907 the La Feuillée priest sought to impose his definition of the sacred on a parish that already held clearly defined ideas about the place of religion in community life. It is significant that in the years following the 1907 incident the *pardon* was reinstituted. At least on this occasion the people of the parish succeeded in making the church bend to their will.

NARRATIVES CONCERNING TRICKS PLAYED BY PRIESTS ON THEIR PARISHIONERS

Folk narratives from the Monts d'Arrée in this category are invariably set in the context of the past. They are generally prefaced with the phrase "*dans le temps*," which refers to some unspecified period in the past, often prior to World War II. In the case of middle-aged or elderly narrators the phrase may refer to the generations of their parents and grandparents.

"*Dans le temps*," priests are accused of "staging" supernatural apparitions to frighten their parishioners and to increase clerical control of community affairs. Such trickery was used to provide visible "proof" of the existence of the other world and its denizens, including lost souls and figures such as the devil.

Marguerite, a La Feuillée woman in her eighties, recounts that in Poullaouen, a neighboring village, the devil himself used to appear at the wakes held for notoriously anticlerical *rouges* from the parish, to claim the body of the deceased for his own. These apparitions frightened the people of Poullaouen. However, after several such cases a group of young men in the community decided to ensure that the incident would not recur. The next time the devil arrived to remove the body from a wake, the young men blocked his way and attacked him. During the course of the struggle it was discovered that the "devil" was none other than the parish curé, dressed in a cowhide and wearing a set of cow's horns attached to his head. By impersonating Satan, Marguerite concludes, the priest had hoped to instill fear into his wayward parishioners and to encourage them to attend mass more regularly.

Although this story might appear implausible, at least one nineteenth-century priest in Poullaouen, famous for his violence and extremism, would have been capable of such an escapade. Jean-Paul Thomas, appointed curé of Poullaouen in 1818, is reputed to have used physical force on numerous occasions to solve parish conflicts: "he strikes with his feet, fists and stick" (Le Gallo 1980:117). In 1824, nineteen inhabitants of Poullaouen, including the church sacristan, petitioned the bishop against Thomas. The sacristan related that "when he [the sacristan] had refused to choose between 30 lashes and two nights of incarceration for having missed evening prayers the previous day, the curé pulled him by the hair and threw him into a cellar below the sacristy" (Le Gallo 1980:117–118). Clearly a priest of this unusual character would have had few scruples about impersonating the devil and stealing bodies from wakes.

Poullaouen has been noted locally as a bastion of anticlericalism since the early nineteenth century. It is equally well known in the Monts d'Arrée for its devotion to music and the dance. Thus, it is not surprising that another narrative concerning a fake supernatural apparition staged by the clergy—this time in an effort to suppress dancing—is set near Poullaouen. The following text was recorded in an interview with Suzanne, a woman in her early sixties who runs a café in a hamlet in the Monts d'Arrée. One of her neighbors, Jeannine, a younger woman, also participated in the conversation, which took place in the kitchen of Suzanne's café.

> Suzanne: *Ben*, that took place during the war there. Directly after the war, it was. They didn't want to see the young people go to balls, you see. So the curé of the village, he paid someone to go and scare the young people, to prevent them [from going dancing]. Because, most likely, they didn't go to mass often enough. And they went dancing too much. It must have been that! And so, *ma foi*, that took place on the road to Poullaouen down there, between Locmaria and Poullaouen. The Lady in Black, we used to call it. And it was a man, disguised in curé's clothes. He had a cassock. And they used to see him all the time, more or less, at the same spot, at the Poullaouen fountain, down there. And when he saw that there were people who weren't scared around him [who were coming too close], he would go into the woods. No one would

go after him. They were scared. Some returned home, others continued along their way; that depended on how it was.

Jeannine: It was on the way to the ball, or on the way home?

Suzanne: Going, often. Me, I only heard tell of it on the way home once. It was on the way to the dance. Another time, it seems, some young people had seen it at Pont-de-Fer, here, next to Moulin d'Argent, too. Me, instead of keeping on, I went back home. *Ah oui!* Turned my bicycle around and then home! Me, I never saw it. Never. I was never all alone in any case. We used to be in a group of girls, you see. Boyfriends and girlfriends. So, me, it never happened that I saw it. But that was the curé who must have given some money to the baker from the station to go and scare us. That was it, because afterwards a group from Huelgoat who had more courage than us went into the woods after him. And then they caught him. They took his costume off. And they saw that it was the baker from the station. . . . The station at Locmaria-Berrien. . . . It happened down there. The Lady in Black, we used to say. The Lady in Black. At least, until the day that we found out from the son of a butcher from Huelgoat, who caught him. And then we knew who it was, and then afterwards he was embarrassed in this area, and so he left. He left the *pays*. He went to work near Trélazé, it seems, he took over a store down there. But that one, he was hand-in-hand with the curé. And so, *voilà*, that's what he did to us, you see, our story!

Breton folklore of the nineteenth and early twentieth centuries is typified by legends concerning *revenants* and other supernatural beings (Le Braz 1928; Le Men 1870–1872; Luzel 1980; Sébillot 1904:136–138, 146–147, 151–159, 162–164, 183–188, 190). Clerical preaching on eschatological themes such as death, the Last Judgment, and damnation also fuelled the Breton preoccupation with death and the otherworld (Croix and Roudaut 1984). By staging apparitions such as the Lady in Black the clergy were able to manipulate traditional fears of the supernatural, to counteract the appeal of the new dances that, together with other aspects of modern popular culture, were becoming commonplace in rural Brittany.

In addition to tricks played by the clergy on their parishioners involving "fake" supernatural apparitions, numerous memorates and legends in the Monts d'Arrée accuse clerics of causing actual manifestations of the supernatural to take place. It is to this fourth category of anticlerical folklore texts from the Monts d'Arrée that we will now turn our consideration.

PRIESTS AND SORCERY

In the Monts d'Arrée it is frequently asserted that in the past—*dans le temps*—priests were taught sorcery, hypnotism, and sleight of hand

Tableau showing the Last Judgment. Paintings like this were used to illustrate preaching at church missions in Brittany until the mid-twentieth century.

tricks during their seminary schooling. These skills were later used, it is claimed, to consolidate clerical control in the rural milieu and to punish those who violated church-approved norms of behavior. As Monts d'Arrée residents explain, "The priests used to do some funny things in the past. They wanted to manage everyone else." Their role within the church made priests privileged intermediators with the supernatural. Logically, if priests could give benedictions, pray for a successful harvest, and perform exorcisms, they could also manipulate the supernatural in a harmful way. In addition, their ability to work deadly magic was perceived to be linked to their superior education. As people explain, "It was only they who knew French and who had been educated." Priests are said to have possessed books of magic formulae enabling them to cast spells. The phrase "they used to have books" is frequently heard in discussions concerning priests and sorcery. The work of Goody (1968:11–20) and others has underlined the ritual and supernatural significance that the printed word may assume in societies of restricted literacy. It is hardly surprising that priests, capable of speaking and reading Latin as well as French in a predominantly Breton-speaking and oral cultural milieu, were suspected of trickery at the very least and black magic at the worst. Moreover, with little difficulty the incantations of the Latin mass, read from a book in a ritual manner, could be construed to resemble magic spells. [13]

According to people in the Monts d'Arrée, the magic books owned by priests were extremely dangerous for lay persons not adept in dealing with the supernatural. "It was forbidden to read them," one La Feuillée woman remarks. Not only was it necessary to read out the appropriate spell or "prayer" for the goal desired but, in addition, it was essential to "unsay" or "undo" the formula by rereading it backwards: "You had to start over again from the end." Those unaccustomed to casting spells who neglected this step risked allowing the magic to run out of control or to turn back upon themselves rather than reaching the intended victim.

One local legend which illustrates the reputed power of the clergy to manipulate the supernatural in order to enforce support for the church concerns the *pardon* at the chapel of Le Relecq. Held annually on 15 August, the *pardon* attracts worshippers from half a dozen neighboring parishes. Formerly the ceremony culminated with a procession in which parish banners and statues were carried around a small lake near the chapel. [14] During this procession on 15 August 1943, it is recounted that a group of young men in small boats on the lake began to make fun of the faithful and to taunt the officiating priests. Suddenly, without warning, one of the boats capsized. Seven young men were drowned as a result of the accident. The catastrophe was interpreted as a retribution by the priests against those who had mocked the ritual and challenged their authority.

In Irish priest tales the clergy generally use their supernatural powers to heal the sick and protect and defend the peasantry (Lawrence Taylor 1985:709; this volume). Likewise, in the Monts d'Arrée region of Brittany priests are sometimes credited with performing magical cures. Most frequently, however, memorates recorded in the Monts d'Arrée express the view that priests in the past manipulated the supernatural to persecute the poor and ignorant, particularly those who attended mass sporadically or voiced opposition to the church. Amélie Le Hir from La Feuillée recalls an experience with the supernatural that she had as a girl of twelve, over fifty years ago, when she was working as a maidservant for a farmer in the neighboring parish of Commana. "The farmer used to sing in the evenings and me, I enjoyed that, because you know, when one is young, one wants to be happy." One evening, she remembers, the farmer told her:

> "Alright. Let's sing. We'll sing for you later, after supper if you go and get the cows. And whatever you do, don't go along the little path. Because one sees things there at night." "Oh," I said, "I'm young"—because the young don't

worry about much, eh? And I didn't listen to my boss. I went by the little path. As soon as night began to fall, *eh ben*, behind the hedgerow, like that, there appeared a hand. Ah, that's what I saw, eh? And it didn't talk, but it went like this [making a waving motion with her hand and forearm]. It waved at me. Well, when I arrived home with the cows I said, "A little bit more and I would have lost my head." It had upset me a bit. "I told you not to go by that route" [the farmer told her]. Because he had seen it already. In the past a lot of things like that used to be seen, you see. And apparently they originated in the scheming of the curés. Because they read books to keep you in line. To frighten people.

This memorate is typical of many others recounted in the Monts d'Arrée that deal with supernatural phenomena such as *revenants*. It is recalled that "*dans le temps* the old people used to talk of nothing but ghosts." The *rouge* attitude toward such traditions is complex. As enlightened Communists and Socialists, they feel obliged to adopt a rational, materialistic interpretation of reality, which disavows belief in any aspect of the supernatural, Catholic or unorthodox. However, like Amélie Le Hir, many *rouges* have had personal experiences which they cannot adequately interpret outside a supernatural frame of reference. This presents a logical contradiction which is resolved, as we see in Amélie's concluding comments, by blaming the clergy for the majority of supernatural manifestations that took place in the past.

To some extent, then, the *rouge* attitude toward the supernatural can be summarized as follows: strange things actually happened in the past, but although they were true supernatural occurrences, they were caused by the clergy. This position is clearly apparent in the following excerpt of a conversation with two Monts d'Arrée couples in their seventies. As the conversation also reveals, folklore dealing with priests and sorcery expresses the class tensions that existed until recently in rural Brittany. The men participating in the conversation and their wives are all *rouges* who, although currently retired, have spent their working lives as peasant small-scale agriculturalists.

Jean: Take the father of Jo Creac'h, for example. He used to have the farm over there.

Yves: At the other end of the village, there.

Jean: Yes. They were really miserable. Here we used to give them things, clothes for the kids, and all, whenever they came. We even used to give them money. Jo knows all that by heart.

My comment: They were very poor?

Jean: Yes, and he was a nice guy too. And one day, going to La Feuillée in the evening, or rather coming home, he said to my mother, "In a moment, Jeanne, you're going to see," he said. "There's something that is going to pass between my legs. Just at sunset." But my mother didn't see a thing. But he saw it. He said, "It has passed between my legs again." The poor guy.

My comment: And what was it, the thing that passed between his legs?

Jean: He didn't know.

My comment: He didn't know?

Jean: No. My mother didn't see it, but he did. It's bizarre. It was *them*. That sort of thing is done to scare people, you see.

My comment: It was the priest who did it?

Jean: Oh yes, in the past, they used to do that. It was them who did it.

Yves: Oh yes, oh yes.

Jean: Whereas now they don't do it any more, because there are other people as well-educated as them, so *ben*, those people prevent it, you see.

Maria: As educated as them.

All: *Voilà, voilà!*

Yves: Whereas in the past there were only poor people. So, *they* [the priests] could do whatever they liked, you see. It's like that! Whereas now there are no more poor people. There aren't any more.

Jean: It's sad, though, even so, eh? Every time, at nightfall. But my mother didn't see a thing.

Lisette: Oh, there aren't so many miserable people any more, like there used to be.

Jean: No, no, no, no. Whereas before there used to be so many miserably poor people. And also it was the miserable ones they used to pick on. It was the one who had a few cows, like that, who was poor, badly off, who had trouble keeping going, you see. Well, it was that guy they'd pick on. It wasn't the big farmer who was comfortably well-off. But that type of guy, well, he went to church, maybe he gave a bit of money as well. . . . Well, because of that they would leave the big farmer alone and pick on the other guy again. It's like that, you see.

This conversation is a forceful condemnation of the former alliance between the church and the prosperous classes of Breton society. According to the *rouge* perception, the church in the past used both natural and supernatural methods to maintain its own privileged social position together with that of the rich. It was not the wealthy *blanc* farmer but a "miserable" peasant who could not afford to donate money to the church who was chosen by the curé as the victim of a magic attack.

Like most *rouges*, Jean and Yves believe that priests no longer use their supernatural powers against lay persons. Jean implies that priests theoretically continue to have the power to practice as sorcerers. However, he holds that they are now prevented from doing so by "other people as well-educated as them." This statement reflects the contemporary demystification of literacy and linguistic skills in French. Jean, Yves, and their wives have children who have completed postsecondary education. The priest is no longer the best-educated figure in the rural community, and this has undermined his status as well as his moral and social authority.

In the conversation just quoted Yves raises a second aspect of social change contributing to the disappearance of sorcerer-priests. As he notes, "Now there are no more poor people." This frequently echoed assertion reflects the fact that in contemporary Brittany, as elsewhere in rural Europe, class distinctions in terms of material possessions and life style are much less apparent than in the past. Land ownership is no longer a necessary precondition to wealth, and as a result of increased government and bank credit, the material goods formerly owned only by the elite are widely accessible.[15]

This blurring of class distinctions together with increased social mobility explains to some extent why folklore dealing with the supernatural powers of the clergy is generally phrased in the past tense. To a large extent the socioeconomic disparities between classes which gave rise to the tensions expressed in such folklore have been alleviated. Moreover, the social power of the Breton clergy and its support for the elite classes have decreased considerably since the 1960s.[16]

While Jean and Yves maintain that it is the presence of other equally well-educated people in rural communities that has forced the clergy to give up their magic practices, other *rouges* suggest that *"la République"* brought an end to this form of clerical repression. This folk explanation stems from the *rouge* allegiance to the French state and their faith in the ultimate triumph of the forces of *liberté*, *égalité*, and *fraternité* against those of privilege and hierarchical authority. According to this explanation, by outlawing the exercise of sorcery by priests, the Republic has safeguarded the rights of its supporters and the poor.

CONCLUSION

Folklore of anticlericalism is by no means a uniquely Breton phenomenon. Jokes and narratives similar to those discussed in this paper have been documented elsewhere in France, as well as for Spain, Portugal, and most of the other countries of Catholic Europe (Brandes 1980:177–204; Cutileiro 1971:265–266; Gilmore 1984; Riegelhaupt 1984:109; McLeod 1981:61; Sébillot 1907:230–272).[17] As in Brittany anticlerical folklore elsewhere in Europe provides a means of expressing tensions between the peasant or working classes and those who are perceived to be in positions of wealth and political power (Gilmore 1984).

Discussions of anticlericalism in other European contexts have often drawn a distinction between its "elite" and "popular" expressions. Cutileiro (1971:265–268), for example, suggests that although popular anticlericalism in southeastern Portugal under the Salazar regime had both "pious" or proreligious and skeptical manifestations it differed from the earlier elite or literate, urban anticlericalism of the Republican period in being essentially nonintellectual and nonideological. Likewise, Pina-Cabral (1986:210–212) comes to a similar conclusion, claiming that unlike "bourgeois" anticlericals, peasants in the northwestern Portuguese province of Minho focus their anticlerical sentiments on the person of the priest, without challenging the legitimacy of the church as an institution. In contrast, Riegelhaupt (1984:98), while retaining Cutileiro's categories, nonetheless cautions that popular anticlericalism should not be dismissed a priori as lacking in ideological content.

In the Monts d'Arrée, elite and popular forms of anticlericalism are not clearly separable. While anticlericalism in this region includes criticism of both priests as a class and individual priests, this is phrased in terms of a larger struggle between the church and the poor, whose interests are represented by the secular Republic. Thus, popular anticlericalism in the Monts d'Arrée is closely integrated into "elite" ideological debates about the positions of church and state in French society. As the emphasis placed in Monts d'Arrée folk narratives on the roles of the Republic and the secular education system in curbing the supernatural powers of the clergy suggests, anticlerical folklore from this region represents a specific, local expression of political attitudes relating to broader, national-level intellectual trends that have existed in France over the past two centuries.

Like certain other European regions noted for their opposition to the church, the Monts d'Arrée is considered by many in the Catholic hierarchy to be "dechristianized" (Croix and Roudaut 1984:198–199; Le Gallo 1980:115–122).[18] Yet the anticlericalism expressed in the Monts d'Arrée does not stem from a fundamental rejection of Christianity. Rather, it is motivated by a perception that the church as a social institution, as well as individual members of the clergy, have failed to live up to the ethical values they profess. The poor, and those who identify with the working class, consider themselves victimized by social injustices for which the church has historically been deemed, at least in part, responsible. Paradoxically, despite their anticlericalism, many rouges in the Monts d'Arrée retain a core of religious faith. Characterizing themselves as "believers but not practicing Catholics," they reject the church and, as in the case of the pardon, clerical norms of appropriate ritual behavior, but not the idea of God as an ultimate moral authority. Moreover, for certain rouges the ideological contradictions between Catholicism and Communism are not insurmountable. In the words of one regional official of the Parti Communiste Français, "To be truly Christian is to be Communist." Echoing these sentiments, another woman from the area comments, "After all, Christ himself was a *résistant*." By focussing on Christ's concern for the poor and his opposition to the religious and social establishment of his time, it is possible for *rouges* to fashion a reinterpretation of Catholicism that justifies their opposition to the authority of the church.

Tales of the Red Monks and sorcerer priests hold continuing appeal for audiences and narrators in the Monts d'Arrée. Memories of the former temporal domination of the Breton clergy have not been erased. The primary message of anticlerical folklore from the Monts d'Arrée is one of class-based resentment toward priests and the elite social groups with which they are identified. The supernatural powers and heightened sexual appetite with which priests are credited stand as metaphors for their actual social power in Brittany prior to the 1960s.

Notes to Chapter 6

I would like to thank the people of La Feuillée for their hospitality during my fieldwork, which was supported by the Social Sciences and Humanities Research Council of Canada, the Wenner-Gren Foundation, as well as a Humanities Research Grant and a Lowie Scholarship from the University of California, Berkeley. This paper was written while visiting the Institute of French Studies, New York University, and I am grateful to Susan Carol Rogers and other colleagues there for useful discussions.

1. See, for example, "*Nobilissima Gallorum Gens*. Encyclical of Pope Leo XIII on the Religious Question in France, February 8, 1884" (Carlen 1981:85–89).

2. From the perspective of Monts d'Arrée peasants the interests of the clergy and those of the elite classes were perfectly matched. In reality, although the upper peasantry consistently supported the church, there were political conflicts in the Léon during the late nineteenth century between the ecclesiastical hierarchy and the nobility, who on occasion supported a more extreme right-wing and royalist position than the clergy (Croix and Roudaut 1984:202). The Léonard clergy were always more influential than the nobility in directing the course of political life in this region (Siegfried 1913:181–183). As Siegfried's (1913:173–180) study shows, in the Léon as in the regions of medium- to large-sized property ownership to the south of the Monts d'Arrée, a strong electoral preference was expressed for right-wing, church-approved political candidates. In contrast, the Monts d'Arrée, where small holdings predominated, voted overwhelmingly in favor of leftist, republican and hence generally anticlerical candidates.

3. In one Monts d'Arrée commune the same mayor, a former *résistant*, held office continuously for thirty-eight years after 1945. Kertzer (1980) describes a parallel case of Resistance leaders emerging as the postwar Communist political elite in a northern Italian context. Kertzer, like Pratt (1984), analyzes the conflict between Communist and Catholic (Christian Democrat) political and religious positions in Italy.

4. For a more detailed ethnography of La Feuillée, focussing on attitudes toward death, see Badone (1989).

5. The term memorate is used by folklorists to describe a genre of narratives about personal experiences with the supernatural which are considered by the narrator to be true. Hence, the memorate is a subcategory of legend (Honko 1964).

6. The *droit de cuissage* is more formally known to folklorists as the *jus primae noctis* (Thompson 1955–1958: Motif T1161).

7. It is not only in the Monts d'Arrée that monastic communities sparked strong anticlerical reactions. McLeod (1981:57) notes that "in France, the best recipe for a long-lasting anti-clerical tradition seems to have been the presence of a large land-owning monastery before the Revolution."

8. See, for example, Brandes (1980:177–204), Gilmore (1984:38–39), Riegelhaupt (1984:109), and Silverman (1975:165–166).

9. Clerical efforts to combat the evils of the dance were not restricted to Brittany, as the Portuguese examples described by Riegelhaupt (1984:110) and Brettell (this volume) attest.

10. See Jorion (1982) on this point.

11. For discussion of the relationships elsewhere in Europe among saints, their festivals and shrines, and local identity or sociocentrism see Christian (1972), Mitchell (1988:30–37), and Riegelhaupt (1973), among others.

12. For discussion of the Christian symbolism of the lamb see Metford (1983:157).

13. Here I do not mean to deny the possibility that actual books of magic formulae, analogous to those mentioned by Goody (1968:16), may have existed in rural Brittany. However, like Favret-Saada (1980:133–135), who has done extensive ethnographic research on magic in Normandy, I have concluded that the role of magic books in Breton sorcery is minimal. Rather, these books have symbolic importance as indicators of the supernatural power of those people who are believed to own them.

As in Brittany, peasants in the Alto Minho of northwestern Portugal link the magical abilities of priests to their educated status, their knowledge of Latin, and their sacramental power (Pina-Cabral 1986:206). Similarly, Devlin (1987:20–21) notes that the identification of priests as sorcerers was common in many parts of rural France during the nineteenth century.

14. The *pardon* continues to be held each year, although it now attracts fewer pilgrims and the procession around the lake no longer takes place.

15. For examples of this development elsewhere in Europe see Silverman (1975:220, 224) and Weingrod and Morin (1971:313).

16. However, opinions differ as to whether or not priests have completely abandoned their magic skills. While priests *as a class* are no longer accused of working spells against the poor, specific individual priests continue to have the reputation of performing nonmalevolent types of magic, primarily healing. These clerics correspond to the *bruxo* priests who practice as "white witches" described for northwestern Portugal by Pina-Cabral (1986:201–202).

17. French examples that present a particularly close parallel to the Monts d'Arrée material are reported by Sébillot (1907:249), who notes that monks in Picardy and Franche-Comté are reputed to have enforced the *droit de cuissage*.

18. Similarly, the Portuguese Estremadura examined by Riegelhaupt (1984:112) is also described as a dechristianized area.

CHAPTER 7

Stories of Power, Powerful Stories: The Drunken Priest in Donegal

Lawrence J. Taylor

"THERE *was a priest here not long ago, and with all respect to his cloth, he had a taste for a wee drop. He was up in the village one day, and he with a drop taken. Well, he went into a pub and asked the boy that was there behind the counter for a drink. The boy said that he wouldn't give him one, that he had had enough as it was. 'Well,' said the priest, 'if I come in to you at this time tomorrow and ask you to give me a drink, you'll get it for me and welcome the sight of it!' He went out the door then and said not another word.*

"*That was fine, the boy went to bed that night, and on the next morning when he arose he was so blind he couldn't dress himself. Well he knew that it was the priest who had brought that upon him with the words he had spoken the evening before. He sent a messenger for the priest, who came to him in his own time.*

"*'What's kept you in your bed there?' the priest said when he went into the room. 'O Priest,' he said, 'Whatever happened to me since I went to bed last night I am blind and I can't put on my clothes.' The priest only put his two fingers on the boy's eyes and in a short while he had his sight back as good as ever before. 'Now,' said the priest as he was leaving, 'when I come again and ask something of you that I want you'll know not to refuse me!' " (Ó'hEochaidh 1945: 43–44, my translation).*

This story is one of twenty-three "priest stories" collected in one notebook by folklorist Sean Ó'hEochaidh from his natal community of Teelin in Donegal, Ireland. The notebook containing these Gaelic tales is dated 1945, but there are also dozens of other priest stories scattered through the more than seventy volumes of oral lore recorded by Ó'hEochaidh in his nearly half century (beginning in the early 1930s) of folklore collecting in the area. The stories relate the exploits of local curates and parish priests—many of them named—in the late nineteenth and early twentieth centuries.

The narratives fall very neatly into two categories. In one, priests, whom I will call "heroic," battle the evil forces of the Protestant ascendancy in their local incarnations: landlords, agents, bailiffs, Protestant farmers, and the rare Catholic collaborator (see Lawrence Taylor 1985). Such clerics are typically armed with the paraphernalia of the church, such as the priest who dons his stole and recites from his book in order to bring a Protestant up from Hell as an object lesson to his unregenerate family. The other category, which includes the story related above, features clerics who "have a taste for the wee drop" or, to translate the Irish euphemism, "drunken priests." These protagonists perform their magic, whether to help or harm, usually unaided by anything but their inherent charisma.

Such legends are not so often heard as in former times. However, they are still told formally and, far more often, informally in various of the households and pubs of southwest Donegal, Ireland.[1] The priest who blinds the boy in the above story, in fact, is still the subject of many stories currently told. I will return below to the question of their performance, but suffice it to say for now that the narratives are rarely if ever presented as "fiction" and that no one laughs when such stories are told (though some may smile in apparent discomfort). Arguments sometimes ensue about whether or not such and such an account or version is strictly accurate, in whole or in part, but the story is "taken seriously" by all tellers and most listeners. Moreover, as we shall see, the powers of such priests are not confined to narratives. Individuals sought, and continue to seek, such clerics for their special powers, particularly for curing.

This essay will explore the stories, beliefs, and practices concerning drunken priests as they operate, historically and currently, in southwest Donegal, Ireland (map). In so doing I hope to shed light on the character of the drunken priest as an element in the local religious world view, as well as on some of the general issues of local versus orthodox religion with which this volume is concerned. The beliefs and stories about drunken priests reveal much about the dynamic, rather than static, relation of local "folk" and imported "orthodox" religious world views. Attention to this corpus also sheds light on the special role of discourse—informal conversation and anecdote as well as formal narrative—in shaping what I will call a chthonic "field of religious experience," that is to say, one of several locally shared perspectives on the meaning of those events, occasions, and experiences which may be called (following local usage) religious.[2]

For most academics who have an interest in such forms priest stories are "legends," with motifs that are in some respects akin to others of similar type found throughout Europe (see Thompson 1955–1958) and in certain special features reminiscent of specifically Irish or perhaps Celtic traditions. As such, they may enjoy various human and social functions: for example, as occasions for moral *exempla* (Ó'hÉalaí 1974), the celebra-

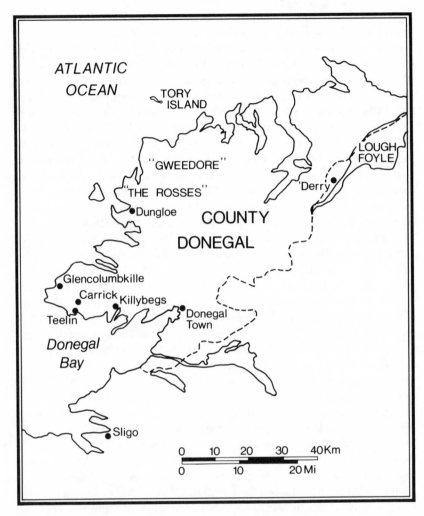

ATLANTIC
OCEAN
TORY
ISLAND

"GWEEDORE"

"THE ROSSES"

●Dungloe   COUNTY

DONEGAL

LOUGH
FOYLE

Derry

Glencolumbkille
Carrick Killybegs
Teelin   ●Donegal
              Town
Donegal
Bay

●Sligo

0   10   20   30   40Km
0   10   20 Mi

Map of Donegal showing details of region.

tion of communal solidarity, or artistic expression (Glassie 1983). The content of these stories and the contexts of their telling, however, suggest that they can also be viewed as both playing a part in, and offering a special insight into, the religious life of the people of the region. Priest stories, and the beliefs and behavior associated with such clergy, are aspects of local religion—collective representations of priests and priesthood, and meditations, as it were, on the nature of religious power.

Anthropologists studying local religious life have considered talk about priests mainly under the rubric of "anticlericalism," and have understood such verbal acts to be manifestations of the distance and hostility between "folk religion" and "orthodoxy." Following historian Bossy's (1970) seminal treatment of the social objectives of the Catholic Counter-Reformation, Riegelhaupt (1973, 1984), Brettell (this volume), and Badone (this volume) have seen anticlerical remarks and stories as an expression of local resentment of and resistance to the anticommunal campaign of the Catholic church which began with the sixteenth-century Council of Trent. From this perspective the local priest is an outsider representative of the ever-extending hegemony of the institutional church. To this political perspective Brandes (1980) and Gilmore (1984) add a psychological consideration of the extremely sexual form of anticlericalism that seems to characterize at least some of the Mediterranean culture area.

While Ireland is by no means devoid of "anticlericalism" in several of its modes, it does not seem to play anything like the central role it does in Portugal (Cutileiro 1971; Riegelhaupt 1984), Spain (e.g., Brandes 1980; Gilmore 1984), or Italy (Silverman 1975). In my experience Irish priests are far more typically praised than damned, and while individual clerics do run into opposition on particular issues, Irish priests are awarded a general respect and even veneration that would be the envy of their Mediterranean colleagues. As for the "stories" as such, only a tiny percentage of those Ó'hEochaidh collected or that I heard could, by any stretch of the term, be called "anticlerical." Yet the stories about drunken priests, as is evident from the opening example, are at least ambivalent, and the nature and roots of that ambivalence require exploration.

It might be argued, with some cogency, that the absence of anticlericalism in rural Ireland is a testament to the total domination of the institutional church. If that is the case, however, it has not produced a static uniformity of religious belief and practice nor an elimination of the difference and tension between local and official religiosity. Stories about both "heroic" and "drunken" priests are certainly not expressions of "orthodox" Catholicism. Rather they are local compositions (though in many cases with much borrowing of elements from other "localities"). They can be understood in this light, along with other elements of local religion, as a people's creative response to their experience of religious power. The stories may thus express a dialectic of opposition between locals and intrusive political, cultural, and psychological forces.

While the priest as sorcerer, using the sacred books and objects of the church, is a familiar enough figure from the folklore of other parts of Catholic Europe, for example Brittany (Hélias 1978; and Badone, this volume), in the case of the heroic priest stories, clerics who might elsewhere in Europe be perceived as part of the problem become, in Ireland, a magical solution to Protestant domination. Although Ó'hEochaidh's stories were of nineteenth-century clerics, I was told one tale of a local parish priest who, with the aid of his stole, froze two Black and Tans (1920s British occupation forces) to their seats overnight. Yet the church in Ireland was never perceived as the unflinching ally of the folk, and less so of their culture. Local clergy were agents of another "civilizing process" (Elias 1978, 1982) aimed at purging folk Catholicism of its heterodoxy and, even more so, folk society of its unruliness. This "civilizing offensive," to use the more appropriate Dutch term (see Verrips 1987), seems to have had a profound psychological effect. By the later nineteenth century the rural Irish seem to have had so well internalized certain forms of religious repression that local resentment rarely took the form of sexual innuendo as it does elsewhere in Europe (and elsewhere in the Catholic world), though comments about clerical avarice were more usual.

Stories and beliefs about drunken priests, however, were and continue to be common. Not only did I hear stories concerning living and recently deceased priests, I have known many individuals, young and old, who sought the efficacious prayers and blessings of such clerics even in the sanitorium. Taken together, such beliefs, stories, and practices may be interpreted as a kind of folk commentary on priestly power in general, as well as a commentary on the people's response to the increasing domination of the institutional church, and perhaps a less conscious way of handling psychological repression. All this will be apparent through a closer inspection of the stories, beliefs, and practices themselves. I will begin with a brief consideration of the historical and contemporary religious scene in the west of Ireland, then proceed to an examination of the content and performance of the stories, and return finally to an assessment of the overall significance of drunken priest beliefs and stories in this Irish case and in the comparative study of local religion.

CATHOLICISM IN THE WEST OF IRELAND

In comparison with other European Catholic countries, such as those treated in this volume, certain basic aspects of local and national religious life in Ireland are striking. Nearly 90 percent of all Irish Catholics attend mass at least once a week. While the figures are lower in cities (mainly Dublin), in areas such as southwest Donegal virtually every able-bodied Catholic man, woman, and child goes to Sunday mass. Women attend other devotional activities in the course of the week and year with far greater regularity than males, but the presence of many men at most regular church functions is in vivid contrast to many other Catholic countries, and particularly those in the Mediterranean (though Malta is an interesting exception in that region). Moreover, the local priest in most of rural Ireland and certainly in southwest Donegal is typically an important and highly visible part of all aspects of local life. Due in part to the relative vacuum of parish political authority—there is nothing like a mayor at the village or small-town level—priests have often played an important role in parish-level politics. They have often been taken as the natural representatives of their parishes by government and other outside officials in addition to acting as "brokers" to the outside world for locals. While such a role is not unique in Catholic Europe, their authority and credibility in Ireland has made them unusually powerful in this regard.

Ironically, much of the strength of the Catholic church in Ireland, and of the diocesan organization in particular, can be credited, directly and indirectly, to the British. Soon after they completed the conquest of Ireland in the late seventeenth century, the English passed a series of "penal laws" persecuting Catholics and the practice of Catholicism. Priests in particular were left in precarious circumstances, and while the various local conditions under which they operated no doubt varied and their difficulties may be exaggerated, the folk memory certainly recalls the "penal days priests" as heroic outlaws performing wilderness masses under constant threat of persecution from "redcoats." Toward the end of the eighteenth century the laws were considerably relaxed, and it would seem that the British, as sociologist Tom Inglis (1987) has put it, decided to turn to the Catholic church for aid in civilizing the "wild Irish."

A critical event in this process was the establishment in 1795 of a state-supported national seminary at Maynooth, outside Dublin, providing an Irish center for the training of a secular clergy. This academy soon supplied curates (assistant priests) as well as parish priests to most parishes. By 1829, when legislation finally removed all remaining legal impediments to the practice of Catholicism in Ireland, the mainly Maynooth-trained bishops were firmly in place. As Inglis points out (1987), their rule was both symbolized and effected through the building of churches throughout the country.

These new, bigger, and far more expensive churches, which in areas like southwest Donegal replaced thatched huts or even open shelters called *scáláin*, provided the institutional setting for what Larkin (1972) called the "devotional revolution." Well provided with priests, the peasantry in these remote areas now began to attend mass regularly and in great numbers. They were also introduced to the revival and expansion of devotional practices then popular on the continent. This was especially so after the arrival of archbishop and papal legate Paul Cullen who, in 1850, convened the first Irish synod since the Middle Ages.

Cullen's church produced an ever-increasing flow of Roman devotional practice and language, aimed particularly at the growing Catholic middle class. Like the Counter-Reformation, the devotional revolution of nineteenth-century Ireland was aimed at the firm establishment of a religious regime. The later movement was, however, far more able to penetrate into local fields of religious experience. From a Weberian perspective the Maynooth-trained diocesan clergy might be seen as poised to accomplish the transition from "magical" to "ethical" religious belief and practice. A step along the historical road toward rationalization, for Weber that general transition was also a means by which true priestly domination was achieved. Indeed, the devotional revolution seems a classic case of the institutionalization of charisma. The weekly mass became the central ritual in a religious field dominated by a discourse and iconography which affirmed the power of the church as institution.

The discourse of the church establishment was in large measure a middle-class Victorian one whose definition of civility and morality did not much differ from that of Protestant England and America, or much of Europe. It linked those more generally held cultural attitudes, however, to a particular institutional matrix—that of the Irish Catholic church. Some idea of the nature of the discourse can be gathered from the pages of the *Irish Catholic Directory*, an almanac of the year's Catholic events published annually from 1836 and distributed among the growing Catholic middle classes. The discourse of the annals through the nineteenth century, mainly authored by well-established clergy, is characterized by two different idioms, often appearing on the very same page: the idiom of opposition/persecution and the idiom of empire.

The idiom of opposition/persecution involved the constant iteration of the theme of British oppression and the consequent moral opposition and superiority of the Irish Catholic people and church. Writers would seize in particular upon occasions with dramatic potential, such as the doomed efforts of Protestant proselytizers in the West, or the eviction of helpless Catholic peasants in West Mayo and Donegal. In such cases the annals would stress the role of heroic clerics as defenders of the oppressed tenantry and the solidarity of the Irish Catholic people in opposition to the British.

Even as they extolled the embattled and famine-stricken peasants resisting the persecution of "bigoted Protestants" and "oppressive landlords," the writers of the annals listed and described in sumptuous detail the achievements and growing power of a Catholic empire whose seat was in Dublin and Maynooth. Not only could the hierarchy provide an alternative state to British Ireland, they could also claim to head an alternative world empire. If Australia was a British colony, then Catholic Australia was increasingly an Irish dominion. Thus the description of yearly events in the directories alternated between the idiom of persecution and the idiom of empire, but increasingly through the middle decades of the century it was the latter that predominated.

The very solidity and growing security of that regime, however, might also have led to a dulling routinization of the charisma so alive under direct British persecution in the eighteenth century. Various forces contributed to the continuing cultural and emotional force of the church in its institutionalizing phase. To return once again to Inglis's apt analysis, the church offered a route to respectable civility and middle-class status. That route, I would add, was through participation in an increasingly rich ritual structure equipped with a veritable myriad of new and revived devotions tying individuals, families, and communities to the sacramental symbols of the church.

In all this, the discourse of middle-class Catholicism, as described above, served a crucial function in structuring the consciousness of those who lived in that cultural world. Peculiarly if not uniquely Irish, the historical and political circumstances allowed the prevailing religious regime to promote middle-class civility and actively oppose various forms of dangerously uncivil behavior, even while it identified itself with the oppressed peasantry. A discourse that managed (and still manages) to link a comfortable clergy to the outlaw prophets of penal times keeps class-conscious anticlericalism at bay even as it revivifies the charisma of dramatic opposition in the face of routinization.

The folk, however, had their own language, a discourse to some extent accessible in the many stories on religious themes contained in the Irish Folklore Archive at U.C. Dublin. In such Gaelic-speaking areas as southwest Donegal the middle-class discourse described above reached most local ears mainly in the contexts of the schoolroom and church, where sermons and pastorals brought this perspective to bear on local experience. The national school system and its teachers warrant further investigation as sources of popular middle-class Catholic discourse as well as manners (see Inglis 1987) in this period. In domestic and other public contexts, however, the idiom was different. The stories recorded in the archives are an invaluable source of this sort of "talk," and the priest stories with which this article is concerned can be viewed within this historical context. They suggest something of the world view which both experienced and responded to the devotional revolution as well as the other social and economic changes that characterized the region (see also Lawrence Taylor 1985).

PRIEST STORIES

The "heroic priest" stories, mentioned earlier, show that the idiom of opposition was as important for the folk as for the hierarchy. In southwest Donegal it was *Gael* (as in Gaelic or Irish) versus *Gall* (foreigner), the latter term designating the substantial minority of Church of Ireland Protestants resident in the area since early in the eighteenth century. Moral and political issues, such as eviction and persecution, are central to these tales in which the priest uses sacramental magic to triumph over his evil enemies.

Drunken priest legends, however, are a very different matter, as one can see from the opening example of the priest who blinded the boy. Such narratives invariably begin with a phrase something like, "there was a priest here and he was fond of a wee drop." Disclaimers such as "with all respect to his cloth" or "though I shouldn't say so" are sometimes inserted for apparently prophylactic purposes. The stories are never set in a church or other ecclesiastical setting; rather the drunken priest is out walking in nature or among his people. Protestants, regular characters in the heroic priest stories, rarely appear in the drunken priest narratives and almost never as enemies; when the priest faces adversaries, they are his own innocent parishioners—guilty only of attempting to deprive him of drink or money.

In a story similar to the priest who blinded the boy, a drunken priest falls asleep at a baptism party, at which point the man of the house hides the one remaining bottle out in the byre. Upon waking the priest asks for a drink, only to be told there is not a drop in the house. "Go out to the byre and get the bottle you hid there" the man is told, and the poor fellow is cursed for his trouble, losing five sons to consumption. In another story a shopgirl refuses a loan of a few shillings for drink and wakes up the next morning with a beard (Ó'hEochaidh 1945: 40–42). The drunken priest is not always malignant, however. There was, for example, the one who found a party of men hesitant to start the haymaking in the face of a threatening storm. "Work away" he told them, reclining against a tree with a jug of whiskey. The rains came in torrents, but not a drop fell on the field where the men labored (Ó'hEochaidh 1945: 23–26).

Most often the benevolent drunken priest cures—either humans or beasts. As mentioned earlier, such miracles are performed without the aid of stole or book, usually with blessings but sometimes with the further action of contagious magic. There was the story, for example, of the time a woman from Teelin, desperate over the decline of her prize sow, finally sought the miraculous Father MacShane, the very same priest, as it turns out, who blinded the boy (and to whom we will be returning at length below). She saw him approaching along the road, but before she could tell him what was wrong he said, "I know what trouble has brought you to me," and with that he scraped a bit of the dirt from the sole of his boot and told her to mix it in the pig's food. A complete recovery ensued (Ó'hEochaidh 1945: 37–39). Religious artifacts may come into play in such cures, but they are natural substances or associated with the landscape, like blessed salt or holy wells.

As the two accounts concerning priest McShane illustrate, cures and curses are attributed in several cases to the same priest; it is not a case of good and bad priests but rather priests whose power is both strong and capricious. They look into mortal minds, they control the forces of nature, and they are as likely to harm (if crossed) as they are to help. Justice doesn't come into these stories, although it is central to the heroic priest stories.

The power of such priests is further illustrated by the manner in which these stories are performed. Folklorist Ó'hEochaidh (1945) has an interesting note prefacing his collection which translates as follows: "Stories about priests are wonderfully difficult to collect because people believe that it is neither right nor proper to be telling such stories for fear that something will befall them for the telling, especially if there is something wrong with the priest in the story." If the old stories were not often told, they were heard frequently enough to be known, and if warnings were included about the danger of telling such stories, then these admonitions, like the phrases "with all due respect for his cloth," only served as extensions of the protagonists' power—they could reach out of the text and blind the narrator. I suspect that such stories were not so willingly told for the collector, not so much because he might be an outsider but because he was writing them down or, worse, recording them and thereby concretizing the event of the telling.

While the formal context of the *seanchaidh* (storyteller) is rarely encountered in southwest Donegal today, I found that many older people knew at least some of the stories Ó'hEochaidh recorded and were quite willing to add others of their own. Whenever I told a story I had heard, listeners would adopt an attentive and apparently believing attitude, shaking their heads at the wonder of the priests' miracles. I was also present at discussions in pubs and homes where a small number of men or women, having raised the topic of priestly power, would relate such stories—sometimes in the "classic" narrative form discussed above and sometimes more in the way of less apparently structured anecdotes. The anecdotal form often related events much more recently transpired.

There was a Father Heany for example, who died only four or five years ago. He was known not only to take a drink but to see patients in the local bar. "Oh Father Heany was very good," a neighbor of mine told me, "my boss John—he's not even a Catholic—had a terrible pain in his neck. He was having a drink in the pub and he told Father Heany about the pain, and Father Heany just put his hand on John's neck and kind of rubbed it. Well the pain just went away and it never came back. Oh Father Heany was a very great priest." I heard another tale, more in the formal style, told of a good Protestant farmer further north in the county who had contributed to the education of a miraculous drinking priest whose father had labored on his farm. Years later the farmer found himself in dire straits with the sheriff threatening to take away his cattle. The young priest commiserated with the old Protestant farmer over a drink and said it would be a shame if his cattle ever strayed past the stream they used to take them to on the edge of the farm. The next day nothing could get the cattle over that barrier.

Of all the local drunken priests, Father McShane, who blinded the boy and cured the pig, certainly figured largest in the local repertoire, and an extended look at McShane stories and how they are told reveals much about the meaning of the stories for their tellers and also about the historical circumstances that may lie behind such legends.

I first encountered the blinded boy story in the archives in the form presented in this paper. Returning to the region, I asked a man of about eighty, in the midst of a general conversation about priests and their powers, if he had ever heard anything about the powers of priests who drink. After a pause and with some small show of discomfort with the topic, he pointed his pipe stem up the road toward the nearby market town. "Sagart [priest] Condy Rua," he began, "he was a McShane from Carrick, from the house there by the post office—you know it—you know the shop there, well that was Johnny Condy Rua's, and Sagart Condy Rua would be his brother. Well he took a drink and once he went into the house [pub] that was there across the road—it was McShane as well—and, whatever happened, he asked the boy who was behind the bar there for a bottle of whiskey that was up on the shelf. And the boy didn't want to give it to him—maybe he owed too much, do you see. Anyway, he said to the priest that he couldn't see the bottle. The priest said to him that he would wish he could see it tomorrow. And he left. Well the boy woke up blind the next morning. So. . . ." Thus the story ended. "And did he ever see again?" I asked. "No."

Some time later I was asking a local school teacher if he knew anything of the priest McShane. "Aye, that would be Sagart [Priest] Condy Rua, Johnny's brother. I grew up next to him there in Carrick. He was already dead when I was born, but I often heard Johnny talk of him, and my mother had great faith in him." He then proceeded to tell me a version of the blinded boy story similar to the one above but without specifying at what point the boy went blind. "Did he go blind right away?" I asked. "I think it must have been maybe six months or a year later," came the reply. At this point the teacher's wife, a very pious, college-educated woman who had married into the community from a far more sophisticated region of Ireland, remarked that of course such a story could not be true. Her husband, also college-educated in Dublin, was visibly upset by her comment. He insisted with stubborn and humorless determination that the story was in fact true, that he knew the parties involved. He went on to relate another incident, closer to home, involving the miraculous Father McShane.

"My mother died last year at the age of ninety, and she often told me the story her mother told her, about when my mother was born with a deformed lip and my grandmother was going to take her to the doctor to have it operated on. Well, she stopped in the McShane house there in Carrick on her way, and Sagart Condy Rua was there at home visiting [his natal family]. He said that he knew she was on the way to the doctor for the baby's lip but that she should not go. 'I'll tell you where you will find a cure for that lip,' he said, 'at the holy well in Kilcar [the next parish and his own curacy]. Just go to the well and do the stations and put a drop of the water on the lip of the child.' Well, she did that, and within days the lip was completely perfect. Now my mother often told me that."

Several months later, Mary, a neighbor woman in her fifties, came to visit me and my wife for tea. Conversation began as it almost always did with a discussion of the immediate neighbors and what they were up to. Her conversation was suggestive of her world view—in the sequence of anecdotes as well as in their individual content. Speaking of one household, she said that she had attended the "stations" (a mass held in the

Nineteenth-century photograph of a Protestant tourist being shown a holy well on a mountain. (From Lawrence Collection, National Library, Dublin)

home with the neighbors as guests) held there by the new parish priest. With that observation she diverted herself to the topic of priests and how some of them were "holier" than others. I then told her that I had recently spoken with the housekeeper of Father Heany (the recently deceased cleric whose barroom curing is described above, who had resided in retirement about fifteen miles away) who had told me of the hundreds of people who would line up for blessings and cures every weekend. Mary was apparently unfamiliar with Father Heany, however, and seemed disinterested in discussing him, but began instead to tell us of her experience with Father O'Donnell (pseudonym), a charismatically inclined priest whose monthly "healing mass" was attended by hundreds of people from all over the county and beyond. She had taken a local minibus to the event the month before (see Taylor 1987b).

"I had this terrible gash in my leg I got when I fell in the house, and it wasn't healing well. And this pain I had in my side—just a terrible sort of ache that would come and go. Well I went to the priest and told him my trouble and he bent his head and listened, and then he put his hand on my side and kind of moved it across me here and prayed over me. And that pain just went away and it hasn't come back since!" Mary then continued, with no provocation from me, to recall the exploits of Father McShane of story fame.

"He had wonderful power. He cured many a one around here. My father went to him once with a very bad eye [here her tone changed to that of serious storytelling], and Father McShane asked him why had he come to him.

'For you to cure my eye,' he told him.

'And do you believe I will cure it?'

'I do.'

And he told my father to kneel down by a table he had there, and he pulled the cloth that was on it over my father's head and said an office [blessing] over him and then my father went home. Well, that eye cleared up and never troubled him again. Oh Father McShane was a very great priest. . . . you know Seamus [her father's brother's son and neighbor]; he has his boot. Ask him and he'll show it to you."

I did on the next day. I found Seamus, a successful small farmer of fifty-six, at home and told him that I had heard he knew something of the priest McShane. Seamus then proceeded to relate how, in his youth, he had come across the boot when cleaning out the byre and had almost thrown it away with the trash.

" 'Boys, oh boys, oh dears, where are you goin' with that boot?' me father asked me.

'Many's the cures that's in that boot,' he told me, and that was the boot of Father McShane. So I put it back in the byre for the cattle like."

"And I keep it shined up," his wife added.

Later on his wife produced the boot for our inspection and asked those present if we "wanted to take a blessing off it" (that is, to touch the boot as one would holy water, blessing oneself after contact).

The same man told me another story about Father McShane: "They say that Father McShane was out walking through the countryside, and he came upon two carters [men who made their living transporting goods in carts to the far-flung small shopkeepers in remote regions]. He would often be out like that and ask someone for money—I guess for drink. Anyway, he asked this one man for money, and he told the priest that he hadn't enough for him. 'Well, you have the money now,' the priest said to him, 'but you won't have money in the future.' And then he came to another carter, a fellow called Boyle—he'd be a cousin of mine—and he asked him for the money, and the Boyle fellow had only half a crown, just enough to feed himself and his horse like, but he said he'd give it to him. And he did. And the priest said he would never have empty pockets, and by God it was true for him. That man never married, but he left a good packet of money to some of his relations—gave them a good start like."

Several days later I was on the other side of the parish on a remote mountain road when I spotted an interesting-looking local man cajoling a donkey up the brae with a cartload of turf. I stopped and we chatted in

Father McShane's boot. (Photograph by V. M. Hickey)

Irish about the place, and he asked where I was staying. I told him, and he asked if I knew a cousin of his who lived nearby: Seamus—the very man with the priest's boot. I asked him if he knew the story of McShane and the carter.

"Indeed I do, wasn't it my own uncle, there, who was in it," he said, nodding toward his own home on the mountainside. "He was carting for that Haughey shop there in Meanacooley and he gave the priest money and prospered for it." He went on to identify the other carter in the story and his townland.

"And a funny thing about that story," he added. "My uncle himself never told us that story, and he lived with us all his life and died when I was twenty years old [about thirty-five years earlier]. And the day he died neighbors who knew him told us what had happened with him and the priest."

This corpus of McShane stories and the contexts of their telling suggest much about the role of the drunken priest in local consciousness. But before proceeding to that analysis we need to take note of the historical circumstances of Father McShane, for he certainly lived, and his local situation suggests some of the reasons both for his suitability for the narrative role of drunken priest and for the historical, cultural, and psychological genesis of this narrative form.

McShane was curate, or assistant priest, under a parish priest named O'Donnell who served the parish of Kilcar from 1893 up until his death in 1910. O'Donnell is memorialized in his parish in two forms. First and foremost is the parish church in the village of Kilcar, which in ornateness is reputedly second only to the diocesan cathedral in Letterkenny. While there is some good agricultural land in the parish, there is far more that is very poor and mountainous, and in most respects Kilcar was a typical west Donegal parish, that is, nothing would lead one to expect the rather impressive parish church there. A local antiquarian told me that in fact the church was built through money raised in America, and, what is more, that it was the curate McShane who was sent there on a number of occasions to collect funds. According to his account (which of course has to be considered as a "story" itself—true or not—rather than simply "history"), O'Donnell was an imperious, egotistical, and crassly materialistic man who resented and exploited the more spiritual and intellectual McShane. According to this account, McShane, exasperated with his constant travels, finally refused to go off to America, and O'Donnell had him "silenced" by the bishop—with drink the legitimating excuse.

The other memorial, which also sheds light on O'Donnell's relation to the parish, is a large concrete "mission cross" dated 1907 (see figure). Such crosses were erected during Redemptorists' parish missions, when representatives of that preaching order took over a parish for several

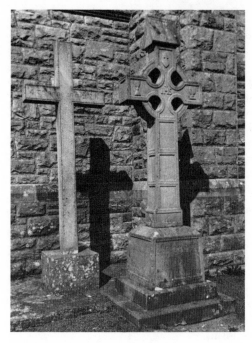

Mission cross, Kilcar. (Photograph by V. M. Hickey)

weeks of intensive sermonizing and confessions. These missions had two chief foci and effects. First, they brought Roman devotionalism to rural Ireland, that is, they were "shock troops" in what Larkin (1972) calls the "devotional revolution." Second, and this was especially so in the west of Ireland in the period in question, the missioners made a special contribution, in particularly dramatic form, to the ongoing clerical attack on uncontrolled drinking and the unsupervised socializing of "big nights" (parties held in houses). A successful mission "campaign" would be concluded with the erection of just such a memorial cross, and indeed such missions often etched themselves into local memory as powerful events (see Taylor 1989, for a full discussion of Irish missions). O'Donnell was for these reasons a perfect representation of the church as oppressor of local life, a point extended in another story I was told wherein he actively opposed the local IRA efforts during the fight for Irish independence.

Thus there is in the O'Donnell/McShane pair a perfect binary opposition between parish priest and curate in terms of politics, temperament, and their respective relationships with the people. Moreover, they have both ascribed and achieved characteristics that lend deeply resonant symbolic dimensions to the opposition. O'Donnell arrived from another part of the diocese and not only ran but actually built a most impressive church. His further association with the Redemptorist mission, memorialized in the cross, makes him the perfect personification of the increasingly successful forces of religious domination and institutional authority that so characterized local experience throughout most of the nineteenth century. On the other hand there is McShane: born locally and thus intimately associated with the sacred landscape—including the local holy well—drunk, wandering through the countryside, and especially so after being "silenced" by the bishop. There is also a wonderful inversion in the types of "begging" the priests do: O'Donnell's is for the church, McShane's is for drink. Clearly there are two kinds of power figured in this opposition, but equally clear is the fact that the conceptual opposition did not originate with these two historical personalities. Rather, the perfect experiential opposition made McShane a particularly appropriate and potent magnet for beliefs about drunken priests.

CONCLUSION

Why, however, do drunken priests have such powers? I found the people with whom I discussed these matters quite willing to talk about the subject but usually unable to come up with an explicit theory; their conceptual schema was both created and embodied in narratives. Typically the response would go something like, "Somehow it's the priests that take a drink that always have the power, the old people always said that, and it's still the way it is—whatever's in it." One old woman ventured a tentative explanation: "Maybe its because when the drink is on them they can't control themselves so much."

The theme of control is an interesting one and consonant with views often expressed concerning that other and closely related type of powerful cleric (combined, in fact, in the case of McShane): the silenced priest. A silenced priest is one who has been removed from the pulpit, in the event very often for excessive drink. Of such clerics it is said, "the *smacht* [control] of the bishop is off them." A local, and sober, priest elaborated: "They think that the priest's miraculous power is under the control of the bishop, so that he is not allowed to work miracles. If the priest is silenced, the power is released." This commentary on the folk theory indicates a marvelous reversal of the official church position conveyed by the term "silenced." Such priests, from the folk religious point of view, have voices indeed. But the uncontained power, no longer channeled into the safe conduits of the sacraments, is both stronger and more dangerous. Following Douglas (1966) and Turner (1969), such priests would be labeled "anomalous" and "liminal." Out of the *smacht* of the bishop—no longer part of the institutional church—the priest is a shaman.

This theme is clearly evinced in the stories of drunken priests as well, who, like McShane, are portrayed away from the church, wandering in

"Nature," and performing their miracles without aid of the symbolic implements of the institutional church. The matter of silencing, already achieved or threatened, indicates that the opposition between drunken priest and parish priest and/or bishop is more than conceptual, it is political. Although the case of McShane makes this particularly clear, it is worth noting that in every case of a historically identifiable "drunken priest" the cleric in question was a curate rather than a parish priest. In nineteenth-century Ireland there was a substantial difference in the power and income of parish priests and curates (see for example O'Shea 1983:315), and the drunken curate was unlikely to rise in the hierarchy and hence was an excellent symbol of political subordination within the authoritarian church. The case of McShane also makes clear the real historical—as well as symbolic—character of such clerics and, potentially, of the situations portrayed in the stories. In that respect such legends offer an indication of the way locals appropriated events to form an ideology that to some extent both defined and framed their perception of local reality (see Lawrence Taylor 1985). Following Turner (1982:72), I would argue that there is a dialectical relation between social dramas like those involving McShane and the stories told about them. The curate's confrontation with O'Donnell was probably real, but it was also particularly meaningful in a cultural sense. Thus the conflict provoked a story. But the narrative that was eventually formed no doubt selectively appropriated the event. Finally, insofar as these stories provide an ideological framework that influences behavior, they may act as both *models of* and *models for* history.

The theme of control, subordination, and release within the church, however, is culturally interesting and resonant to the people who tell and hear the stories because it draws upon a variety of rich experiential sources and has the metaphorical potential to stand for similar themes, consciously or unconsciously understood, in their own lives.

In culturally constructing the type of the drunken priest the people have availed themselves of a variety of potent traditions. Within the non-Christian Irish and Celtic tradition one is reminded especially of the *file*, the poet whose words have magical efficacy to curse or help prosper. Drunkenness turns out to be one of the important ways and signs of inspiration/possession for such poets and thus provides one line of cultural resonance for the drunken priest character (see Ó'hÓgáin 1983). Moreover, the image of drunkenness has long been a central feature of the national-ethnic stereotype, and in my field experience it is still a highly ambivalent aspect of corporate and/or individual self-image. As such it is related to a whole series of attributes forged in the binary opposition of "reasonable" (read dull) Anglo-Saxon with "emotional" (read creative) Celt.

There is a tradition of internal symbolic opposition within the Catholic church as well, embodied in the dichotomy of the political/worldly versus the spiritual/natural. The latter form was of course rooted in the image of Christ and his disciples, a troop of prophetic mendicants who cured without tools or emblems of office. This charisma of poverty and anti-institutionality periodically re-emerged in the history of the church in the shape of several religious orders, such as the Franciscans, who appropriated that sort of image and power. Ireland, in fact, was home to one of the earlier forms of this monastic tradition, and most Irish saints (and all local ones) originate in the Celtic eremetic tradition of the early Middle Ages. Although Irish monasteries were certainly important and occasionally wealthy institutions acting directly in the political world, the stories of the early saints, which form another subgenre of folk religious tales, all feature lone, wandering figures.

These saints are clearly identified with Christ, about whom similar legends are told. They wander, they are poor, even mendicant. They are also intimately connected to the landscape, especially to the holy wells which retain associated curing power, but also in the place names of more ordinary features of the local terrain. Their magic defies natural processes (growth, death, rain), and they have tempers. Associating the saints with Christ in this way serves to extend the foundation myth of the church in time, but more importantly, in space; it makes the local landscape sacred and thus symbolically associated with the Holy Land.

It is through this sacred landscape that the drunken priest wanders, and in this characteristic, as well as in his mendicant, holy, but dangerous ways, he is linked with these local saints, especially the major one, Columcille (St. Columba), who behaves very similarly in many narratives. In this context the relic of Father McShane's boot hanging in the byre makes sense, as does his linkage with St. Cartha's holy well. People speak of having "great faith" in a particular priest, with the same language used to discuss devotions to saints. Priests can be associated directly with both the poetic and saintly traditions by displaying such "natural" characteristics as insanity, drunkenness, and unpredictability, and especially if they run into trouble with "authority." Christ, in their stories, is more a shaman than a prophet, as is Columcille, neither of whom, as noted, uses the paraphernalia of the church in performing miracles nor uses his magic against political authorities. Further, the drunken priest begs and punishes those who do not recognize him, as do both Columcille and even Christ in the folk if not biblical version of his exploits.

The folk construction of the drunken priest, and the theory of "control and release" elicited to explain him, can be read as a commentary on the process of becoming a priest but also on the longer historical process of the growth of institutional church power through priestly domination.

From this perspective the priest's charisma, whether natural (as some people indicate) or achieved through the rite of passage of ordination, is not augmented through religious training. What the priest learns is self-control; his charisma is institutionalized (see Weber 1963). The further a cleric rises in the church, the less sacred power he manifests. Another sort of royal charismatic power emerges at the top in the Pope, but the bishops are perceived more as politicians than princes; no one goes to bishops for cures.

Analogously, this figuring of priestly power can also be read as a metaphor for the church's attempt to civilize and contain the natural power of local folk religion and indeed of those elements of local folk life perceived as uncivilized. In Larkin's (1972) "devotional revolution" mid-nineteenth-century Irish Catholics were subject to the steadily increasing domination of the clergy. Mass attendence became regular, and official religious objects such as scapulars, miraculous medals, and rosary beads provided concrete foci of sacred power and devotion. Through the same period the church also represented the most active agency of general social control (see Connolly 1982). The people were not silent, however. There was and is power in the Word as well, and if they recognized the force of priestly language, the tellers of priest stories thereby exercised their own linguistic power by appropriating the clergy as actors in the very folk religion they typically opposed. In this sense the stories both react to and create history not only as event but as process. For the people the drunken priest represented, and to some extent still represents, a kind of chthonic power, less controlled or contained than that of the ordinary clergy: a force released beyond the walls of the church, in the mountains, or in stories of his parish.

There may well also be a less conscious, psychologically motivated metaphor at work in the priest stories, though one materially connected to the historical circumstances discussed above. As mentioned in our brief discussion of the Redemptorist mission, it was not only—or even mainly—heterodox religious practice that the nineteenth-century church sought to control. Rather, powerful religious dramatics were brought to the task of suppressing sexual and violent behavior. It is interesting in this regard that there are not in Ireland the sexual stories of priests that abound in other areas of the Catholic world. A Freudian addendum to our thus far historical, structural, and symbolic analysis of the drunken priest would suggest that perhaps the actual or implied opposition of drunken and ordinary priest metaphorically represents aspects of *self* with which that very church and its personnel have been, and are, intimately concerned. That is, the potent but capriciously destructive drunken priest may represent the *libido* "when the *smacht* of the church—and its internalized aspects of the self—is off it." This interpretation does not seem arbitrary in light of both the actual historic role of the church in repressing sexuality and the evidence of its success in the high rate of celibacy that has long characterized the region. As noted, the rarity of sexual motifs in the Irish stories is in stark contrast with priest narratives from such regions as Spain. If the stories and beliefs do have this psychological aspect, then their telling and hearing might provide opportunities for "release," albeit in a more sublimated form than, for example, the sexual stories of the Spanish priest discussed in this way by Brandes (1980). If such were the case, it would make sense that these stories are both compelling and dangerous to tell.

The drunken priest, when put into historical as well as folkloric context, illustrates the dynamic nature of the relationship between local and official religion. The stories and beliefs examined here constitute part of an ever-changing field of local religious experience, which adapts to changing conditions—political, cultural, and psychological. Indeed, the degree to which these categories, in their conscious and unconscious forms, can be linked in such stories makes them powerful. The special role of discourse in this formation and maintenance of religious experience is also well exampled here, for like religious symbols or rituals, discourse can be borrowed and applied in both directions. It is likely, for example, that the use of the idiom of opposition by the church in its publications rises from the folk use of the same idiom.

Finally, these beliefs continue to operate not just in stories but in behavior. The search for relief from affliction continues to motivate much religious behavior, and if alcoholic priests are not as popular as in the past, they are certainly still sought by individuals young and old. The reputations, in this regard, of contemporary clerics such as Father Heaney rise and fall like those of holy wells, saints, and particular devotions. In all cases proof of efficacy is conveyed in narrative form, so that the power of the story is critical to the perceived power of the curer. Medicine shows no sign of obviating such needs, and even if their form shifts, such beliefs have a future. Mary, the woman who went to see the healing priest looking for a cure found herself at a Charismatic mass, a novel religious form imported to the region from America, home of the "Pentecostal Catholic" or "Charismatic Renewal" movement. There is a chance that her experience there may lead her, as it has others of her neighbors, to join a local prayer group. In the context of such a charismatic or pentecostal "community of affliction" she would, as in the storytelling sessions, take part in the corporate construction of experience. In such contexts, however, narrative serves a more radical enterprise. An idiom foreign to the ordinary situations of local life is adopted and the search for a cure becomes a quest for "healing," a key notion at the heart of a new discourse and a new field of religious experience.

Notes to Chapter 7

This paper is based on field and archival research conducted in Ireland for eleven months in 1973 and 1976 and twelve months in 1986/1987. Fieldwork was generously supported by grants from the National Endowment for the Humanities and Lafayette College. I wish to thank the many individuals of the region that spoke with me on these matters (none of whom are identified by actual name in the text), and several scholars whose advice or comments on this and earlier versions of the paper were especially helpful, including Tom Inglis, Father Brendan McConvery CssR, Sean White, and Gearóid Ó'Crualaoich in Ireland and Dan Bauer, Susan Niles, Stanley Brandes, and Ellen Badone in North America. A great debt is owed to the Folklore Archives in Dublin and the generous assistance there of Séamus Ó'Catháin and Bairbre O'Floinn. Special thanks are due to my wife, Maeve Hickey Taylor, without whom the research for this paper would not have been possible.

1. This paper is part of a more general work, in progress, on forms of Catholicism in this region. For relevant accounts of other aspects of historical and local life see Lawrence Taylor (1980a, 1980b, 1981, 1987a, and especially 1985, 1987b, and 1989). A nearby parish is the subject of Shanklin (1985).

2. The theoretical concept "fields of religious experience" is an attempt to provide a mode of analyzing the multiplicity of meaning systems that can be discovered within a population of believers. In the region under consideration it is possible to distinguish such distinct if overlapping fields as "chthonic," "middle-class," and "charismatic." This notion is elaborated in the longer work in progress referred to in note 1.

CHAPTER 8

Conclusion: Reflections on the Study of Religious Orthodoxy and Popular Faith in Europe

Stanley Brandes

THE ANTHROPOLOGICAL STUDY OF EUROPEAN RELIGION

THE anthropological study of European religion has developed in the context of the anthropology of complex societies. No matter where we go in Europe, no matter how large or small our unit of analysis, we inevitably discover the coexistence of several competing, mutually derivative systems of religious beliefs and practices. If it would be oversimplifying matters to speak of Australian aboriginal religion, Trobriand religion, or Ife religion, then it is an even graver injustice to refer to Roman Catholicism or Eastern Orthodoxy as if these each reflected homogeneous, undifferentiated cosmologies, world views, and sets of ritual behavior. European religious systems are intricately patterned and highly elaborated; they have emerged over the course of centuries in response to an infinite variety of social, economic, political, and cultural circumstances. How, then, can anthropologists, with their usual focus on highly localized traditions, contribute to the more general understanding of religion in Europe?

In the main I would say that anthropologists, as well as historians who utilize anthropological modes of analysis, have relied on often very fragmentary evidence to reconstruct the religious beliefs and practices of the poorer, less literate peoples in Europe. In this volume Jane Schneider correctly points out that peasants (and, by extension, other dependent segments of European society) were hardly unreflective members of the religious communities to which they belonged. The growing corpus of microhistories to which she refers more than substantiates the sometimes thoughtful manner in which these peoples approached their relation to God and the supernatural. However, these peoples tended not to record their religious conceptions. Nor, with few exceptions, were their ideas systematized and codified into some internally consistent, all-encompassing cosmology, such as clerics, philosophers, and other intellectual specialists might have the time and inclination to develop.

Whether dealing with people past or present, the anthropological mandate is to resuscitate religious beliefs and practices such as those of the masses that would otherwise be lost to history. It is for this reason that anthropologists of Europe feel so closely allied with social historians like Natalie Davis, Carlo Ginzburg, and Emmanuel Le Roy Ladurie.[1] These scholars, like most of the anthropologists included in this volume, have retrieved for history a host of ideas that might have permanently disappeared. For convenience we may lump these ideas under the rubric "popular faith" in contrast to "religious orthodoxy," the domain of the specialized religious elite. It is the relationship between these two overlapping religious systems that, of course, forms the main theme of this book.

Probably the first scholars to study European religion in what we might call a cultural anthropological framework were Sir Edward B. Tylor and Sir James George Frazer. These men, like other writers of the late nineteenth century, were social evolutionists, who believed that societies progressed through regular stages of development, from savagery to barbarism and, finally, to civilization, a stage quintessentially represented in these men's minds by England of the day. In the course of their investigations they uncovered many previously undescribed folk beliefs dealing with the supernatural. However, they implicitly discredited these beliefs by labelling them superstitions and, as indicated in the Introduction to this volume, survivals—superstitions because they seemed, in their departure from official, elite religion, to be hopelessly irrational; and survivals because they could only be explained as anachronistic leftovers of some earlier stage of societal development. Evolutionists such as Tylor and Frazer dealt only implicitly with the relationship between religious orthodoxy and popular faith in Europe. Though they failed to delineate official religious tenets and practices presumably characteristic of civilized peoples, they used these as ethnocentric standards by which to identify superstitions. For this reason it might be said that they implicitly perceived a wide gap between official and folk religion, the two coexisting but representing discrete stratigraphic layers in the great societal march from savagery through barbarism to civilization.

Not until after World War II, when anthropologists began to debate the definition of peasantry and to examine complex societies *qua* complex societies, did the discussion of religious orthodoxy and popular faith become explicit in anthropological discourse. Robert Redfield (1956) coined the terms "great tradition" and "little tradition" to differentiate between recognizably divergent aspects of the same overall culture that could be identified within any high civilization, past or present. Great traditions, he believed, were characteristic of the reflective, literate elite, who invented, elaborated, and refined with infinite subtlety a wide range of laws and philosophical-religious tenets. These products of the great tradition were said to diffuse over time to the supposedly nonreflective, nonliterate, and, as Ellen Badone points out in the Introduction, rural masses, who selected from among the great tradition elements, reinterpreted them, and arrived at a simplified, localized, somewhat distorted version of the great tradition, known as the little tradition. Because diffusion from the elite to the masses was considered to take a long time, elements of the little tradition were considered to have experienced a process of "cultural lag" (see, for example, Foster 1967a:12); in other words, by definition the little tradition lagged behind the great tradition.

The inestimable contribution of the Redfieldian perspective was to focus anthropological attention on the complexity of religious traditions in places like Europe, Asia, the Middle East, and Latin America. It sought to demonstrate structural contours and historical connections among the rich panoply of beliefs and practices that characterize any given people. The Redfieldian point of view also increased our awareness of intracultural variation by postulating that different segments of society bear slightly or substantially different religious ideas. Finally, I would say that the anthropological study of European religion, largely ignored until the 1960s, earned a place in American anthropology through the dissemination of Redfields's notions of great and little tradition. For the presence of great and little traditions was something that non-Western and Western peoples alike shared. Europe could now be seen as a valid, defensible arena within which to understand the religious dynamics of complex societies generally.

Despite these theoretical advances, Redfield and his followers—like the evolutionists before them—implicitly denigrated the religion of the masses. Not only did they view popular religion as less reflective and creative—in other words, more reactive—than that of the elite but they also believed that popular religion lagged behind elite religion temporally; elite beliefs and practices of one century might be discovered among the peasantry of the next. There was also the built-in ethnocentric bias of referring to elite religion as "great" and peasant religion as "little."

Yet another difficulty with the study of religion through a great and little traditional framework was the reification of culture. Religious beliefs and practices, though perceived as characteristic of one segment of society or the other, were analyzed as if they had a superorganic existence, as if they floated through time and space independent of human carriers. Anthropologists were interested in demonstrating the origin of a particular popular belief, usually among the elite of an earlier historical epoch. The social context and symbolic meaning of religious ideas to concrete individuals in specific settings were for the most part ignored in anthropological studies of the day.

In this volume, by contrast, authors demonstrate an admirably refined sensitivity to the particular circumstances in which rituals occur, legends are narrated, beliefs are expressed, and the like. Whether through field

188 · Stanley Brandes

data or historical documentation, we get a picture of people whose religious actions and ideas derive from a combination of spatially and temporally specific situations. Religion in this volume is decidedly not reified. Like the authors, we can identify with both the living informants and document-writers whose ideas are conveyed in these pages. In good anthropological tradition the people here portrayed are for the most part economically and politically weak; to this extent the articles in this book conform to the basic anthropological mandate mentioned above.

As Ellen Badone indicates in the introductory chapter, these articles (with the possible exception of Schneider's) share a specific interest in Roman Catholicism and Eastern Orthodoxy rather than Protestantism. In part this emphasis reflects the generally greater anthropological attention that has been paid to Ireland and southern Europe than to the rest of the continent. More is involved, however. To speak of religious orthodoxy and popular faith is automatically to invoke the image of a multilayered religious hierarchy and cultural tradition. Not only are the Roman Catholic and Eastern Orthodox churches themselves highly stratified but, at least until recently, they have fostered the differentiation (through costume, custom, and canon law) of clergy from laity. In addition, Catholic and Orthodox clergy have for centuries debated questions of religious orthodoxy and defined that orthodoxy for all lay adherents of the religion.

It is for this reason that we can more easily speak about folk Catholicism than folk Presbyterianism or folk Unitarianism. Protestant sects tend to be differentiated, in terms of ritual and belief, more from one another than internally. Over the course of history serious dissensions within Protestantism have resulted in the formation of new churches in which orthodoxy and popular belief are virtually indistinguishable. Protestants who object to one set of ideas need not feel bound to a given sect; they move on to join or found another. Catholics, on the other hand, often remain formally contained within the bounds of the church, while privately espousing ideologies and enacting rituals that are at least partially contrary to it. Within Roman Catholicism and, perhaps to a lesser extent, Eastern Orthodoxy, there exists an authoritative clerical standard, an orthodox version of faith. It is the stable, long-term coexistence of such a formal religious standard with a plethora of rebellious but essentially loyal heterodoxies that produces the kind of layered division of religion to which this book is devoted.

IMAGES OF THE CHURCH AND CLERGY

Let us now turn to the way the authors of this volume treat the religious standard bearers, the church and clergy. For the most part we can say that the church and clergy here, as in almost all anthropological analyses of European religion, are analyzed not on their own terms but rather through the eyes of the laity. The overall picture that emerges from these highly sensitive, detailed field accounts is one in which parishioners are engaged in a relentless struggle, whether overt or disguised, against priests. In the Portuguese cases that Brettell presents, for example, there clearly exists a contest of wills between priests and parishioners over ritual activities. When confronted by clerical opposition to particular *festas*, the villagers simply take matters into their own hands and, in what amounts to a minirebellion, perform ceremonies on their own time and in their own way. We know of similar occurrences elsewhere in southern Europe as well; Lope de Vega's (1978) theatrical rendition of the rebellion at Fuenteovejuna is but an extreme manifestation of the same phenomenon. Throughout history Iberian peasants, such as the ones Behar writes about, have considered themselves even more religious, more orthodox, than the clergy. This posture has afforded them the moral justification to depart occasionally from priestly commands and take control over religious ritual.

The rural peoples portrayed in this volume not only compete with priests for ritual control but also undermine clerical status through gossip and slander. In Portugal (Brettell), Brittany (Badone), and Spain (Behar), villagers seem to pursue every narrative form in the folkloristic repertoire in order to foster an image of hypocritical, greedy, and oversexed priests. The social conditions that give rise to these anticlerical images no doubt vary slightly from country to country, or even region to region. But, taken as a whole, they reflect what I think is a very Mediterranean view of human nature and therefore not a view shared, for example, by the Irish as described in Taylor's paper.

Consider, first, the popular concern over hypocrisy. The people of southern Europe seem to believe that appearances belie reality. The struggle between appearance and reality often reaches dramatic heights in accounts of Mediterranean life, where people often seem to spend a lot more time preparing for and acting out elaborate religious ritual than contemplating and verbalizing religious ideas. This theme has been played out extensively in the anthropology of Greece, for example. We may reiterate here Dubisch's perceptive observation that "popular religion in Greece, like popular religion in Portugal, . . . is more outward than inward looking, more concerned with external images, with the public and communal than with the interior or the mystic." The same preoccupation with external images has been a major concern in Spanish literature from Fernando de Rojas' (1955) portrayal of *La Celestina* in the sixteenth century to Miguel de Unamuno's (1979) characterization of *San Manuel Bueno, Mártir* in the twentieth. In the Mediterranean area reality is said to lie deep beneath the surface. And priests are believed to possess no thinner façade than anybody else. Where they diverge is in their alleged pretense that they are different; for this presumably hypocritical posturing they are mercilessly criticized.

As to clerical greed, I would trace this popular stereotype in large measure to another theme that emerges repeatedly in this volume: the historically recurrent alliance between the church and clergy, on the one hand, and the political and economic elite, on the other. Brettell, Behar, and Badone all trace anticlerical sentiments in Portugal, Spain, and Brittany, respectively, at least in part to what we might call right-wing biases of the church and clergy. Like the powerful landowners and urban politicians with whom they are said to be in cahoots, priests are reputed to act deviously in the interests of themselves and their upper-class allies. Devious behavior might consist of siphoning off local funds and communal assets (like antique religious images), or be conceived in terms of larger issues such as control over jobs and education, hence over children's futures.

Whatever the specific charge, it is clear that throughout southern Europe, greed is hardly thought to be limited to individual clerics. To many humble rural people, this quality is inherent in the clerical role, an automatic derivative of class interests and alliances. The image of the greedy priest amounts to a popular protest against privilege. Although priests portray Christianity as the enemy of privilege, church policies and clerical alliances have often redounded to the benefit of the elite. It is this kind of discrepancy between religious ideals and worldly behavior that heightens popular animosity toward church and clergy. It reinforces the dual stereotypes of greed and hypocrisy.

The third clerical stereotype, illicit sexuality, also emerges in our authors' discussions of rural Brittany, Portugal, and Spain. Behar and Brettell, speaking respectively about Spain and Portugal, emphasize what to my mind is a quintessentially Iberian notion: the radical equality of mankind. In rural Andalusia and Castile, where I carried out fieldwork, there prevails a noteworthy insistence on the existential similarity among all people, despite obvious signs of socioeconomic stratification. All people have to die, it is said. (An important Spanish literary theme, according to Brodman [1976:28], is the "democratizing force of death.") And nobody, including priests, is immune from sexual drives. Even celibate priests may be suspect. People claim that priests relish parishioners' confessions for their prurient value and that they derive vicarious pleasure from listening to detailed erotica. In thoughts as well as action priests are therefore just like all men. Their error is not inescapable conformity to the human condition but, again, hypocrisy, pretending to be above other humans in sexual drives and involvements. If we accept Badone's reasonable interpretation that sexual stereotypes of the clergy are symbolic commentaries on priestly power, we may perceive a further correspondence between the images of sexuality and greed. With powerful, privileged personae like priests, society can exert almost no sanctions against the illicit pursuit of material gain and libidinal gratification.

All these clerical stereotypes in one way or another speak to the overriding issue of control—both societal control over powerholders and the control that powerholders may be expected to exercise over themselves. Taylor's discussion of the metaphoric significances of the drunken priest shows how this theme emerges even in a society like Ireland, in which clerics are highly esteemed. In the Irish narratives drunken priests—who are regularly portrayed as occupying a subordinate rank within the church hierarchy—are able to produce miraculous cures. These tales, which claim that drunken priests break away from and rise above church authority in order to perform good deeds, are actually commentaries on lay society; we may speculate, with Taylor, that they provide vicarious, temporary release from social and affective constraints normally binding both narrators and audience. It is important to recognize, however, that release comes through the relatively safe channel of storytelling. The storytelling context, we might say, provides the very boundaries that contain the extraordinary, unpredictable powers invoked through the tales.

There is a parallel between this phenomenon and Dubisch's sensitive interpretation of the Greek pilgrimage to the shrine of the *Panayía* on the island of Tinos. Although the pilgrims themselves act in unpredictable and unorthodox fashion in order (like the drunken priests) to effect miraculous cures, they are constrained by the pilgrimage occasion itself. Dubisch interprets "major official events such as the festival of the Dormition as ways of counteracting this antistructure, as occasions in which official religion seeks to contain and control the massive and individualized religious behavior of the thousands of pilgrims who have descended upon the island at this time." The pilgrimage, in this regard, is analogous to the Irish storytelling session, the major difference being that in the Greek case the structure is presumably imposed by outside powerholders (the Greek Orthodox church), while the Irish impose the limiting social framework (the storytelling session) upon themselves.

The papers in this volume hint at a possible geographic continuum in Roman Catholic attitudes toward the clergy. In the north—Ireland—there exists a basically positive, almost adulatory view of priests. To the south—Portugal and Spain—the opposite pole, hard-core anticlericalism, manifests itself. Brittany, situated as it is midway between Ireland and Iberia, seems to harbor a mixture of positive and negative attitudes toward the clergy. In the stories that Badone's informants related to her, priests certainly appear unlike ordinary men in that they have access to miraculous power. Unlike the Irish priests, however, who heal the sick, in these Breton narratives priests use their power primarily to punish those who transgress church norms. Hence, in the Monts d'Arrée region of Brittany priests are not adulated. For the most part they are feared, although occasionally, as in Ireland, clerics are credited with the ability to perform supernatural cures. As Badone notes, the clergy are viewed favorably in certain regions of Brittany. However, in the Monts d'Arrée, tales of clerical sorcery are just one expression of a more general anticlericalism, which is a social posture that *rouges* Bretons share with their Mediterranean neighbors.

RECOGNIZING INTRACULTURAL VARIATION

The attitudes toward the clergy represented in this volume raise questions regarding possible connections between observers and the observed. For one thing, it is evident that our authors omit discussing popular attitudes toward female clerics. It may indeed be the case that folk beliefs dwell more on male than female clergy; nonetheless, if my own field experience in eastern Andalusia is at all representative, Catholics express quite definite feelings about nuns. Indeed, many people have relatives who are nuns and formulate opinions about them. In my experience most Spaniards express more positive feelings toward nuns than priests. This attitude is probably related to ideas about female sexuality—celibacy being more acceptable for women than men—and to the relatively low position of nuns in the church hierarchy, hence their inability to wield destructive power. Nuns may also seem less threatening than priests simply because they are women, hence perceived as relatively innocuous, at least in the public arena. In any event, our collective focus as anthropologists on male clergy says as much about our own selective observations, influenced by our own culturally determined research priorities, as it does about the societies under investigation.

By paying closer attention to narratives and other statements about nuns, a softer anticlerical picture might well emerge in the southern countries than the one here presented. Information from a wide range of informants must inevitably reveal a diversity of feelings, both positive and negative, about male and female clergy. These feelings can then be discussed in the context of not only the history and culture of the region in question but also the specific circumstances of each individual's life, including age cohort, gender identity, marital status, ethnic affiliation, and the like. This effort should yield a much rounder portrait of religious attitudes than we have hitherto produced.

By raising the issue of intracultural variation I do not mean to suggest that this theme has been entirely ignored in this volume (or, for that matter, elsewhere [for example, Bax 1983, 1985b]). Badone, for example, touches on regional differentiation both within Brittany and between Brittany and the rest of France, and Dubisch argues that Greek Orthodox rituals, like pilgrimages, may disguise highly diverse motives for individual participation. But Taylor is the only author here actually to take substantive account of different types of clergy, namely parish priests and curates, and to incorporate this differentiation into his analysis. In our authors' field accounts we find consistent attention to class and gender differences among the lay populace. Both these phenomena are certainly intrinsic to any consideration of European religion. But, as evidenced in part by the absence of attention to female clergy, we have generally ignored clerical variation and church administration.

This blind spot is understandable if not entirely justifiable. If our mandate is, as Malinowski put it (1922:25), to see the world through the eyes of our informants, and if our informants are the rural laity rather than the clergy, then to portray the priests, the clergy, or the church as undifferentiated entities may very well reflect native categories. In fact, my own experiences in village Castile and Andalusia, together with informant quotations from Behar, indicate that this way of thinking is common in Spain, as it may well be elsewhere in Europe. Nonetheless, it has become necessary to reach beyond lay categories and carry the anthropological study of religion to the European clergy as such. This means transforming priests, nuns, and the church hierarchy and administration themselves into subjects of investigation; Judith Shapiro (1981), among others, has been successful in doing just that in lowland South America, and I expect that with some limitations the task could be accomplished in Europe as well. This endeavor would be analogous to the medical anthropological study of hospitals and the health service establishment. Just as no medical anthropologist could hope to understand primary medical care without examining both doctors and patients, so we should begin to understand European religion by analyzing the attitudes and actions of particular clergy in the specific social arenas that they share with parishioners.

FAITH AS AN OBJECT OF ANTHROPOLOGICAL RESEARCH

In addition to focussing on the clergy as objects of study we need to refine our understanding of popular belief systems. This is part of an agenda that Susan Tax Freeman proposed for hispanic research about a decade ago. Since several of our authors invoke her ideas, she is worth quoting directly (Freeman 1978:120):

> Belief as well as observance is crucial to any definition of religion, and belief, or faith, may be relatively constant even though it is only sporadically ex-

pressed in officially sanctioned collective action. Spain has, over the centuries, been christianized . . . to the extent that officially sanctioned collective ritual in sacred space has virtually no unofficial rivals—no major pagan rites, no reformed churches. The real rival is the insistence that faith may be expressed through communication with the divine outside of the collective context as well as within it. This includes much of what goes on at shrines, apart from the periodic collective festivals at them, and also what goes on within the person, as a believer, privately. . . . Secularization is hardly at issue; what must be recognized in many cases is, rather, a withdrawal of willingness to recognize the Church as an acceptable arena for the exercise of faith, at least at a given moment.

Freeman laments the tendency to allow the church implicitly to make the anthropological decision of what is or is not religion. "The weight of the great traditions may have deterred the study of popular belief systems in Europe," she claims (1978:122), so that the anthropologist's job is to look beyond formal to more private forms of religious expression.

In another important and more recent policy statement on the study of Christianity Talal Asad reaffirms Freeman's assertion that religious studies should include a consideration of beliefs as well as ceremonial behavior. "[W]e must examine not only the ritual itself," he says (1983:249), "but the entire range of disciplinary activities, of instrumental forms of knowledge and practice, within which selves are formed, and the possibilities of 'attaining to faith' are marked out." Indeed, anthropologists of European religion have been remiss in the study of faith as such. Most of the essays in this volume happily go a long way toward rectifying the imbalance of emphasis. Several of them (for example, Badone, Behar, and Brettell) illustrate the insight, proposed by Riegelhaupt (1984), that even anticlericalism displays elements of religiosity. After all, if we ignore anticlericalism and private faith as objects of study, then we are likely to dismiss many southern European men as completely irreligious simply because they refuse to participate in the sacraments or attend church-sponsored events.

As important to anthropological study as private religious beliefs may be, investigators should try to distinguish between idiosyncratic beliefs and those that are shared and transmitted. In Andalusia I had a friend who never would step inside a church but who nonetheless claimed to believe in God. To justify this posture, he stated, "If they charged a quarter (*cinco duros*) a day to believe in God, I probably wouldn't, but since it's free, I might as well believe." Yet another nonchurchgoing man stated flatly, "I don't believe in God, but I do believe in the Señor del Consuelo [the principal miraculous image in town]." Here is evidence of two private religious beliefs. Whether they form part of a larger popular religious ideology, or even represent two competing ideologies, could only be determined by further investigation.

In the study of faith, anthropologists also should be attentive to evidence for the absence of faith. Freeman's enthusiastic call for the study of private religious beliefs leads her to deemphasize secularization as an object of investigation: "Secularization is hardly at issue," she states (1978:120); "what must be recognized in many cases is, rather, a withdrawal of willingness to recognize the Church as an acceptable arena for the exercise of faith, at least at a given moment." True, Spaniards and other Catholics have always harbored religious beliefs that depart from official dogma and engaged in sacred rituals that are independent of the clergy. Nonetheless, when rural people persistently claim, as those in the small Castilian village of Becedas did to me in the early 1970s, that "they themselves—the priests—are taking religion away from us," we should respect the people's own recognition of the secularization process. Behar's analysis of the impact of the Second Vatican Council on the religious atmosphere in Spain is relevant here: "Since religion has become contestable, since one can say yes or no, many in Spain today, especially the young, are saying no to religion and declaring it irrelevant to their lives. . . ." Similarly, the marketplace of religious ideas to which Behar alludes has produced in many older Spaniards a cynicism that we can easily read as a kind of secularism. Much as we anthropologists of religion may appreciate religion, let us allow rural European villagers the option to let go of it. The loss of faith should interest us as much as the adoption or transformation of faith.[2]

We should also build into our analyses a recognition that when dealing with Roman Catholicism and Eastern Orthodoxy the religious power structure has always exerted a tremendous influence not only on public but also on private manifestations of faith. These power structures have undoubtedly even molded popular definitions of religion. Speaking of early Christianity, Asad states (1983:243): "It was not the mind that moved spontaneously to religious truths, but power that imposed the conditions for experiencing that truth. Particular discourses and practices were to be systematically excluded, forbidden, denounced—made as much as possible unthinkable; others were to be included, allowed, praised, and even drawn into the narrative of sacred truth." This is a process, I would contend, that persisted and became more acute through time, particularly in Spain and other countries in which religious power-holders long enjoyed special treatment in the economic, educational, and political domains. In the Catholic and Orthodox worlds, if not in Protestant Europe, there is good reason to emphasize the study of public rather than private faith; for private faith is something cultivated in Protestantism but suppressed—often with brutal success—in traditional Catholicism.

Private faith among Catholics is likely either to derive from or be a reaction to established religious teachings; the establishment, in other words, sets the religious agenda and is directly relevant to private belief systems. Hence, I agree with Talal Asad (1983:252) that in the anthropological study of European religion—both public and private—we should ask: "How does power create religion?" As he says, "To ask this question is to seek an answer in terms of the social disciplines and social forces which come together at particular historical moments, to make particular religious discourses, practices and spaces possible. What requires systematic investigation therefore are the ways in which, in each society, social disciplines produce and authorise knowledges, the ways in which knowledges are accumulated and distributed."

Although they do not specifically invoke Asad's theoretical framework, a number of the authors in this volume in fact follow his program. Certainly in their historical contextualization of popular religious beliefs Behar, Badone, and Taylor all demonstrate the relation between national political and religious power structures, on the one hand, and local belief systems, on the other. Jane Schneider does the same, only with respect to much larger-scale historical processes than the others discuss. In this respect she perhaps comes closest—at least in terms of intellectual scope—to the kind of endeavor that Asad advocates and that any complete study of European religion must include.

Conclusion

In summary I wish briefly to comment on just two of the important topical themes that this volume addresses: first, religion and the problem of order and, second, religion and change.

In anthropological discourse religion has long been perceived as both perpetuating and reflecting social processes of order and control. The authors of this volume show how these processes are played out with specific respect to local varieties of Roman Catholicism and Eastern Orthodoxy.

Social order and control are portrayed here, first, as consequences of self-interested clerical and church policies. Throughout southern Europe the church and clergy have allied themselves during critical historical moments with one social class or national group over another. As perceived by the Breton, Spanish, Portuguese, and other informants cited in this book, economic and political elites have been the great beneficiaries of these alliances; the church has thereby earned the reputation of being a powerful, conservative supporter of existing social hierarchies.

A second aspect of order prominently represented here involves religion as a safety valve. For example, in Ireland, according to Taylor, innocuous but effective release comes not through ritual but through storytelling. Narration permits what I have elsewhere called "peaceful protest" (Brandes 1977), thereby stifling potentially more serious social rebelliousness. Gossip, rather than storytelling or ritual, is the form of deflected protest that Brettell discusses for northern Portugal. And, finally, Dubisch provides an example of how religious ritual in Greece allows individuals temporarily to relax their normal corporal and emotional defenses in a process which then allows these constraints successfully to reassert themselves. She suggests that festivals such as the one she studied are "ways of counteracting this antistructure" and means "to contain and control . . . individualized religious behavior."

This book's treatment of order and control, then, extends to relationships between religion and the individual as well as between religion and society. Our authors portray the popular classes in Europe, past and present, as both dominated by the orthodox religious hierarchy and engaging in symbolic rebellion against that hierarchy. The people of rural Europe, who are the principal subjects of this volume, are pictured as both collapsing under the weight of religious reform and struggling against that reform. They are above all a religiously creative people, forging their own brands of Roman Catholicism and Eastern Orthodoxy, yet always remaining within the confines of the overarching sacred tradition into which they were born and raised.

A second major theme in this book is religious change. Several of our authors—Badone on Brittany and Taylor on Ireland, for example—discuss change implicitly within the broader context of the relationship between national political and religious power structures, on the one hand, and local rituals and beliefs, on the other. It is in the Spanish and Portuguese material, however, that a focussed concern with local-level change is most evident in this volume. One of Behar's main concerns is the impact of Vatican II reforms on the belief systems of her northern Spanish informants. When she states (accurately, I believe) that "Vatican II is still symbolic of the church's power to create religion, . . . to change the meaning of religion," she has defined a major issue for the anthropology of sacred symbolism in contemporary Europe. Many of the reactions of villagers in Santa María to Vatican II—including anger, disenchantment, confusion, even loss of faith—echo what I observed nearly twenty years ago in Becedas, another northern Spanish village (Brandes 1976). For most people in this part of Iberia religion expresses eternal verities; abruptly to change longstanding religious premises and ritual requirements is inevitably to evoke skepticism and, for many, a feeling that formal, official religion is either irrelevant or wrong.

As for Portugal, a concern with change emerges in the discussion of power struggles between priests and parishioners. The Portuguese-Canadian priest whom Brettell interviewed would have liked to suspend the feast of the Holy Ghost in his parish but realized that his opposition to the people's will was futile, even contrary to interests of the church. The Catholic church, for all its bureaucratic immensity and political strength, has always had to make this sort of accommodation to popular Christian beliefs.

Such accommodation, however, is nothing when compared with the sweeping religious and economic changes that Schneider discusses in her chapter. In fact, of all the authors, she alone makes change her primary subject of investigation and does so, as I believe Asad would have it, in a political economy framework. Where she departs significantly from Asad is in causal analysis. Asad sees religious ideology as deriving from (in his words) social disciplines and social forces, while Schneider tries to demonstrate how a change in religious ideology—namely the ascendency of the concept of "brotherly love"—produced ideological conditions compatible with the rise of capitalism. For Schneider it seems that religious change arises simultaneously and in interaction with economic change. Precapitalist societies, as Schneider following Collier and Rosaldo (1981) envisions them, were dominated by animistic thinking in which social relationships among people, as well as between people and spirits, were designed "to achieve not dominance but parity." Schneider suggests that in such societies inequities are a potential source of violence, so that "it is important to mask them, be generous with goods," and to "avoid the provocation of undue assertion."

Schneider's rendition of these societies is reminiscent of George Foster's description of contemporary peasant communities governed by what he calls the "Image of Limited Good" (Foster 1967b). Like Foster's peasants, Schneider's precapitalists are people whose social rules tend more toward anarchy than toward the sacred solidarity that romantics would have us construct. Within such societies the quest for social and economic equality, manifested in the application of religious and social sanctions against people who become too financially successful, impedes capitalist development. According to Schneider, by substituting the abstract value of brotherly love for the ideal of actual material reciprocity, salvationist Christianity was responsible for freeing individuals to act in a more frankly selfish way—a prerequisite of capitalism. Schneider's analysis, like Max Weber's earlier this century, tries to demonstrate that religious values are not merely derivative of material circumstances but can effectively influence large-scale economic processes through interaction with them.

Even cursory familiarity with Spain, France, Portugal, Greece, and Ireland—the main countries represented here—is sufficient to show the relevance of religion to everyday life. These are peoples for whom place names and personal names operate as constant reminders of the sacred domain. Their landscapes, replete with shrines and churches; their calendar, punctuated by saints' days and periods of special religious observance; and their political leaders and parties, often identified by formal religious affiliation—all of these pervasive phenomena impart to religion, if not greater significance than it has in the United States, certainly a different significance. For the general Roman Catholic and Eastern Orthodox populace in Europe religion and the clergy are an absolutely primary point of departure, an inescapable frame of reference. The main contribution of this volume is to recognize in anthropological terms how and why that is the case.

Notes to Chapter 8

1. Among their works see Davis (1975a, 1975b, 1975c), Ginzburg (1980, 1983), and Le Roy Ladurie (1979).

2. However, it is also important to note that religious change can proceed in different directions depending upon the social and cultural context. In Malta, for example, Boissevain (1984) notes that in contrast to his earlier predictions, popular ritual underwent an "escalation" rather than a decline between the early 1960s and the late 1970s. He concludes that the increased importance of popular religious celebrations corresponds to the need in Malta for ongoing foci of local identity in a situation of rapid social change.

References Cited

Almeida, João Ferreira de
1986 Classes sociais nos campos: camponeses parciais numa região do noroeste. Lisbon: Instituto de Ciências Sociais.
Anderson, Bonnie S., and Judith P. Zinsser
1988 A History of Their Own: Women in Europe. Volume I: From Prehistory to the Present. New York: Harper and Row.
Anderson, Robert
1970 The Conflict in Education. Catholic Secondary Schools (1850–1870): A Reappraisal. *In* Conflicts in French Society: Anticlericalism, Education, and Morals in the Nineteenth Century. Theodore Zeldin, ed. Pp. 51–93. London: George Allen and Unwin.
Angel, Juan
1985 Domund 85: tiempo para una iglesia joven. Boletín oficial del Obispado de León 132:267–271.
1987 Arciprestazgo y evangelización: propuestas para seguir en al camino. Suplemento oficial del Obispado de León, marzo 1987:27–33.
Appel, Willa
1982 Idioms of Power in Southern Italy. Dialectical Anthropology 7:74–80.
Arensberg, Conrad M.
[1937] 1959 The Irish Countryman: An Anthropological Study. Gloucester, Mass.: Peter Smith.
Ariès, Philippe
1982 The Hour of Our Death. Translated by Helen Weaver. New York: Random House.
Asad, Talal
1983 Anthropological Conceptions of Religion: Reflections on Geertz. Man 18:237–259.
Badone, Ellen
1989 The Appointed Hour: Death, Worldview, and Social Change in Brittany. Berkeley: University of California Press.
Bax, Mart
1983 "Us" Catholics and "Them" Catholics in Dutch Brabant: The Dialectics of a Religious Factional Process. Anthropological Quarterly 56:167–178.
1985a Religious Infighting and the Formation of a Dominant Catholic Regime in Southern Dutch Society. Social Compass 32:57–72.
1985b Popular Devotions, Power, and Religious Regimes in Catholic Dutch Brabant. Ethnology 24:215–227.
1987 Religious Regimes and State Formation: Towards a Research Perspective. Anthropological Quarterly 60:1–12.
1988 Return to Mission Status? Religious Reality and Priestly Perception in Catholic Dutch Brabant. Ethnologia Europaea 18:73–79.

Behar, Ruth
    1986 Santa María del Monte: The Presence of the Past in a Spanish Village.
    Princeton, N.J.: Princeton University Press.
Beidelman, T. O.
    1986 Moral Imagination in Kaguru Modes of Thought. Bloomington: Indiana
    University Press.
Bellah, Robert N.
    1964 Religious Evolution. American Sociological Review 29:358–374.
Bent, James Theodore
    [1884] 1965 Aegean Islands: The Cyclades, or Life Among the Insular Greeks.
    Chicago: Argonaut.
Benz, Ernst
    1963 The Eastern Orthodox Church: Its Life and Thought. New York: Double-
    day Anchor Books.
Bernstein, Richard
    1987 A French Parish Takes to Barricades. New York Times, April 26, p. 3.
Blum, Richard, and Eva Blum
    1970 The Dangerous Hour: The Lore of Crisis and Mystery in Rural Greece.
    New York: Charles Scribner's Sons.
Boff, Leonardo
    1985 Church, Charism, and Power: Liberation Theology and the Institutional
    Church. London: SCM Press.
Boissevain, Jeremy
    1965 Saints and Fireworks: Religion and Politics in Rural Malta. London: The
    Athlone Press.
    1977 When the Saints Go Marching Out: Reflections on the Decline of Patron-
    age in Malta. In Patrons and Clients in Mediterranean Societies. E. Gellner
    and J. Waterbury, eds. Pp. 81–96. London: Duckworth.
    1984 Ritual Escalation in Malta. In Religion, Power, and Protest in Local Com-
    munities: The Northern Shore of the Mediterranean. Eric R. Wolf, ed. Pp.
    163–183. Berlin: Mouton.
Borker, Ruth
    1978 'To Honor Her Head': Hats as a Symbol of Women's Position in Three
    Evangelical Churches in Edinburgh, Scotland. In Women in Ritual and
    Symbolic Roles. J. Hoch-Smith and A. Spring, eds. Pp. 55–73. New York:
    Plenum Press.
    1986 'Moved by the Spirit': Constructive Meaning in a Brethren Breaking of
    Bread Service. Text 6:317–337.
Bossy, John
    1970 The Counter-Reformation and the People of Catholic Europe. Past and
    Present 47:51–70.
    1973 Blood and Baptism: Kinship, Community, and Christianity in Western
    Europe from the Fourteenth to the Seventeenth Centuries. Studies in
    Church History 10:129–143.
    1983 The Mass as a Social Institution, 1200–1700. Past and Present 100:29–62.
    1985 Christianity in the West, 1400–1700. Oxford: Oxford University Press.

Bourdieu, Pierre
1977 Outline of a Theory of Practice. Cambridge: Cambridge University Press.
Braga, A. Vieira
1943 Curiosidades de Guimarães, cercos e clamores. Braga: Oficinas Gráficas Pax.
Brandes, Stanley H.
1975 Migration, Kinship, and Community: Tradition and Transition in a Spanish Village. New York: Academic Press.
1976 The Priest as Agent of Secularization in Rural Spain. In Economic Transformations and Steady-State Values: Essays in the Ethnography of Spain. J. B. Aceves, E. C. Hansen, and G. Levitas, eds. Pp. 22–29. Flushing, N.Y.: Queen's College Press.
1977 Peaceful Protest: Spanish Political Humor in a Time of Crisis. Western Folklore 36:331–346.
1980 Metaphors of Masculinity. Philadelphia: University of Pennsylvania Press.
Brettell, Caroline B.
1983 Emigração, a igreja e a festa religiosa do norte de Portugal: estudo de um caso. Estudos contemporâneos 5:175–204.
Brodman, Barbara L. C.
1976 The Mexican Cult of Death in Myth and Literature. Gainesville: University Presses of Florida.
Brögger, Jan
1986 Belief and Experience among the Sidamo: A Case Study towards an Anthropology of Knowledge. London: Norwegian University Press.
Brooke, Rosalind, and Christopher Brooke
1984 Popular Religion in the Middle Ages: Western Europe, 1000–1300. London: Thames and Hudson.
Brown, Peter
1981 The Cult of the Saints: Its Rise and Function in Latin Christianity. Chicago: University of Chicago Press.
Burke, Peter
1978 Popular Culture in Early Modern Europe. London: Temple Smith.
Campbell, John
1964 Honour, Family, and Patronage: A Study of Institutions and Moral Values in a Greek Mountain Community. Oxford: Clarendon Press.
1966 Honour and the Devil. In Honour and Shame: The Values of Mediterranean Society. J. G. Peristiany, ed. Pp. 139–170. Chicago: University of Chicago Press.
———, and Philip Sherrard
1968 Modern Greece. London: Ernest Benn.
Cancian, Frank
1965 Economics and Prestige in a Maya Community: The Religious Cargo System in Zinacantan. Stanford, Calif.: Stanford University Press.
Caraveli, Anna
1986 The Bitter Wounding: The Lament as Social Protest in Rural Greece. In

Gender and Power in Rural Greece. Jill Dubisch, ed. Pp. 169–194. Princeton, N.J.: Princeton University Press.

Carlen, Claudia, ed.
1981 The Papal Encyclicals, 1878–1903. Raleigh: McGrath Publishing Company.

Carr, Raymond, and Juan Pablo Fusi Aizpurua
1979 Spain: Dictatorship to Democracy. London: George Allen and Unwin.

Cases, Cesare
1973 Introduzione. In Il mondo magico: Prolegomeni a una storia del magismo. Ernesto de Martino. Pp. vii–xlviii. Torino: Editore Boringhieri.

Centro de Investigaciones Sociológicas
1984 Iglesia, religión, y política. Revista Española de investigaciones sociológicas 27:295–328.

Chadwick, Nora K.
1969 Early Brittany. Cardiff: University of Wales Press.

Chaussy, M., R. Emeillat, and G. Messager
1976 Monographie communale: La Feuillée. Angers: Ecole supérieure d'agriculture.

Christian, William A., Jr.
1972 Person and God in a Spanish Valley. New York: Seminar Press.
1981a Local Religion in Sixteenth-Century Spain. Princeton, N.J.: Princeton University Press.
1981b Apparitions in Late Medieval and Renaissance Spain. Princeton, N.J.: Princeton University Press.
1984 Religious Apparitions and the Cold War in Southern Europe. In Religion, Power, and Protest in Local Communities: The Northern Shore of the Mediterranean. Eric R. Wolf, ed. Pp. 239–266. Berlin: Mouton.
1987a Tapping and Defining New Power: The First Month of Visions at Ezquioga, July 1931. American Ethnologist 14:140–167.
1987b Folk Religion: An Overview. In The Encyclopedia of Religion. Mircea Eliade, ed. Vol. 5, pp. 270–274. New York: Macmillan.

Christiansen, Reidar Thorwald
1964 Introduction. In Folktales of Norway. Reidar Christiansen, ed. Pp. v–xlv. Translated by Shaw Iversen. Chicago: University of Chicago Press.

Clark, David
1982 Between Pulpit and Pew: Folk Religion in a North Yorkshire Fishing Village. Cambridge: Cambridge University Press.

Cohn, Norman
1961 The Pursuit of the Millennium: Revolutionary Messianism in Medieval and Reformation Europe and its Bearing on Modern Totalitarian Movements. 2d ed. New York: Harper Torchbooks.
1975 Europe's Inner Demons: An Inquiry Inspired by the Great Witch-Hunt. London: Sussex University Press.

Collier, Jane F., and Michelle Z. Rosaldo
1981 Politics and Gender in Simple Societies. In Sexual Meanings: The Cul-

tural Construction of Gender and Sexuality. Sherry B. Ortner and Harriet Whitehead, eds. Pp. 275–329. Cambridge: Cambridge University Press.

Congreso de Evangelización y Hombre de Hoy
1985 Documento final del Congreso. Boletin oficial del Obispado de León 132:300–310.

Connolly, Sean
1982 Priest and People in Pre-Famine Ireland. Dublin: Gill and Macmillan.

Croix, Alain
1981 La Bretagne aux 16e et 17e siècles: La vie, la mort, la foi. Paris: Maloine.

Croix, Alain, and Fanch Roudaut
1984 Les bretons, la mort et Dieu: De 1600 à nos jours. Paris: Messidor-Temps Actuels.

Cucchiari, Salvatore
1985 Sicilian Pentecostalism: An Interpretive Study in Cultural Discontinuity. (Dissertation, University of Michigan, Ann Arbor.) Ann Arbor: University Microfilms.

1987 Between Sanctification and Shame: Patriarchy and its Transformations in Sicilian Pentecostalism. Paper presented at the Annual Meeting of the American Anthropological Association, Chicago, November 18–22, 1987.

1988 "Adapted for Heaven": Culture and Conversion in Western Sicily. American Ethnologist 15:417–441.

Cutileiro, José
1971 A Portuguese Rural Society. Oxford: Clarendon Press.

Danforth, Loring, and Alexander Tsiaras
1982 The Death Rituals of Rural Greece. Princeton, N.J.: Princeton University Press.

Dansette, Adrien
1961 Religious History of Modern France. Vol. 2. New York: Herder and Herder.

Davis, Natalie Zemon
1974 Some Tasks and Themes in the Study of Popular Religion. In The Pursuit of Holiness in Late Medieval and Renaissance Religion. Charles Trinkaus and H. A. Oberman, eds. Pp. 307–336. Leiden: E. J. Brill.

1975a Strikes and Salvation at Lyon. In Society and Culture in Early Modern France: Eight Essays by Natalie Zemon Davis. Pp. 1–16. Stanford, Calif.: Stanford University Press.

1975b City Women and Religious Change. In Society and Culture in Early Modern France: Eight Essays by Natalie Zemon Davis. Pp. 65–95. Stanford, Calif.: Stanford University Press.

1975c The Rites of Violence. In Society and Culture in Early Modern France: Eight Essays by Natalie Zemon Davis. Pp. 152–187. Stanford, Calif.: Stanford University Press.

1977 Ghosts, Kin, and Progeny: Some Features of Family Life in Early Modern France. Daedalus 106(2):87–114.

1981 The Sacred and the Body Social in Sixteenth-Century Lyon. Past and Present 90:40–70.

1982 From "Popular Religion" to Religious Cultures. *In* Reformation Europe: A Guide to Research. Steven Ozment, ed. Pp. 321–341. St. Louis: Center for Reformation Research.

Delaruelle, Etienne
1975 La piété populaire au moyen âge. Turin: Bottega d'Erasmo.

Delumeau, Jean
1977 Catholicism between Luther and Voltaire: A New View of the Counter-Reformation. Translated by Jeremy Moiser. Philadelphia: Westminster Press.
1983 Le péché et la peur. La culpabilisation en Occident (XIIIe–XVIIIe siècles). Paris: Fayard.

Deng, Francis Mading
1972 The Dinka of the Sudan. New York: Holt, Rinehart and Winston.

De Rosa, Gabriele
1977 Religione e religiositá popolare. Ricerche de storia sociale e religiosa 11:177–192.

Devlin, Judith
1987 The Superstitious Mind: French Peasants and the Supernatural in the Nineteenth Century. New Haven, Conn.: Yale University Press.

Dias, Jorge
1961 Os elementos fundamentais da cultura Portuguesa. *In* Ensaios etnológicos, by Jorge Dias. Lisboa: Estudos de ciências políticas e sociais 52:97–120.
[1953] 1981 Rio de Onor: Comunitarismo agro-pastoril. Lisbon: Editorial Presença.

Di Tota, Mia
1981 Saint Cults and Political Alignments in Southern Italy. Dialectical Anthropology 5:317–329.

Douglas, Mary
1966 Purity and Danger. New York: Praeger.

Douglass, William A.
1969 Death in Murelaga: Funerary Ritual in a Spanish Basque Village. Seattle: University of Washington Press.

Driessen, Henk
1984 Religious Brotherhoods: Class and Politics in an Andalusian Town. *In* Religion, Power, and Protest in Local Communities: The Northern Shore of the Mediterranean. Eric R. Wolf, ed. Pp. 73–91. Berlin: Mouton.

Dubisch, Jill
1983 Greek Women: Sacred or Profane? Journal of Modern Greek Studies 1:185–202.
1986 Culture Enters through the Kitchen: Women, Food, and Social Boundaries in Rural Greece. *In* Gender and Power in Rural Greece. Jill Dubisch, ed. Pp. 195–214. Princeton, N.J.: Princeton University Press.
1987 What Mother is Crying? Suffering and the "Poetics of Womanhood" in Greece. Paper presented at the Spring Meeting of the American Ethnological Society, San Antonio, Texas, May 1987.
1988 Golden Oranges and Silver Ships: An Interpretive Approach to a Greek Holy Shrine. Journal of Modern Greek Studies 6:117–134.

du Boulay, Juliet
  1974 Portrait of a Greek Mountain Village. Oxford: Clarendon Press.
  1976 Lies, Mockery, and Family Integrity. In Mediterranean Family Struc-
    tures. J. G. Peristiany, ed. Pp. 389–406. Cambridge: Cambridge University
    Press.
  1982 The Greek Vampire: A Study of Cyclic Symbolism in Marriage and
    Death. Man 17:219–238.
  1984 The Blood: Symbolic Relationships between Descent, Marriage, Incest
    Prohibitions, and Spiritual Kinship in Greece. Man 19:533–556.
  1986 Women—Images of Their Nature and Destiny in Rural Greece. In Gen-
    der and Power in Rural Greece. Jill Dubisch, ed. Pp. 139–168. Princeton,
    N.J.: Princeton University Press.
Durkheim, Emile
  [1915] 1965 The Elementary Forms of the Religious Life. Translated by Joseph
    Ward Swain. New York: The Free Press.
Eliade, Mircea
  1964 Shamanism: Archaic Techniques of Ecstasy. New York: Pantheon.
Elias, Norbert
  1978, 1982 The Civilizing Process. 2 vols. Oxford: Basil Blackwell.
Elliott, John H.
  1963 Imperial Spain, 1469–1716. New York: Penguin.
Evans, E. Estyn
  1957 Irish Folk Ways. New York: Devin-Adair.
Favret-Saada, Jeanne
  1980 Deadly Words: Witchcraft in the Bocage. Translated by Catherine Cul-
    len. Cambridge: Cambridge University Press.
Fernandez, James W.
  1986 Persuasions and Performances: The Play of Tropes in Culture. Blooming-
    ton: Indiana University Press.
Firth, Raymond
  1963 Offering and Sacrifice: Problems of Organization. Journal of the Royal
    Anthropological Institute 93:12–24.
Florakis, Alekos
  1982 Ship Ex-Votos and the Practice of Marine Offerings in the Aegean [In
    Greek.] Athens: Filipotti.
Fortes, Meyer
  1965 Some Reflections on Ancestor Worship in Africa. In African Systems of
    Thought. M. Fortes and G. Dieterlen, eds. Pp. 122–142. London: Oxford
    University Press.
Fortier, David H.
  1980 Brittany: "Breiz Atao." In Nations without a State: Ethnic Minorities in
    Western Europe. Charles R. Foster, ed. Pp. 136–152. New York: Praeger.
Foster, George M.
  1967a What is a Peasant? In Peasant Society: A Reader. Jack M. Potter, May
    N. Diaz, and George M. Foster, eds. Pp. 2–14. Boston: Little Brown.
  1967b Peasant Society and the Image of Limited Good. In Peasant Society: A
    Reader. Jack M. Potter, May N. Diaz, and George M. Foster, eds. Pp. 300–
    323. Boston: Little Brown.

Frazee, Charles

1969 The Orthodox Church and Independent Greece, 1821–1852. Cambridge: Cambridge University Press.

1977 Church and State in Greece. In Greece in Transition. J.T.A. Lomoulides, ed. Pp. 128–152. London: Zeno.

1979 The Greek Catholic Islanders and the Revolution of 1821. East European Quarterly 12:315–326.

Frazer, Sir James George

[1922] 1963 The Golden Bough. A Study in Magic and Religion. Vol. 1, abridged ed. New York: Macmillan.

Freeman, Susan Tax

1968 Religious Aspects of the Social Organization of a Castilian Village. American Anthropologist 70:34–49.

1970 Neighbors: The Social Contract in a Castilian Hamlet. Chicago: University of Chicago Press.

1978 Faith and Fashion in Spanish Religion: Notes on the Observance of Observance. Peasant Studies 7:101–123.

1987 Egalitarian Structures in Iberian Social Systems: The Contexts of Turn-Taking in Town and Country. American Ethnologist 14:470–490.

Gaines, Atwood D.

1985 Faith, Fashion, and Family: Religion, Aesthetics, Identity, and Social Organization in Strasbourg. Anthropological Quarterly 58:47–62.

Gallaghar, Tom

1987 The Catholic Church and the Estado Novo of Portugal. In Disciplines of Faith: Studies in Religion, Politics, and Patriarchy. Jim Obelkevich, Lyndal Roper, and Raphael Samuel, eds. Pp. 518–536. London: Routledge and Kegan Paul.

Gallini, Clara

1977 Introduzione. In La fine del mondo: Contributo all'analisi delle apocalissi culturali. Ernesto de Martino. Pp. ix–xciii. Torino: Giuliano Einaudi.

Geertz, Clifford

1960 The Religion of Java. London: The Free Press of Glencoe.

Geertz, Hildred

1975 An Anthropology of Religion and Magic, I. Journal of Interdisciplinary History 6:71–89.

Gilmore, David

1984 Andalusian Anti-Clericalism: An Eroticized Rural Protest. Anthropology 7:31–42.

Ginzburg, Carlo

1980 The Cheese and the Worms: The Cosmos of a Sixteenth-Century Miller. Translated by John and Anne Tedeschi. Baltimore: The Johns Hopkins University Press.

1983 The Night Battles: Witchcraft and Agrarian Cults in the Sixteenth and Seventeenth Centuries. Translated by John and Anne Tedeschi. London: Routledge and Kegan Paul.

1989 The Inquisitor as Anthropologist. In Clues, Myths, and the Historical

Method, by Carlo Ginzburg. Baltimore: The Johns Hopkins University Press.

Giovannini, Maureen J.
1981 Women: A Dominant Symbol within the Cultural System of a Sicilian Town. Man 16(3):408–426.

Glassie, Henry
1983 Passing the Time in Ballymenone. Philadelphia: University of Pennsylvania Press.

Golde, Gunter
1975 Catholics and Protestants—Agricultural Modernization in Two German Villages. New York: Academic Press.

Goldey, Patricia
1983 The Good Death: Personal Salvation and Community Identity. In Death in Portugal. Rui Feijó, Herminio Martins, and João de Pina-Cabral, eds. Pp. 1–16. Oxford: Journal of the Anthropological Society of Oxford Occasional Papers No. 2.

Goody, Jack
1968 Introduction. In Literacy in Traditional Societies. Jack Goody, ed. Pp. 1–26. Cambridge: Cambridge University Press.
1983 The Development of the Family and Marriage in Europe. Cambridge: Cambridge University Press.

Greenhouse, Steven
1988 Archbishop Defies Pope on Bishops. New York Times, July 1, pp. 1, 6.

Grelot, Pierre
1988 Mgr Marcel Lefebvre et la foi catholique. Etudes 368(1):93–107.

Gudeman, Stephen
1976 Saints, Symbols, and Ceremonies. American Ethnologist 3(4):709–730.

Guthrie, Stewart
1980 A Cognitive Theory of Religion. Current Anthropology 21:181–203.

Gutiérrez, Gustavo
1973 A Theology of Liberation: History, Politics, and Salvation. Translated and edited by Sister Caridad Inda and John Eagleson. Maryknoll, N.Y.: Orbis Books.

Hallowell, A. Irving
1960 Ojibwa Ontology: Behavior and World View. In Culture in History: Essays in Honor of Paul Radin. Stanley Diamond, ed. Pp. 19–53. Columbia University Press.

Harding, Susan
1988 Narrative Resistance: The Village Version of the Spanish Civil War. In Meanings and Memories. Pp. 24–32. Cambridge, Mass.: Harvard University, Center for European Studies, Working Paper Series, 1936–1986: From Civil War to Contemporary Spain.

Hauschild, Thomas
1982 Der Böse Blick: Ideengeschichtliche und Sozialpsychologische Untersuchungen. (Unpublished translation by Robert Weiner.) Berlin: Verlag Mensch und Leben.

Hélias, Pierre-Jakez
  1978 The Horse of Pride. New Haven, Conn.: Yale University Press.
Henningsen, Gustav
  1980 The Witch's Advocate: Basque Witchcraft and the Spanish Inquisition. Reno, Nev.: University of Nevada Press.
  1984 "The Ladies from Outside": Fairies, Witches, and Poverty in Early Modern Sicily. In Witchhunting in Early Modern Europe: Centers and Peripheries. Bengt Ankarloo and Gustav Henningsen, eds. Pp. 1–26. Stockholm: Proceedings from the Olin-Foundation Symposium.
Herr, Richard
  1974 An Historical Essay on Modern Spain. Berkeley: University of California Press.
Hertz, Robert
  1960 Death and the Right Hand. Glencoe, Ill.: The Free Press.
Herzfeld, Michael
  1982 Ours Once More: Folklore, Ideology, and the Making of Modern Greece. Austin: University of Texas Press.
  1985 The Poetics of Manhood: Contest and Identity in a Cretan Mountain Village. Princeton, N.J.: Princeton University Press.
  1986 Within and Without: The Category of "Female" in the Ethnography of Modern Greece. In Gender and Power in Rural Greece. Jill Dubisch, ed. Pp. 215–233. Princeton, N.J.: Princeton University Press.
  1987 Anthropology through the Looking-Glass: Critical Ethnography in the Margins of Europe. Cambridge: Cambridge University Press.
Heschel, Abraham J.
  [1962] 1975 The Prophets. Vol. 2. New York: Harper Torchbooks.
Hirschon, Renée
  1978 Open Body/Closed Space: The Transformation of Female Sexuality. In Defining Females. S. Ardener, ed. Pp. 66–88. New York: John Wiley and Sons.
  1983 Women, the Aged, and Religious Activity: Oppositions and Complementarity in an Urban Locality. Journal of Modern Greek Studies 1:113–130.
Hobart, Mark
  1985 Is God Evil? In The Anthropology of Evil. David Parkin, ed. Pp. 165–193. Oxford: Basil Blackwell.
Hoffman, Susannah
  1976 The Ethnography of the Islands: Thera. In Regional Variation in Modern Greece and Cyprus. M. Dimen and E. Friedl, eds. Annals of the New York Academy of Sciences 268:328–340.
Honko, Lauri
  1964 Memorates and the Study of Folk Beliefs. Journal of the Folklore Institute 1:5–19.
Horsley, Richard A.
  1979 Who Were the Witches? The Social Roles of the Accused in the European Witch Trials. Journal of Interdisciplinary History 9:689–717.

Horton, Robin
1960 A Definition of Religion and Its Uses. Journal of the Royal Anthropological Institute 90:201–225.
1962 The Kalabari World View: An Outline and Interpretation. Africa 32:197–219.
Hubert, Henri, and Marcel Mauss
[1898] 1964 Sacrifice: Its Nature and Functions. London: Cohen and West.
Hume David
[1757] 1956 The Natural History of Religion. Edited with an Introduction by H. E. Root. London: Adam and Charles Black.
Hurlbutt, Ralph
1985 The Phenomenology of Proskinitária. Master of Arts Project, Hamline University.
Idowu, E. Bolaji
1962 Olodumare: God in Yoruba Belief. London: Longmans.
Inglis, Tom
1987 Moral Monopoly: The Catholic Church in Modern Irish Society. Dublin: Gill and Macmillan.
Isambert, François A.
1972 France. In Western Religion: A Country by Country Sociological Inquiry. Hans Mol, ed. Pp. 175–187. The Hague: Mouton.
Jackson, Michael
1977 Sacrifice and Social Structure among the Kuranko. Africa 47:123–140.
Johnson, H. B., Jr.
1983 Portrait of a Portuguese Parish: Santa Maria de Alvarenga in 1719. Estudos de história de Portugal, vol. 2, Séculos XVI–XX. Pp.181–201. Lisbon: Editorial Estampa Limitada.
Jorion, P.
1982 The Priest and the Fishermen: Sundays and Weekdays in a Former 'Theocracy.' Man 17:275–286.
Keesing, Roger M.
1982 Kwaio Religion: The Living and the Dead in a Solomon Island Society. New York: Columbia University Press.
Kenna, Margaret
1977 Greek Urban Migrants and Their Rural Patron Saint. Ethnic Studies 1:14–23.
Kertzer, David I.
1974 Politics and Ritual: The Communist Festa in Italy. Anthropological Quarterly 47:374–389.
1980 Comrades and Christians: Religion and Political Struggles in Communist Italy. Cambridge: Cambridge University Press.
Kieckhefer, Richard
1976 European Witch Trials: Their Foundations in Popular and Learned Culture, 1300–1500. Berkeley: University of California Press.
1979 Repression of Heresy in Medieval Germany. Philadelphia: University of Pennsylvania Press.

Kilmartin, Edward
    1979 Toward Reunion: The Roman Catholic and Orthodox Churches. New York: Paulist Press.
Klaits, Joseph
    1985 Servants of Satan: The Age of the Witch Hunts. Bloomington: Indiana University Press.
Klaniczay, Gabor
    1983 Le culte des saints dans la Hongrie médiévale. (Problèmes de recherche.) Acta Historica Academiae Scientiarum Hungaricae 29:57–78.
    1984 Shamanistic Elements in Central European Witchcraft. In Shamanism in Eurasia. Mihaly Hoppal, ed. Pp. 404–422. Gottingen: Herodot.
    1987 Decline of Witches and Rise of Vampires in Eighteenth-Century Habsburg Monarchy. Ethnologia Europaea 17:165–180.
Kligman, Gail
    1988 The Wedding of the Dead: Ritual, Poetics, and Popular Culture in Transylvania. Berkeley: University of California Press.
Kokosalakis, Nikos
    1982 Ethnic Identity and Religion: Tradition and Change in Liverpool Jewry. Washington, D.C.: University Press of America.
    1987 The Political Significance of Popular Religion in Greece. Archives de sciences sociales des religions 64:37–52.
Kors, Alan C., and Edward Peters
    1972 Witchcraft in Europe, 1100–1700: A Documentary History. Alan C. Kors and Edward Peters, eds. Philadelphia: University of Pennsylvania Press.
Kramer, Heinrich, and Jacob Sprenger
    [1486] 1972 The Malleus Maleficarum. (Excerpts.) In Witchcraft in Europe, 1100–1700: A Documentary History. Alan C. Kors and Edward Peters, eds. Pp. 113–190. Philadelphia: University of Pennsylvania Press.
Kselman, Thomas
    1983 Miracles and Prophecies in Nineteenth-Century France. New Brunswick, N.J.: Rutgers University Press.
La Barre, Weston
    1969 They Shall Take Up Serpents: Psychology of the Southern Snake-Handling Cult. New York: Schocken Books.
Lambert, M. D.
    1977 Medieval Heresy: Popular Movements from Bogomil to Hus. London: Edward Arnold.
Lambert, Yves
    1985 Dieu change en Bretagne. Paris: Cerf.
Lanternari, Vittorio
    1982 La religion populaire: perspective historique et anthropologique. Archives de sciences sociales des religions 27:121–143.
Larkin, Emmett
    1972 The Devotional Revolution in Ireland. American Historical Review 77:625–652.

Larner, Christina
1981 Enemies of God: The Witch-Hunt in Scotland. Baltimore: The Johns
Hopkins University Press.
1984 Witchcraft and Religion: The Politics of Popular Belief. Oxford: Basil
Blackwell.
Latoche, John
1875 Travels in Portugal. London: Ward, Lock.
Le Bras, Gabriel
1955–1956 Etudes de sociologie religieuse. 2 vols. Paris: Presses Universitaires
de France.
1976 L'Eglise et le village. Paris: Flammarion.
Le Braz, Anatole
1928 La légende de la mort chez les bretons armoricains. 5th ed., 2 vols. Paris:
Honoré Champion.
Leff, Gordon
1967 Heresy in the Later Middle Ages: The Relation of Heterodoxy to Dissent,
c. 1250–c. 1450. New York: Barnes and Noble.
Le Gallo, Yves
1980 Prêtres et prélats du diocèse de Quimper, de la fin du 18e siècle à 1830.
(Thèse d'Etat, Université de Paris; available in library of the Centre de re-
cherche bretonne et celtique at the Université de Bretagne occidentale,
Brest.)
Le Goff, Jacques
1984 The Birth of Purgatory. Translated by Arthur Goldhammer. Chicago:
University of Chicago Press.
Le Guirriec, Patrick
1984 Parents, paysans, partisans. (Thèse de Troisème Cycle, Université de
Paris X, Nanterre.)
1986 Communisme local, Résistance, et PCF: Les trois éléments du pouvoir
dans une commune bretonne. Etudes rurales 101–102:219–230.
Le Men, R. F.
1870–1872 Traditions et superstitions de la Basse-Bretagne. Revue celtique
1:226–242, 414–435.
Le Roy Ladurie, Emmanuel
1979 Montaillou: The Promised Land of Error. Translated by Barbara Bray.
New York: Vintage Books.
Lincoln, Bruce
1985 Revolutionary Exhumations in Spain, July 1936. Comparative Studies in
Society and History 27:241–260.
Lisón-Tolosana, Carmelo
1979 Brujería, estructura social, y simbolismo en Galicia. Madrid: Akal Editor.
[1966] 1983 Belmonte de los Caballeros: Anthropology and History in an Aragonese Community. Princeton, N.J.: Princeton University Press.
Lope de Vega
[1619] 1978 Fuenteovejuna. Maria Grazia Profet, ed. Madrid: Capsa.

Luzel, François-Marie
    [1879] 1980 Veillées bretonnes. Paris: Jean Picollec.
Macfarlane, Alan
    1970 Witchcraft in Tudor and Stuart England. New York: Harper Torchbooks.
    1985 The Root of All Evil. In The Anthropology of Evil. David Parkin, ed. Pp.
        57–76. London: Basil Blackwell.
MacFarlane, Charles
    1846 Popular Customs of the South of Italy. London: C. Knight.
Machin, Barrie
    1983 St. George and the Virgin: Cultural Codes, Religion, and Attitudes to the
        Body in a Cretan Mountain Village. Social Analysis 14:107–126.
Macklin, June
    1974 Folk Saints, Healers, and Spiritist Cults in Northern Mexico. Revista/
        Review Interamericana 3:351–367.
McLeod, Hugh
    1981 Religion and the People of Western Europe, 1789–1970. Oxford: Oxford
        University Press.
MacNeill, Máire
    1962 The Festival of Lughnasa. London: Oxford University Press.
Maddox, Richard Frederick
    1986 Religion, Honor, and Patronage: A Study of Culture and Power in an
        Andalusian Town. (Dissertation, Stanford University.) Ann Arbor: Univer-
        sity Microfilms.
Magraw, Roger
    1970 The Conflict in the Village. Popular Anticlericalism in the Isère (1852–
        1870). In Conflicts in French Society. Anticlericalism, Education, and Mor-
        als in the Nineteenth Century. Theodore Zeldin, ed. Pp. 169–227. London:
        George Allen and Unwin.
Malinowski, Bronislaw
    1922 Argonauts of the Western Pacific. New York: E. P. Dutton.
Maltz, Daniel N.
    1978 The Bride of Christ Is Filled with His Spirit. In Women in Ritual and
        Symbolic Roles. J. Hoch-Smith and A. Spring, eds. Pp. 27–44. New York:
        Plenum Press.
    1985 Joyful Noise and Reverent Silence: The Significance of Noise in Pente-
        costal Worship. In Perspectives on Silence. D. Tannen and M. Saville-
        Troike, eds. Pp. 113–137. Norwood, N.J.: Ablex.
Meeks, Wayne A.
    1983 The First Urban Christians: The Social World of the Apostle Paul. New
        Haven, Conn.: Yale University Press.
Melia, Daniel F.
    1978 The Grande Troménie at Locronan: A Major Breton Lughnasa Celebra-
        tion. Journal of American Folklore 91:528–542.
Metford, J.C.J.
    1983 Dictionary of Christian Lore and Legend. London: Thames and Hudson.

Midelfort, H. C. Erik
1972 Witch Hunting in Southwestern Germany, 1562–1684: The Social and Intellectual Foundations. Stanford, Calif.: Stanford University Press.

Mintz, Jerome R.
1982 The Anarchists of Casas Viejas. Chicago: University of Chicago Press.

Mitchell, Timothy
1988 Violence and Piety in Spanish Folklore. Philadelphia: University of Pennsylvania Press.

Moeller, B.
1971 Piety in Germany around 1500. In The Reformation in Medieval Perspective. S. E. Ozment, ed. Pp. 50–75. Chicago: Quadrangle Books.

Monter, William
1976 Witchcraft in France and Switzerland. Ithaca, N.Y.: Cornell University Press.
1983 Ritual, Myth, and Magic in Early Modern Europe. Brighton: The Harvester Press.

Moore, Brian
1972 Catholics. New York: E. P. Dutton.

Moore, Kenneth
1976 Those of the Street. The Catholic-Jews of Mallorca. Notre Dame, Ind.: University of Notre Dame Press.

Moore, Robert
1974 Pit Men, Preachers, and Politics. Cambridge: Cambridge University Press.

Muchembled, Robert
1979 The Witches of Cambrésis: The Acculturation of the Rural World in the Sixteenth and Seventeenth Centuries. In Religion and the People, 800–1700. James Obelkevich, ed. Pp. 221–277. Chapel Hill: University of North Carolina Press.

Murphy, Michael
1987 The Cultural Framing of a Chaotic Ritual in Andalusia. Paper presented at the Spring Meeting of the American Ethnological Society, San Antonio, Texas, April 30–May 3, 1987.

Nadel, Jane H.
1986 Burning with the Fire of God: Calvinism and Community in Scottish Fishing Villages. Ethnology 25:49–60.

Neville, Gwen Kennedy
1979 Community Form and Ceremonial Life in Three Regions of Scotland. American Ethnologist 6:93–109.
1980 Protestant Pilgrims and Inter-Urban Linkages: The American South and Scotland. In Cities in a Larger Context. T. Collins, ed. Pp. 97–109. Athens: University of Georgia Press.
1987 Religious Symbols and Secular Ritual: Cultural Construction in the Scottish Borders. Paper presented at the Spring Meeting of the American Ethnological Society, San Antonio, Texas, April 30–May 3, 1987.

Obelkevich, James
1976 Religion and Rural Society: South Lindsey, 1825–1875. Oxford: Clarendon Press.
Obelkevich, James, ed.
1979 Religion and the People, 800–1700. Chapel Hill: University of North Carolina Press.
Ó'hÉalaí, Pádraig
1974 Moral Values in Irish Religious Tales. Beáloideas 42–44:176–212.
1977 Cumhact an tSagairt sa bheáloideas. Leachtai Cholm Cille 8:109–131.
Ó'hÉochaidh, Sean
1945 Notebook of Priest Stories. (In Irish.) Folklore Archive v. 989. Dublin: Department of Irish Folklore, University College.
Ó'hÓgáin, Dáithí
1983 An file. Dublin: University College Dublin.
Oliveira, Ernesto Veiga de
1984 Festividades cíclicas em Portugal. Lisbon: Publicações Dom Quixote.
Oliveira, Pedro A. Ribeiro de
1979 Catholicisme populaire et hégémonie bourgeoise au Brésil. Archives de sciences sociales des religions 24:53–79.
O'Malley, J. W.
1974 Vatican II. In New Catholic Encyclopedia. Vol. 14, pp. 688–690. New York: McGraw Hill.
O'Neil, Mary R.
1984 Sacerdote ovvero strione: Ecclesiastical and Superstitious Remedies in 16th Century Italy. In Understanding Popular Culture: Europe from the Middle Ages to the Nineteenth Century. Steven Kaplan, ed. Pp. 53–83. Berlin: Mouton.
Orsi, Robert Anthony
1985 The Madonna of 115th Street: Faith and Community in Italian Harlem, 1880–1950. New Haven, Conn.: Yale University Press.
Ortner, Sherry
1973 On Key Symbols. American Anthropologist 75:1338–1346.
O'Shea, James
1983 Priest, Politics, and Society in Post-Famine Ireland. Dublin: Wolfhound Press.
Ott, Sandra
1981 The Circle of Mountains: A Basque Shepherding Community. Oxford: Clarendon Press.
Ozment, Steven
1980 The Age of Reform, 1250–1550: An Intellectual and Religious History of Late Medieval and Reformation Europe. New Haven, Conn.: Yale University Press.
Pace, Enzo
1979 The Debate on Popular Religion in Italy. Sociological Analysis 40:71–75.
Parkin, David
1985 Introduction. In The Anthropology of Evil. David Parkin, ed. Pp. 1–25. Oxford: Basil Blackwell.

Parsons, Talcott
1963 Introduction. *In* The Sociology of Religion. Max Weber. Pp. xix–lxvii. Boston: Beacon Press.
Payne, Stanley G.
1984 Spanish Catholicism: An Historical Overview. Madison: University of Wisconsin Press.
Pérez-Díaz, Víctor
1987 El retorno de la sociedad civil. Madrid: Instituto de Estudios Económicos.
Pina-Cabral, João de
1980 Cults of Death in Northwestern Portugal. Journal of the Anthropological Society of Oxford 11(1):1–14.
1981 O pároco rural e o conflito entre visões do mundo no Minho. Estudos contemporâneos 2/3:75–110.
1986 Sons of Adam, Daughters of Eve: The Peasant Worldview of the Alto Minho. Oxford: Clarendon Press.
Pina-Cabral, João de, and Rui Feijó
1983 Conflicting Attitudes to Death in Modern Portugal: The Question of Cemeteries. *In* Death in Portugal. Rui Feijó, Herminio Martins, and João de Pina-Cabral, eds. Pp. 17–43. Oxford: Journal of the Anthropological Society of Oxford Occasional Papers No. 2.
Pinto, Manuel
1979 A igreja e a insurreição popular do Minho de 1846. Estudos contemporâneos 0:83–135.
Pirgos, Dionisios
1865 Description of the Island of Tinos. . . . (In Greek.) Book available in Gennadian Library, Athens.
Pitt-Rivers, Julian
1954 The People of the Sierra. London: Weidenfeld and Nicolson.
Pocock, David
1973 Mind, Body, and Wealth: A Study of Belief and Practice in an Indian Village. Totowa, N.J.: Rowman and Littlefield.
1985 Unruly Evil. *In* The Anthropology of Evil. David Parkin, ed. Pp. 42–56. Oxford: Basil Blackwell.
Potter, Jack
1974 Cantonese Shamanism. *In* Religion and Ritual in Chinese Society. Arthur P. Wolf, ed. Pp. 207–233. Stanford, Calif.: Stanford University Press.
Prandi, Carlo
1977 Religion et classes subalternes en Italie. Archives de sciences sociales des religions 22:93–139.
Pratt, Jeffrey
1984 Christian-Democrat Ideology in the Cold War. *In* Religion, Power, and Protest in Local Communities: The Northern Shore of the Mediterranean. Eric R. Wolf, ed. Pp. 213–238. Berlin: Mouton.
Rapp, Rayna
1986 Ritual of Reversion: On Fieldwork and Festivity in Haute Provence. Critique of Anthropology 6:35–48.

Redfield, Robert

1956 The Social Organization of Tradition. *In* Peasant Society and Culture: An Anthropological Approach to Civilization, by Robert Redfield. Pp. 67–104. Chicago: University of Chicago Press.

Riegelhaupt, Joyce

1973 Festas and Padres: The Organization of Religious Action in a Portuguese Parish. American Anthropologist 75:835–852.

1981 Camponeses e estado liberal: A revolta de Maria da Fonte. Estudos contemporâneos 2/3:129–142.

1982 O significado religioso do anticlericalismo popular. Análise social 18:1213–1229.

1984 Popular Anti-Clericalism and Religiosity in Pre-1974 Portugal. *In* Religion, Power, and Protest in Local Communities: The Northern Shore of the Mediterranean. Eric R. Wolf, ed. Pp. 93–114. Berlin: Mouton.

1985 Review of The Holy Greyhound: Guinefort, Healer of Children since the Thirteenth Century, by Jean-Claude Schmitt. American Ethnologist 12:153–154.

Rojas, Fernando de

1955 La Celestina. Lesley Byrd Simpson, ed. Berkeley: University of California Press.

Rothkrug, Lionel

1979 Popular Religion and Holy Shrines: Their Influence on the Origins of the German Reformation and their Role in German Cultural Development. *In* Religion and the People, 800–1700. James Obelkevich, ed. Pp. 20–87. Chapel Hill: University of North Carolina Press.

Russell, Jeffrey Burton

1972 Witchcraft in the Middle Ages. Ithaca, N.Y.: Cornell University Press.

Sabean, David

1984 Power in the Blood: Popular Culture and Village Discourse in Early Modern Germany. Cambridge: Cambridge University Press.

Saler, Benson

1977 Supernatural as a Western Category. Ethos 5:31–54.

Sanchis, Pierre

1983 Arraial: Festa de um povo. Lisbon: Publicações Dom Quixote.

Scheper-Hughes, Nancy

1979 Saints, Scholars, and Schizophrenics. Berkeley: University of California Press.

Schmitt, Jean-Claude

1976 "Religion populaire" et culture folklorique. Annales: Economies, sociétés, civilisations 31:941–953.

1983 The Holy Greyhound: Guinefort, Healer of Children since the Thirteenth Century. Translated by Martin Thom. Cambridge: Cambridge University Press.

Schneider, Jane, and Peter Schneider

1984 Mafia Burlesque: The Profane Mass as a Peacemaking Ritual. *In* Religion, Power, and Protest in Local Communities: The Northern Shore of the Mediterranean. Eric R. Wolf, ed. Pp. 117–136. Berlin: Mouton.

Schneider, Jane, and Shirley Lindenbaum
  1987 Introduction. Frontiers of Christian Evangelism: Essays in Honor of Joyce Riegelhaupt. American Ethnologist 14:1–8.
Scribner, R. W.
  1984 Popular Religion in Catholic Germany at the Time of the Reformation. Journal of Ecclesiastical History 35:47–77.
Sébillot, Paul
  1904 Le folk-lore de France. Tome premier: le ciel et la terre. Paris: Guilmoto.
  1907 Le folk-lore de France. Tome quatrième: le peuple et l'histoire. Paris: Guilmoto.
Second Vatican Council
  1966 The Teachings of the Second Vatican Council: Complete Texts of the Constitutions, Decrees, and Declarations. Westminster, Md.: The Newman Press.
Segundo, Juan Luis
  1976 Liberation of Theology. Translated by John Drury. Maryknoll, N.Y.: Orbis Books.
  1985 Theology and the Church: A Response to Cardinal Ratzinger and a Warning to the Whole Church. Translated by John W. Diercksmeier. Minneapolis: Winston Press.
Seligman, Kurt
  1948 Magic, Supernaturalism, and Religion. New York: Pantheon.
La Semaine Religieuse du Diocèse de Quimper et de Léon
  1907a La Feuillée—paroisse sans prêtres. Pp. 461–462.
  1907b La Feuillée—réception du nouveau Recteur. Pp. 875–876.
Sen Rodríguez, Luis Carlos
  1987 Hacia un nuevo comportamiento social? Diario de León. Series on La guerra civil española en León, II, fascículo 12.
Serrador, Ana M.
  1983 A festa do santo padroeiro numa comunidade rural. Estudos contemporâneos 5:205–240.
Shanklin, Eugenia
  1985 Donegal's Changing Traditions. New York: Gordon and Breach.
Shapiro, Judith
  1981 Ideologies of Catholic Missionary Practice in a Postcolonial Era. Comparative Studies in Society and History 23:130–149.
Siegfried, André
  1913 Tableau politique de la France de l'ouest sous la Troisième République. Paris: Armand Colin.
Silverman, Sydel
  1975 Three Bells of Civilization. New York: Columbia University Press.
  1976 On the Uses of History in Anthropology: The Palio of Siena. American Ethnologist 6:413–436.
  1981 Rituals of Inequality: Stratification and Symbol in Central Italy. In Social Inequality: Comparative and Developmental Approaches. Gerald Berreman, ed. Pp. 163–181. New York: Academic Press.

Slater, Candace
  1986 Trail of Miracles: Stories from a Pilgrimage in Northeast Brazil. Berkeley: University of California Press.
  In press. City Steeple, City Streets: Saints' Lives in Granada and a Changing Spain. Berkeley: University of California Press.
Soares, Antonio Franquelím Sampaio Neiva
  1975 O distrito de Viana do Castelo nos inquéritos paroquiais de 1775, 1825, e 1845. Arquivo do Alto Minho 21:1–27.
  1977 O distrito de Viana do Castelo nos inquéritos paroquiais de 1775, 1825, e 1845. Arquivo do Alto Minho 22:108–177.
  1980 O distrito de Viana do Castelo nos inquéritos paroquiais de 1775, 1825, e 1845. Arquivo do Alto Minho 25:99–133.
  1982 A sociedade de Ponteliminse na primeira metade do século XIX: o inquérito de arciprestado de 1845–1846. Arquivo de Ponte de Lima 3:201–252.
Sousa, D. Agostinho de Jesus e
  1943 Pastoral sobre festas. Porto: Tipografia Porto Médico.
Sperber, Jonathan
  1984 Popular Catholicism in Nineteenth-Century Germany. Princeton, N.J.: Princeton University Press.
Spring, David, and Eileen Spring, eds.
  1974 Ecology and Religion in History. New York: Harper Torchbooks.
Steinfels, Peter
  1988 A Champion of Tradition, Marcel Lefebvre. New York Times, July 1, p. 6.
Stocking, George
  1987 Victorian Anthropology. New York: The Free Press.
Stromberg, Peter G.
  1981 Variation and Consensus in the Interpretation of Religious Symbolism: A Swedish Example. American Ethnologist 8:544–559.
  1986 Symbols of Community. The Cultural System of a Swedish Church. Tucson: University of Arizona Press.
Swiderski, Richard M.
  1986 Voices: An Anthropologist's Dialogue with an Italian-American Festival. Bowling Green: Bowling Green University Popular Press.
Tackett, Timothy
  1977 Priest and Parish in Eighteenth-Century France. Princeton, N.J.: Princeton University Press.
Tambiah, Stanley J.
  1970 Buddhism and the Spirit Cults in North-East Thailand. Cambridge: Cambridge University Press.
Taylor, Donald
  1985 Theological Thoughts About Evil. In The Anthropology of Evil. David Parkin, ed. Pp. 26–41. Oxford: Basil Blackwell.
Taylor, Lawrence
  1980a Colonialism and Community Structure in the West of Ireland. Ethnohistory 27:169–181.

1980b The Merchant in Peripheral Ireland: A Case from Donegal. Anthropology 4(2):63–76.

1981 Man the Fisher: Fishing and Community in a Rural Irish Settlement. American Ethnologist 8:774–788.

1985 The Priest and the Agent: Social Drama and Class Consciousness in the West of Ireland. Comparative Studies in Society and History 27:696–712.

1987a The River Would Run Red with Blood: Commons and Community in Donegal. In The Question of the Commons. B. McCay and J. Acheson, eds. Pp. 290–307. Tucson: The University of Arizona Press.

1987b The Healing Mass: Regimes and Fields of Religious Experience in Ireland. Paper presented at a Conference on Religious Regimes and State Formation, Free University Amsterdam, June 27, 1987.

1989 The Mission: An Anthropological View of an Irish Religious Occasion. In Ireland from Below. Chris Curtin and T. W. Wilson, eds. Galway: University College Galway Press.

Tezanos, José Félix
1986 Transformaciones en la estructura social española. In Estructuras sociales y cuestión nacional en España. Francesc Hernández and Francesc Mercadé, eds. Pp. 28–69. Barcelona: Ariel.

Thomas, Keith
1971 Religion and the Decline of Magic. New York: Charles Scribner's Sons.

Thompson, Stith
1955–1958 Motif-Index of Folk Literature. Bloomington: Indiana University Press.

Trachtenberg, Joshua
[1939] 1977 Jewish Magic and Superstition: A Study in Folk Religion. New York: Atheneum.

Trevor-Roper, Hugh
1969 The European Witch-Craze. Harmondsworth: Penguin Books.

Turner, Victor
1969 The Ritual Process: Structure and Anti-Structure. Ithaca, N.Y.: Cornell University Press.

1974 Dramas, Fields, and Metaphors. Ithaca, N.Y.: Cornell University Press.

1982 Social Dramas and Stories About Them. In From Ritual to Theatre: The Human Seriousness of Play, by Victor Turner. Pp. 61–88. New York: Performing Arts Journal Publications.

Turner, Victor, and Edith Turner
1978 Image and Pilgrimage in Christian Culture. New York: Columbia University Press.

Unamuno, Miguel de
1911 Por tierras de Portugal y de España. Madrid: V. Prieto y Coma.

1930 La agonía del cristianismo. Madrid: Compañía Ibero-Americana de Publicaciones.

[1931] 1979 San Manuel Bueno, Mártir. Mario J. Valdés, ed. Madrid: Ediciones Cátedra.

Vallée, Francis Gerald
  1955 Burial and Mourning Customs in a Hebridean Community. Journal of the Royal Anthropological Institute 85:119–130.
van Binsbergen, Wim M. J.
  1976 The Dynamics of Religious Change in Western Zambia. Ufahamu 6:69–87.
van Velzen, H. U. E. Thoden, and W. van Wetering
  1982 Female Religious Responses to Male Prosperity in Turn-of-the-Century Bush Negro Societies. New West Indian Guide 56:43–68.
Vasconcellos, Dr. J. Leite de
  1958 Etnografia portuguesa, Volume IV. Lisbon: Imprensa Nacional.
Verdery, Katherine
  1988 Comment on Goody's Development of the Family and Marriage in Europe. Journal of Family History 13:265–270.
Verrips, Jojada
  1973 The Preacher and the Farmers: The Church as a Political Arena in a Dutch Community. American Anthropologist 75:852–867.
Verrips, Kitty
  1987 Noblemen, Farmers, and Labourers: A Civilizing Offensive in a Dutch Village. Netherlands Journal of Sociology 23:3–16.
Vieira, Padre Alves
  1923 Vieira do Minho. Vieira: Hospital da Torre.
Vovelle, Michel
  1973 Piété baroque et déchristianisation en Provence au XVIIIe siècle. Paris: Plon.
Ware, Timothy
  1963 The Orthodox Church. London: Penguin Books. (Reprinted with revisions 1984.)
Weber, Eugen
  1976 Peasants into Frenchmen: The Modernization of Rural France, 1870–1914. Stanford, Calif.: Stanford University Press.
Weber, Max
  1958a The Protestant Ethic and the Spirit of Capitalism. Translated by Talcott Parsons. New York: Charles Scribner's Sons.
  1958b From Max Weber: Essays in Sociology. Translated and edited by H. H. Gerth and C. Wright Mills. New York: Oxford University Press.
  [1922] 1963 The Sociology of Religion. Boston: Beacon Press.
Weingrod, A., and E. Morin
  1971 Post-Peasants: The Character of Contemporary Sardinian Society. Comparative Studies in Society and History 13:301–324.
Weissler, Chava
  1987a The Religion of Traditional Ashkenazic Women: Some Methodological Issues. AJS Review 12:73–94.
  1987b The Traditional Piety of Ashkenazic Women. In Jewish Spirituality, vol. 2, From the Sixteenth-Century Revival to the Present. Arthur Green, ed.

Pp. 245–275. (World Spirituality: An Encyclopedic History of the Religious Quest, vol. 14.) New York: Crossroad.

White, Lynn, Jr.
1974 The Historical Roots of Our Ecological Crisis. *In* Ecology and Religion in History. David and Eileen Spring, eds. Pp. 15–32. New York: Harper Torchbooks.

Williams, Peter
1980 Popular Religion in America. Englewood Cliffs, N.J.: Prentice-Hall.

Wolf, Eric R.
1982 Europe and the People without History. Berkeley: University of California Press.
1987 Cycles of Violence: The Anthropology of War and Peace. *In* Waymarks: The Notre Dame Inaugural Lectures in Anthropology. Pp. 127–151. Notre Dame, Ind.: University of Notre Dame Press.
————, ed. 1984 Religion, Power, and Protest in Local Communities: The Northern Shore of the Mediterranean. Berlin: Mouton.

Zeldin, Theodore
1970 The Conflict of Moralities. *In* Conflicts in French Society: Anticlericalism, Education, and Morals in the Nineteenth Century. Theodore Zeldin, ed. Pp. 13–50. London: George Allen and Unwin.

Zernov, Nicolas
1961 Eastern Christendom. New York: G. P. Putnam's Sons.

Zuesse, Evan M.
1985 Ritual Cosmos: The Sanctification of Life in African Religions. Athens: Ohio University Press.

Index

Greek independence, 137n.5; symbolism of woman's body in, 138n.11

Edict of Nantes (1685), 140

Education: Irish Catholicism and, 170; as priestly activity, 71, 81

Enlightenment, 48; French religion and, 140

Equity-consciousness: vs. "brotherly love," 37–38; capitalism and, 53; elaboration and suppression of, 31–35; empathy and, 28; between peasants and earth spirits, 44–45; salvationist religions and, 52–53; suppression of by reform movements, 37–38

Ethics: of animism, 27–31; equity-based and rationalizing ethics, 15–16; popular vs. learned religion, 8–9, 15

Eucharist: concept of brotherly love and, 45–46; and Franco, 87–88; priest's power to provide, 93; ritual of, 36

Evil, 46–47; moral responsibility and, 32. *See also* Satan

Exorcism and demonic possession, 124–26; gender aspects of, 132; at Panayía Shrine, 120–24; sacred and profane dichotomy and, 127–28

Fairies, European belief in, 43–44

Faith: anthropological aspects of, 97, 193–96; individual vs. community religion, 56–60; pilgrimage and, 129; public vs. private, 195–96

Fátima, shrine of, 73, 75 nn. 9 and 13

Festas: anticlericalism and, 64; *arraials* and, 61–64; community identity and, 59–60; disputes over control of, 12–13, 57–58, 61–63, 65, 189; importance of saints in, 63–64; lay operation of, in rural Portugal, 70; tourism value of, 73

Festivals, political role of, 74n.2

Fires of Saint John, 42–43

Folk religion, defined, 55

Food-sharing customs, rotation and, 101–2, 111n.15

Foster, George, 198

France: church-state relations in, 140–41; Integrist movement in, 19–20; popular religion in, 8, 74n.3; priests as sorcerers in, 162n.13

Franciscan Order, 25

Franco regime: glorification of rural life un-

der, 88–89; impact on Catholic Church in Spain, 83–90

Frazer, James George (Sir), 29–30, 186

Freeman, Susan Tax, 8–9, 60, 68, 97, 193–94

Galicia (Spain), religious beliefs in, 108n.3

Gender and religion, 11–12, 14–15, 21, 68, 111n.16, 132, 147–48, 167–68, 192–93

Ginzburg, Carlo, 6, 23n.3, 25, 186; study of Menocchio, 40, 78; on witch-hunts, 48–49

Gossip: anticlericalism and, 189; as form of protest, 197

Great tradition–little tradition dichotomy, 6–7, 133, 186–87

Greed, stereotypes about priests and, 65, 189–90

Greek nationalism: Greek Orthodox Church and, 23 nn. 8 and 11, 113; icon of Tinos and, 115–16

"Green" movements, equity-consciousness and, 53

Greyhound, Holy, 12, 44–45

Gypsies, 88, 132, 134–35; and intervention in Panayía exorcism, 123–24; proportion of men visiting Panayía shrine among, 139n.23

Hauschild, Thomas, 25, 28, 48

Healing miracles: at Panayía, 120; role of in Irish drunken priest stories, 171–72, 175–76, 183

Hellenism, impact on Greek religion, 114–15, 137n.6

Henningsen, Gustav, 25

Heroic priest stories, 163–64, 170–71; British oppression and, 169–70

Holy wells, sites of in Ireland, 174, 181

"Image of Limited Good," 198

Images (religious), popularity of, in rural Spain, 80–81, 109n.4

Individual faith: vs. community religion, 56–60; pilgrimages and, 128–31

Inheritance rules, witch-hunts and, 50–51

Inquisition: 39, 47, 48; Spanish, 86–87

Integrist movement, 19–20

Ireland: Catholicism in, 18–19, 166–70; popular religion in, 15, 18–19

Islam, 33–34